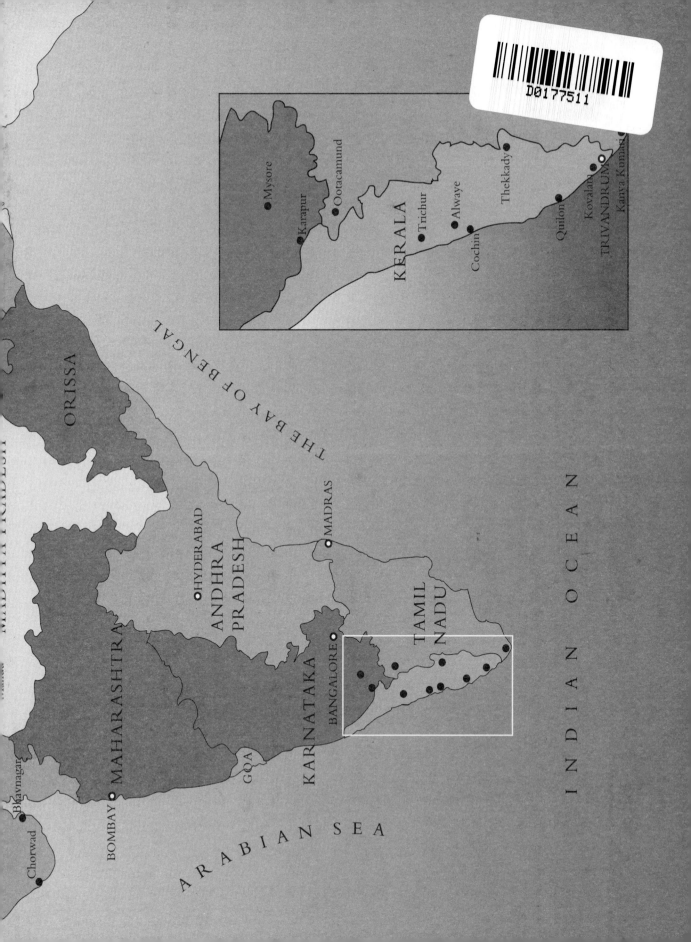

Palaces of
INDIA

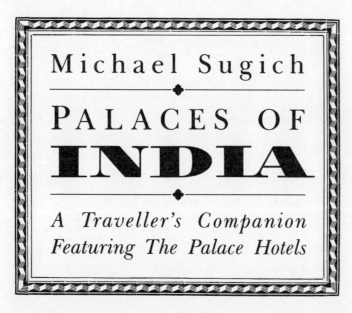

Michael Sugich

PALACES OF

INDIA

A Traveller's Companion
Featuring The Palace Hotels

PHOTOGRAPHS BY MOHAMMED AKRAM

PAVILION

For
HELEN SUGICH
with love

First published in Great Britain in 1992 by
PAVILION BOOKS LIMITED
196 Shaftesbury Avenue, London WC2H 8JL

Text Copyright © Michael Sugich 1992
Illustrations copyright © Mohammed Akram 1992

A CIP catalogue record for this book is
available from the British Library

ISBN 1 85145 5205
10 9 8 7 6 5 4 3 2

Printed and bound in Great Britain by
Butler & Tanner Ltd, Frome and London

CONTENTS

ACKNOWLEDGEMENTS

This book was made possible by the unstinting assistance extended to us by the Ministry of Tourism of the Government of India in coordination with the state tourist authorities throughout the country. In each state we were accommodated and given the use of a car and driver, the most precious research aid in India. Therefore, I would like to begin by thanking Sri B.K. Goswami, Director General of Tourism of the Government of India, who godfathered this project through from start to finish and Sri A.N. Chaturvedi, Director of the India Tourist Offices in the Near and Far East, for his crucial help in launching us. My thanks also to the Secretary of Tourism, Sri S.K. Misra, for his support. And to the tourist departments of all the state governments who helped us on the way, specifically Rajasthan Tourism, Himachal Pradesh Tourism, Gujarat Tourism, Andhra Pradesh Tourism, Karnataka Tourism, Tamil Nadu Tourism and Kerala Tourism, our sincere thanks.

We are also indebted to Air India for flying us to and from Jeddah and facilitating our arrivals and departures, particularly management and staff in Jeddah: D.W. Shembavanekar, Guru Benegal, Sadat Khan, Sarwar Aziz and Hafiz Sarang.

ENGLAND

Ovidio and Pat Salazar extended constant friendship and support during my prolonged research periods in London. Without their kindness and hospitality this book would have been nigh on impossible to pull off. Heartfelt thanks to Abdel Wahed El Wakil, my architectural mentor, for his genius and his generosity and to Grigoris and Christa Arzoglu for their good company and open house. Dr Giles Tillotson and his wife Sarah have been extremely helpful in sharing their time and knowledge of India and architecture which has deepened my own understanding immeasurably. Thanks also to Dr Robert Skelton and Philip Davies for some telephonic advice in the early days.

Much of my research was carried out in the India Office Library, the School of Oriental and African Studies Library at the University of London, and the British Library. I am grateful to those great institutions for access to their literary treasures.

And to Ann Dewe, my literary agent at Andrew Mann Ltd, for her hard work and encouragement.

INDIA

So many people in this wonderful country have extended their help as to make even fleeting mention of their individual services impossible within this limited space. I hope they will forgive me for simply listing their names and understand that my gratitude far exceeds anything that could be set down in any case:

Rajmata Gayatri Devi of Jaipur, Maharaj Jai Singh of Jaipur, Shriji Arvind Singh Mewar of Udaipur, Maharaja Gaj Singh of Jodhpur, Sobha Kanwar Baiji of Jodhpur, M.K. Brij Raj Singh of Kota, Maharana Pratap Sinh, Maharaja Rama Kumari and Yuvraj Dr Digvijay Sinh of Wankaner, Maharaja Virbadhrasinh and Maharaj Shivbadrah Sinh of Bhavnagar, Maharaja Madhav Rao Scindia of Gwalior, Maharaja Dr Karan Singh of Kashmir, Nawab Mujib Yar Jung Bahadur of Hyderabad, S.K.N. Wadiyar of Mysore, Raja Malvinder Singh of Patiala.

Rawal Raghuvender Singh and Yuvrawal Yaduvender Singh of Samode, Lt. Col. Raghuvir Singh Dundlod, Thakur Mohan Singh of Kanota, Thakur Onkar Singh of Khimsar, Maharaj Swaroop Singh and Maharaj Sobhag Singh of Jodhpur, Rawal Madan Singh of Nawalgarh, Kumar Sangram Singh of Nawalgarh, Kumar Devi Singh of Mandawa, Kesri Singh of Mandawa, Sidharth Singh of Rohet, Sanjai Singh of Bissau, Ranbir Singh of Dundlod, Nawabzada Aimaduddin Ahmad Khan of Loharu, Th. Onkar Singh Katoch, Th. Sajjan Singh of Ghanerao, Th. Sunder Singh and Mahendra Singh of Achrol, Sardar S.C. Angre of Gwalior, Kanwar Udai Singh of Jubbal, Kanwar Rajinder Singh of Kapurthala.

Monisha Mukundan, Aman Nath, Francis Wacziarg, M. Yunnus Kunju, Didi Contractor, Laxman Subedi, L.K. Kasliwal, Dr Ashok Das, Ajit Cheema, Dr S. Nagaraja Rao, Rashid and Haseeb Shaw and the staff of Cottage Arts Emporium.

Divyabhanusinh Chavda, Shushi Wadhwan, K.B. Kachru, Vikram Madhok, Raju Shahani, Mahendra Singh Rathore, Surjit Dhillon, Mahendra Ahluwalia, Ashok Chauhan, Alok Jain, Col. A.K. Shivpuri, Ms Umaima Mulla-Feroze, Ms Neeta Helms, Jagat Mastaram, R. Sheshadri, P.K. Gopinath, R.E. Smith.

Shantunu Consul, Vittal Rai, K. Jayakumar, Imtiaz, R. Narasimha Rao, B.S. Palaksha, Col. John Wakefield, A.S. Sunder Raj, P. Ramaraj.

Ishani Majumdar, S.K. Sivanandan, Martand Singh, Prem Subramaniam, Mrs Happy Singh, Salim Kedwai, K.C. Katoch, Professor S.N. Wakhlu, Pronoti Deoi, Sudhir Kasliwal, Nand Kishore Pareek, Pandit Misraji, S.K. Saxena, Jai Singh, Dalip Singh, Devi Singh Rathore, Nelima Jauhary, Surender Singh Chauhan, Dharm Veer Agarwal, Hemant Kumar, Devdutt Pandya, Ashok Desai, Mr Agnihotri, Sri Gangadhara, Mrs Neomi Meadows, Dr M. Vellayadha Nair, Ramesh Menon, Ravi Kuttikadu, Justice T. C. Menon.

And to our patient, first-rate Rajput driver Sita Ram who put up with us for one gruelling month in Rajasthan through elections, strikes, rioting, breakdowns (automotive and low-grade nervous), etc.

SAUDI ARABIA

I would like to thank Willy Koilpillai for his many and sundry services, Talmiz Ahmad, Consul General of India, for his interest and assistance, and Javed Akhtar for his translations. Dennis Danchik gave me invaluable midstream feedback on the text, as did Sultan Ghalib Al Qu'aiti, who also provided me with rare and precious background literature.

AMERICA

Mrs Lillian Keyes allowed me the use of her peaceful beach retreat to write my first chapters in solitude. Any writer with five boisterous young children will appreciate the inestimable value of such a gift. My mother, another inestimably precious gift, has been more than maternally generous during this project and I have dedicated this book to her.

Finally, deepest love and thanks to my beloved wife Shadiya for cliff-hanging with me.

You soon find your long-ago dreams of India rising in a sort of vague and luscious moonlight above the horizon-rim of your opaque consciousness, and softly lighting up a thousand forgotten details which were parts of a vision that had once been vivid to you when you were a boy, and steeped your spirit in tales of the East. The barbaric gorgeousness, for instance; and the princely titles, the sumptuous titles, the sounding titles, – how good they taste in the mouth!

Following the Equator
MARK TWAIN

INTRODUCTION

This is a book for travellers, armchair and actual, presenting the history and description of thirty-eight former princely palaces in India which have been opened in one form or another to paying guests – as luxury resorts, tourist bungalows or roadside rest-stops. These castles are scattered across India from Kashmir to Kerala and range from medieval desert fortifications with ramparts and battlements to twentieth-century neo-classical pleasure domes with ballrooms and banqueting halls. Each has a tale to tell – of love and chivalry, of intrigue and murder, of passion and scandal, of heroism and infamy, of piety and stupidity, of stupendous wealth, staggering pageantry and sudden humiliation – of an India that has irrevocably disappeared.

My original aim in undertaking this project was simply to provide a historic and architectural context for each palace considered so that visitors might better appreciate where on earth they actually are when they sojourn in one of these bewildering, unfamiliar buildings, created for a lifestyle almost inconceivable in this present democratic age. I set out to discover when each property was first constructed, for what it was originally intended, its architectural peculiarities and how it evolved in use and structure.

In the process it dawned on me that these palaces offer a strange, arresting reflection of the flamboyant and convoluted history that produced them. The following pages form a narrative collage of records, chronicles, anecdotes, local folklore, tribal mythology, scholarly commentary, eyewitness description and oral tradition which collectively renders a multiform image of princely India in much of its exotic fascination and barbaric gorgeousness.

It also became clear to me that for all the diversity of circumstance, and the unbridled, seemingly lunatic, eclecticism of Indian palace building in the nineteenth and early twentieth centuries (most of the properties presented here are products of this period), an overriding pattern and rationale did exist which was determined as much by tradition and British Imperial policy as by princely caprice.

In the beginning there were war-lords and fortifications. Before British dominion in India – that is to say, before the beginning of the nineteenth century – Indian princes were fundamentally clan chiefs who, in the words of Robert W. Stern:

Wherever it was possible and in every possible combination and permutation . . . did violence to one another and on behalf of one another. They seized one another's lands and defended them, laid waste to one another's estates and died protecting them, honoured and defamed one another, rescued and betrayed one another and in glorious battle met and mangled one another. They fought over land and honour and because they were warriors.

So intrinsic was this martial heritage to these tribal fighters of the *Kshatriya*, or warrior caste of Hinduism, that a science of fortress-building evolved which was enshrined in the *Shastras* – canons of Hindu craftsmanship – and consecrated in the Vedas and Puranas and the sacred Hindu epics. Hindu war-lords built their fortifications according to these canonic archetypes to protect themselves and their clansmen from the depredations of their neighbours.

The Muslim conquest of India culminating in the Mughal Empire did little to change this ancient system. The Mughals simply co-opted Hindu martial traditions in their empire-building. A profound architectural transformation did take place in the synthesis of Persian and Central Asian forms introduced by the Mughals with indigenous Hindu architecture, but Indian princes still lived as war-lords and continued to build fortifications, basically according to their ancient canons.

With the decline of Mughal power following the death of the Emperor Aurangzeb in 1707 and the consequent chaos throughout the eighteenth century as liberated vassals campaigned to expand their territories and Maratha armies rose up with imperial ambitions of their own, the war-lord princes of India needed their fortresses more than ever.

This was all to change with the arrival of the British.

The fighting-instinct thrown back upon itself must have some sort of outlet; and a merciful Providence wisely ordains that the Kings of the East in the

nineteenth century shall take pleasure in shopping on an imperial scale. Dresden china snuff-boxes, mechanical engines, electro-plated fish-slicers, musical boxes, and gilt blown-glass Christmas-tree balls do not go well with the splendours of a Palace that might have been built by Titans and coloured by the morning sun. But there are excuses to be made for Kings who have no fighting to do.
Rudyard Kipling, *Letters of Marque*, 1887-9

By the beginning of the nineteenth century, following the defeat of Tippu Sultan in the south and the Marathas in the north, British East India Company forces had emerged as the most powerful army in India. The beleaguered war-lord princes, driven by military defeat and Maratha onslaught, signed treaties of protection with the Honourable East India Company, one by one, recognizing Britain as the Paramount Power in India and relinquishing territorial ambitions in exchange for the enforced territorial integrity of their now delimited dominions. With the stroke of a pen two separate Indias were created: the India of the Princes (what became known as 'Indian India'), comprising two-fifths of the subcontinent divided into 565 individual states; and the remainder of the land under direct Company rule, known thereafter as British India.

The entire traditional dynamic was thus arrested. Suddenly kings who, as Professor Stern wrote, 'derived their cultural identity from their profession as conquerors and warriors', had, as Kipling pointed out, no fighting left to do. At first these erstwhile war-lords simply went shopping on an imperial scale and filled up their titanic hereditary castles with incongruous gadgetry and Victorian bric-à-brac, but gradually as time passed in Pax Britannia it began to seem as if it was the traditional palace that was incongruous rather than the other way around and the princes of India began to build homes in harmony with their newly acquired customs and accoutrements. In his recent study *The Tradition of Indian Architecture* G.H.R. Tillotson described the ultimate impact of pacification upon the princely lifestyle and palace architecture:

The reduction in warfare saved the maharajas not only energy but considerable amounts of money,

and both could now be spent on another long-favoured pastime: building. Traditional Indian palaces are fortified, but the treaties had obviated the need for defences, so many maharajas began to build a new kind of palace: not hilltop retreats but mansions on the plains. The treaties also brought the maharajas into contact with Britons, and gave rise to occasions when they had to entertain the new overlords. In the nineteenth century, few Britons were adventurous enough to want entertainment in the Indian fashion, and some maharajas were happy to provide ballrooms and billiard rooms instead. The small cramped apartments of traditional palaces where one sat on the floor strewn with quilts and velvet bolsters were abandoned in favour of spacious halls where one could sit on European furniture. Apart from satisfying guests these new amenities also suited the increasingly Westernized tastes of the maharajas themselves.

These increasingly Westernized tastes were not merely an accident of association but the result of a long-term policy of acculturation first established in the 1830s by rationalists and evangelicals within the Company contemptuous of Indian civilization and strenuously dedicated to its reformation according to Western principles and prototypes. By the end of the nineteenth century this policy had produced a generation of Western-educated (by British tutors or regional Princes' Colleges set up for the purpose) 'progressive' rulers living an Anglicized lifestyle within fantastically elaborate but essentially European palaces built primarily for recreation and entertainment. Once established, the English system perpetuated itself so that the prince became (in most cases) a proper Anglo-Oriental gentleman and his palace a fabulous baronial manor (and sometimes more) with traditional embellishments serving as a reminder that, yes, this was still the East.

Suddenly in 1947, with the creation of democratic (socialist) India, the princely order was eclipsed. Between 1947 and 1949 the princely states were subsumed, voluntarily or by force, into the Indian Union. Former ruling princes were promised privy purses, tax exemptions, the retention of titles and other privileges in perpetuity in exchange for handing over their dominions to newly established state governments. These promises were guaranteed in three constitutional amendments (and in 1970

broken by presidential order when the princes of India were formally de-recognized). Nevertheless, the immediate loss of revenue, power, prestige and purpose turned these men who had been raised to rule into dinosaurs overnight and their palaces, built for pageantry and entertainment on an imperial scale, into gradually dilapidating white elephants.

These palaces, as Rajmata Vijayaraje Scindia of Gwalior wrote:

had been built almost as monuments, with full-dress levees and Viceregal visits in mind; they were stuffed with chandeliers, carpets, carved furniture and decorative statuary bought without thought of cost. They were about as impracticable as family residences as elephants were as a means of transport; and these too we happened to possess in embarrassingly large numbers. When was I or my son ever going to give a party that could fill out durbar hall, or host a sit-down dinner for over a hundred guests and dazzle them with our special silver plate and crystal? We could neither put down our elephants nor demolish our palaces. The only thing to do was let the poor beasts live out their days in diminishing comfort and watch the palaces sag and crumble and their exotic gardens wither and become dustbowls.

But of course this is when the traveller arrives – the foreigner, the tourist, the globetrotter – with restorative prosperity and dreams of India rising . . .

And this is where our book begins – to steep your spirit in tales of the East.

NORTHERN INDIA

UDAIPUR

SUN CITY

*It was worth a night's discomfort, and revolver-
beds to sleep upon – this city of the Suryavansi,
hidden among the hills that encompass the great
Pichola lake. Truly, the King who governs to-day
is wise in his determination to have no railroad to
his capital. His predecessor was more or less
enlightened, and, had he lived a few years longer,
would have brought the iron horse through the
Dobarri – the green gate which is the entrance of
the Girwa or girdle of hills around Udaipur; and,
with the train, would have come the tourist who
would have scratched his name upon the Temple
of Garuda and laughed horse-laughs upon the lake.
Let us, therefore, be thankful that the capital of
Mewar is hard to reach.*

Rudyard Kipling, *Letters of Marque*, 1887-9

The 'iron horse' eventually did intrude
upon the tranquillity of Mewar and
Pichola lake has surely heard its share
of horse-laughs, but Udaipur
remained remote for a very long time
after Maharana Fateh Singh held sway over
his ancient state when Kipling took his tour.
Fateh Singh was a fiercely independent chief
who refused to attend the durbar of the
King-Emperor, kept his distance from Delhi
and brandished Mewar tradition with a
truculent disdain for imperial priorities.

G.E.C. Wakefield, who served in
Udaipur as a colonial officer during the
reign of this proud, recalcitrant prince,
remembered taking to the Maharana:

*. . . a long letter, written by Lord Curzon himself,
in which he stated that His Highness should be
made to realize that in these modern days kings
were the servants of the people and not the people
the servants of the kings.*

*His Highness sprang out of his chair when he
heard this and said he could not understand anybody
having such an insane belief.*

The Mewars had been vanquished by
Akbar and forced to remove from Chittor
to Udaipur but as the proudest princes in
India, revelling in their sacred descent from
the sun, they never relinquished a sense of
independence and gladly exchanged blood
for the dignity of their lineage.

Udaipur, the capital of Mewar, was
founded by the Rana Udai Singh after the
fall of Chittor to the Mughal forces of Akbar
in 1568. The Rana had previously been
drawn to the site of his new city and had
formed an artificial lake named Udai Sagar
in honour of himself. He later came upon
a pond said to have been created in the
fifteenth century by a *banjara* (one who
transports grain) who raised a dyke across
a mountain stream for his bullocks to walk
over, damming up its waters. Udai Singh
extended this pond, creating the most
beautiful of man-made lakes, named
Pichola after the neighbouring village of
Picholi. Upon an overlooking ridge he built
a small palace in 1559, and other structures
soon clustered round it. With the establishment of his new capital the Rana's marble
and granite palace spread magisterially
across the rise over several generations,
retaining an architectural integrity unique
to the kings of Mewar.

The Sisodias did little to assimilate
themselves into Mughal India. Unlike other
Rajput princes to the north, the kings of
Mewar never willingly submitted to
Mughal authority. Udaipur remained as
unadulterated in its aesthetics and religious
devotion as an overmastered state could be,
changing only late in the nineteenth century
with the insinuation of European influences.
Even then, no Maharana of Udaipur ever
visited Europe until after the Native States
were subsumed into democratic India.
Udaipur retained its dream-struck quality
and Rosita Forbes, who passed through this
land in the twilight of the Raj, described it
as 'like no other place on earth'.

... The Children of the Sun must indeed reign here, for a more beautiful light I have never seen than that which bathes these palaces, makes the trees glow as if cut out of emerald, and throws shadows as blue as the deep sky on those white walls. It is an enchantment and a benediction in one, and on the vast sweep of water guarded by the hills, float the islands, each the wonder of the whole ... We swept out of the dark creek, under the bridge, into a world of tremulous beauty, flame palaces floating on the waters of an enchanted sea, at once so amazing and so lovely as to drive the despairing biographer to blasphemy or silence ... Udaipur is becoming a literary torment.

Yvonne Fitzroy, *Courts and Camps in India,* 1926

JAG NIWAS

The Lake Palace Hotel

The Pichola lake lies to the immediate west of the ridge on which the City Palace of Udaipur stands. It is two and a quarter miles long and one and a quarter miles wide. The dam that captures its waters is 334 yards across and its height above the water is thirty-seven feet. One day's hard rain is sufficient to fill the lake for a year.

Two pleasure palaces – one white and one weathered – seem to float upon these still and steely waters, dominating the lake and lending an almost mythical quality to the opulent capital of Mewar.

The earliest of the island palaces was developed by Rana Karan Singh (1620-28) following an extension and raising of the dam in the first year of his reign. In 1626 Karan Singh's water palace became the temporary exile of Sultan Khurram, the second son of Jahanghir, who was to ascend the Mughal throne as Shah Jahan upon his father's death the following year. Khurram had set himself against his father in intrigue and rebellion, and had fled to Udaipur where the Rana gave him refuge, first in his City Palace and later, when the Sultan's Muslim retainers failed to respect Rajput customs, on the island in Pichola.

Ironically, it was Prince Khurram who had led the Mughal armies which had in 1614 subjugated Rana Amar Singh, the father of his host. Jahangir had been ecstat-ically gratified by the fact that 'the Rana Amar Singh and his fathers, proud in the strength of the hilly country and their abodes, had never seen or obeyed any of the kings of Hindustan, [and that] this should be brought about in my reign', and ordered his son Khurram to extend every kindness and solicitation to the Rana in his defeat.

Prince Karan was called upon to save his proud father's face by serving as emissary to the Mughal court and it was during this period that a rapport evolved between the two princes based, the Sisodias say, upon Khurram's Rajput blood as much as upon his magnanimity in triumph. It could also be said that Mewar hospitality to the rebel prince was a golden opportunity to retaliate against the king who vassalized their dynasty.

However mixed his motives may have been, Rana Karan Singh treated his royal guest with tremendous generosity, raising a domed pavilion upon the island, crowned by the Muslim crescent, the interiors of which were lavishly ornamented. The Rana had a throne sculpted from a single block of serpentine for his royal guest and a mosque built in honour of a venerated Muslim saint for the prayers of the Mughal prince and his partisans. Sultan Khurram resided in his island exile in great comfort until removing to Golconda in the Deccan, shortly before his father's death.

His sojourn was fortuitous for Udaipur, for on his ascension to the throne of Hindustan, Shah Jahan favoured the Sisodias and the recently humiliated kingdom was able to regain a measure of its dignity and independence.

Rana Karan Singh died in 1628 just before the death of Jahanghir and the ascension of his friend, and was succeeded by his son Rana Jagat Singh I (1628-52) who added to the island palace a zenana (women's quarters) and named the island Jag Mandir, in honour of himself.

For more than a century Jag Mandir remained alone upon the Pichola as the principal pleasure palace of the Sisodia kings. During the reign of Maharana Sangram Singh II (1710-34) his son and heir-apparent Jagat Singh II applied for permission to sojourn upon Jag Mandir but,

for unknown reasons, his father refused, setting aside the adjacent island for his son's use.

The original pavilions on this undeveloped island were constructed sometime before 1734 and upon his ascension to the Gadi Rana Jagat Singh II (1734-51) continued to expand the white-marble water palace, calling it Jag Niwas, in honour of himself.

During this period the main pavilions were built: Bara Mahal, Khush Mahal, Phool Mahal, Dhola Mahal, as well as the Dilaram Palace and the Canal. In 1829 Colonel James Tod, the British East India Company's representative in Rajputana, who had during his long tenure in India fallen under the hypnotic sway of Mewar, wrote of the land and its lake palaces in his meticulous history *Annals and Antiquities of Rajast'han*:

Nothing but marble enters into their composition; columns, baths, reservoirs, fountains, all are of this material, often inlaid with mosaics, and the uniformity pleasingly diversified by the light passing through glass of every hue. The apartments are decorated with historical paintings in water colours, almost meriting the term fresco from their deep absorption in the wall, though the darker tints have blended with and in part obscured the more delicate shades, from atmospheric causes. The walls, both here and in the grand palace, contain many medallions, in considerable relief, in gypsum, portraying the principal historical events of the family, from early periods even to the marriage pomp of the present Rana. Parterres of flowers, orange and lemon groves, intervene to dispel the monotony of the buildings, shaded by the wide-spreading tamarind and magnificent evergreen khirni; while the graceful palmyra and coco wave their plume-like branches over the dark cypress or cooling plantain. Detached colonnaded refectories are placed on the water's edge for the chiefs, and the extensive baths for their use. Here they listened to the tale of the bard, and slept off their noonday opiate amidst the cool breezes of the lake, wafting delicious odours from myriads of lotus-flower which covered the surface of the waters; and as the fumes of the potion evaporated, they opened their eyes on a landscape to which not even its inspirations could frame an equal: the broad waters of the Peshola, with its indented and well-wooded margin receding to the terminating point of sight, at which the temple of the Brimpoori opened on the pass of the gigantic Aravulli, the fields of the exploits of their forefathers. Amid such scenes did the Seesodia princes and chieftains recreate during two generations, exchanging the din of arms for voluptuous inactivity.

Later in the century the traveller Louis Rousselet experienced at first hand this 'voluptuous inactivity' as a guest of the Maharana on a royal excursion to Jag Niwas:

We started very early the next morning, and, driving through town, embarked at the quay of the Tripolia Derwaza; a few moments brought us to the island of Jugnavas. This island, usually so quiet and deserted, was now the scene of bustle and excitement; the servants of the Rana ran hither and thither, landing the provisions from the boats, and arranging everything for our short stay. The apartments were quickly furnished, awnings and blinds being hung from the verandahs, and the floors covered with carpets and cushions.

Close at hand, the cooks were busy preparing a substantial breakfast, and the banghy-coolies arrived with such a profusion of champagne and still hock that I began to have suspicions that the Rana had some design upon our lives. Nothing was forgotten. In a kiosk on the water's edge we found a bevy of young and laughing girls assembled, their dresses sparkling with jewels. These were the Nautch girls of the Court, sent here by the Rana to amuse us with their songs and dancing.

We breakfasted in a saloon, the balconies of which overlooked the lake, and passed our siesta on sofas, watching the Nautch girls dancing . . . The Rana did not join us until two o'clock. We received him at the landing-place of the island, where he arrived with great pomp, accompanied by the Rao of Baidlah and the Rao of Pursoli. We chatted together until the preparations for the expedition were completed, when, the guards and the choubdars [mace-bearers and court heralds who announce arrival of state guests] with their golden staves forming lines, the procession advanced, and we embarked with great solemnity in half-a-dozen boats. These flat-bottomed boats or punts are admirably adapted to these marshes, where the water is very shallow.

Having crossed the lake, we agreed to follow Doctor Cunningham, the acknowledged Nimrod of Oudeypoor, into a labyrinth of canals, which intersect the great marsh lying at the foot of the mountains; where we found ourselves in the midst of reeds and water-plants of a prodigious height,

from which, as we advanced, rose immense flocks of wild-fowl and flamingoes. Shooting soon commenced, and lasted about an hour. The bag was large, including numbers of snipe and other game. At four o'clock we left the marsh and betook ourselves to the boats, where the Rana again went through the ceremony of the pan, and threw round each of our necks a most lovely garland of roses.

The crocodile found here, as in other inland lakes of India, is a formidable animal. It attains a great size, and the people who inhabit the shores of the lake occasionally fall victims to its savage attacks . . . Since the English Residency has been established at Oudeypoor, and the Rana, overcoming the ridiculous religious prejudices which protect these reptiles, has allowed Europeans to hunt them down, these formidable animals have abandoned the neighbourhood of the town, and have taken refuge on the opposite banks. Pitilessly pursued into their retreats, they have become very wary. As soon as a boat appears upon the lake, they dive to the bottom, and, on rising again, only show the tips of their muzzles above the surface. That, however, is sufficient for the hunter, and our rifle-balls soon found them out under water. A violent commotion immediately ensued, which, with the blood-stained water, was the only visible result of the encounter, as the alligator, when killed, sinks at once to the bottom . . .

We returned to our enchanting island, where we were greeted by the songs of the Nautch girls. After dinner we re-embarked and sailed for hours about the lake. The moon rose, flooding with her soft light the cupolas of the palace; and the water scintillated in her rays, while the notes of the Taza-bi-Taza [a popular song] sung by the Nautch girls, were wafted to us by the soft night air. We were at length, however, forced to depart, and mounting our elephants, which awaited us at the Tripolia, we returned to the Residency; and thus concluded, as we all agreed, the happiest days of our life in India.

During the reign of Rousellet's host, the Maharana Shambhu Singh (1861-74), the Victorian-style Shambhu Prakash was added to the Jag Niwas complex and, in the decade of his successor, Sajjan Singh (1874-84) the Sajjan Vilas was completed. By the end of the nineteenth century, time was beginning to take its toll upon Udaipur's water palaces. French writer Pierre Loti described Jag Niwas as 'slowly mouldering in the damp emanations of the lake'. At roughly the same time William Hunter Workman and

his wife Fanny, two inveterate colonial bicyclists, registered their disappointment in the 'cheap and tasteless style' of the interiors of the island palaces with 'an assortment of infirm European furniture, wooden clocks, coloured glass ornaments, and children's toys, all of which seems to the visitor quite out of place, where he would naturally expect a dignified display of Eastern splendour'.

During the reign of Bhopal Singh (1930-55) another pavilion, the Chandra Prakash, was built but otherwise Jag Niwas remained unchanged, beautiful, mouldering, infirm and increasingly silent until Geoffrey Kendall described it on a visit during the 1950s as 'totally deserted, the stillness broken only by the humming of clouds of mosquitoes'.

When Maharana Bhagwat Singh ascended to the Gadi in 1955 he had already witnessed the end of the rarified life led by his ancestors. Although traditionally educated he was among the first of princes to come to terms with the new order in India. In Udaipur the pressures to accommodate change were even greater than in many other princely states in India. Their refusal to bend to Mughal or British imperial will had kept them their dignity but cost them their fortunes. Whereas other Maharajas had, through the establishment of strong relations with their imperial overlords, reaped the rewards of enormous, overflowing wealth, the Sisodias had only their properties to fall back on. Even in the 1960s Udaipur had no industry or business to speak of. The only industry in Kipling's time was that of sword-making and little had changed since then.

Bhagwat Singh saw this clearly and set about preparing his dynasty and domains for the future. To this end, in 1961 he set about converting Jag Niwas Palace into Udaipur's first luxury hotel.

It was at this point that Didi Contractor, an American artist married to a Bombay-based Parsi engineer, became a design-consultant to the project:

I worked from 1961 to 1969 and what an adventure! His Highness, you know, was a real monarch – really like kings always were. So one had a sense of being one of the last people to be an artist for

the king. It felt the way one imagines it was like working in the courts of the Renaissance. It was an experience of going back in time to an entirely different era, a different world.

His Highness was actually working on a shoe-string. He wasn't in dire straits, mind you, but when he came to the throne he inherited big problems, like what to do with the 300 dancing girls that belonged to his predecessor [Maharana Bhopal Singh]. He tried to offer them scholarships to become nurses but they didn't want to move out of the palace so what could he do? He had to keep them. They were old crones by this time and on state occasions I remember that they would come to sing and dance with their ghunghats *[face veils] down and occasionally one would lift hers to show a wizened old face underneath. And he had something like twelve state elephants. When you have twelve elephants you have either got to feed them or give them away. Finding a home for a kitten is one thing but finding a home for an elephant is kind of difficult. And he had all these properties which were deteriorating. The buildings on Jag Niwas were starting to fall down and basically the Lake Palace was turned into a hotel because it seemed the only viable way that it could be maintained . . . It was really a job of conservation.*

Kipling said that 'All palaces in India excepting dead ones . . . are full of eyes', and Didi Contractor found this to be the case with Jag Niwas. The place was riddled with peep-holes, secret passages, and secret rooms. 'There was this room that you could only enter through a trap door at the top.' All these openings had to be sealed off or exposed and changed.

There was another problem: few tourists came to Udaipur in those days. The Maharana's second son, Arvind, who now controls the Sisodia properties, remembers that he did not think his father's idea would ever work:

Udaipur was too isolated for anybody to come; it was inaccessible so you can appreciate my apprehension. We didn't even have a flight here. In '61 there was no regular flight to Udaipur. It was a question of putting the horse before the cart and my father did put the hotel in first and the rest of the infrastructure followed.

But the Lake Palace Hotel caught on very quickly, hosting a parade of celebrated guests including Her Majesty Queen Elizabeth II, America's First Lady Mrs Jacqueline Kennedy, the Shah of Iran and the King of Nepal.

In 1971 the management was taken over by India's oldest hoteliers, the Tatas, as the first hotel in the Taj luxury chain which has since spread across India and beyond.

For travellers the Lake Palace Hotel is an undeniable boon, providing an incomparable and voluptuous glimpse of the pleasures that once were the preserve of princes. To open one's eyes in dreamy freedom upon the broad waters of the Pichola as the Ranas were wont to do is a privilege not to be missed.

Architects and conservationists, however, have greeted the commercial development of Jag Niwas with less felicity. A major renovation and extension was made of the property during the 1970s which has elicited serious criticism. Most of the palaces in India that have been converted into hotels are nineteenth and early-twentieth-century structures built on the European model, with service areas, guest rooms, reception halls, salons and dining rooms, for all intents and purpose just like hotels. Jag Niwas, by contrast, was basically a garden with a number of open pavilions, built mostly in the eighteenth century. This was part of the beauty which arrested visitors and the first renovation did little to undermine it. A single bank of twenty rooms was added at the back of the island.

The most recent development of the island has almost entirely engulfed the original structure and turned the more ornamental open areas into public rooms. Most of the additional guest rooms are modern in style and indistinguishable from those in any city hotel. The architectural additions, say some critics, are utilitarian and without architectural distinction. Other critics agree with the Workmans' turn-of-the-century assessment that the architecture of Jag Niwas is 'not sufficiently good or varied to hold the attention for long', and does not warrant conservation.

The opposite side of the argument is simply that, given the dearth of government funds for archaeological preservation, most of these properties would be falling into utter ruin if they were not put to some form of commercial use, and that whatever

sacrifices have been made in the development of Jag Niwas are far outweighed by the pleasure this dream palace has given countless thousands of travellers.

Whether it is better to appreciate a palace like Jag Niwas as a ruin or as a transmogrified luxury hotel is a question that will probably never be answered rationally in modern India. The Lake Palace, for all its changes, retains an hypnotic impact that magnetizes and enchants.

SHIV NIWAS

It would seem that even in these days of change there are still Indian princes who plan dwellings such as their forefathers dreamt of in the bygone days of splendour.
Pierre Loti, *c.* 1900

Each successive generation of rulers in Udaipur made its architectural mark on the City Palace complex. The original structure was built in the sixteenth century. By the end of the nineteenth century the Maharana's palace was a city in itself, with farms, storehouses, wells and stables within its walls, capable of withstanding months of siege.

As the nineteenth century wore on, the European influence increasingly seeped into the design of the palace buildings. The Shambhu Niwas, constructed in the time of Maharana Shambhu Singh (1861-74), probably in the 1870s in the final phase of his reign, was the first blatant departure from the traditional Rajput style which had been so strictly observed in Udaipur. In 1888 *The Handbook of Meywar* characterized Shambhu Niwas as a '. . . modern villa . . . which was built in the time of the late Maharana's predecessor, Maharana Shambhu Sing, after the European fashion, commanding a very fine view of the lake beneath on the west'. The French writer Pierre Loti described Shambhu Niwas on his turn-of-the-century visit as '. . . modern, with European drawing-rooms, looking-glasses, sideboards laden with silver, and billiard-rooms, appointments which we had been far from expecting to see in so indigenous a town'.

It was for the Shambhu Niwas Palace that the celebrated suite of Belgian crystal furniture was initially purchased by Shambhu Singh's successor, the Maharana Sajjan Singh (1874-84). Fateh Lal Mehta observed in 1888 that the drawing room of Shambhu Niwas Palace was 'thoroughly furnished, having a crystal throne, chairs, table and bed. The punkha rods are cut glass with blue and purple velvet fringes.' Only later, in the reign of Maharana Fateh Singh (1884-1930), was the crystal suite moved to the newly constructed Shiv Niwas Palace.

Despite the rage for European architecture in the Raj, the effect of Shambhu Niwas was jarring, set as it was against the ravishing backdrop of Rajput traditional building. It was designed by an Englishman who, in the words of a member of the Indian press of the period, ' . . . should have been tenderly dropped into the lake at the foot of its walls'.

Although Fateh Singh did not himself live at Shambhu Niwas, his descendants have found its rococo comforts less resistible. Maharana Bhagwat Singh (1955-84), his son's successor, was in permanent residence there until his death in 1984 and his own son, Shriji Arvind Singh, has undertaken to totally restore the fading 'modern villa' to its former gorgeousness as his own princely residence.

Shiv Niwas Palace was a semicircular annexe contiguous to the larger Shambhu Niwas, overlooking a garden and the southern end of the Pichola lake, built sometime near the turn of the century by Maharana Fateh Singh at a cost of nearly six lakhs (a lakh equals 100,000) of rupees. Although it maintained many of the distinctive traditional Hindu elements that characterized the architecture of Udaipur (such as the *chajja* – an overhanging dripstone or blade which can be traced back to eleventh-century temple architecture), the spatial proportions, the arrangement of rooms and the curve of the building are distinctly European, albeit more graceful in design than its predecessor, the Shambhu Niwas. The Maharana had even sent two of his court artisans, Master Kundan Lal and Khaja Ustadh, to England; the first to study the fine art of fresco painting and the second to learn the demanding and delicate craft of glass-mosaic design. The latter, more than any other element, has given the interiors of Shiv Niwas their dazzling

aspect. When the Prince of Wales visited Udaipur in 1903, his party was enchanted by the crescent shape of Shiv Niwas and described it as 'the Diadem of the Palace'.

Following a private audience with Maharana Fateh Singh, Pierre Loti was treated to a tour of the ruler's uncompleted palace, 'perched loftily on a flat and circular space that juts out upon the lake'.

It is composed of a number of white halls and white kiosks, almost covered with festoons, and traceries of stone and marble, so placed as to overlook the varied aspects of the lake. A sumptuous staircase, lined by elephants of stone, leads down to the waters which lie embosomed amidst high and savage mountains and gloomy virgin forests. Within, mosaics of glass and porcelains of twenty different colours; in another room, aquatic plants, water-lilies, herons, and kingfishers. One room has just been finished. Here rose-coloured lotus flowers wander over the moss-green walls in a simple, antique, and formal design, which reminds us of what we call 'the new art'. In the middle of this room there is a crystal bedstead, with satin cushions of the same tone of green as the walls and velvet mattresses that match the rosy colour of the lotus flowers.

The Shiv Niwas Palace was used briefly by the Maharana Fateh Singh as his personal residence. During the reign of the Maharana Bhopal Singh (1931-55) it was employed as a palace of entertainment for royal house guests. When his adopted son Bhagwat Singh married in 1939, Shiv Niwas was given to the heir-apparent as his private residence, which he used until his ascension to the Gadi in 1955. In the late 1950s the palace was modernized and converted by Maharana Bhagwat Singh for the use of his personal guests.

There were only nine 'kiosks' or suites in the original palace, all curving round a courtyard. The first suite is adorned with many paintings. The second, third, seventh and eighth are without embellishment. The fourth, fifth, sixth and ninth were ornamented with inlaid glass mosaics. The fifth suite, which until recently housed the suite of Belgian crystal furniture, has the most intricate and beautiful of the glass-mosaic work.

Following the success of the Lake Palace Hotel, Shiv Niwas was converted by

Bhagwat Singh in 1982, and further developed by his son and heir, Arvind Singh, into what is possibly India's most luxurious and exclusive hotel. Other suites were added on a second level overlooking the courtyard and marble swimming pool, each with an open terrace facing the lake. It is one of the rare instances in India of both taste and restraint in the commercial expansion of a palace property, and it is entirely successful. Arvind Singh lived on the premises for many years in the fabulously ornate Imperial Suite until his recent move to Shambhu Niwas, personally entertaining hotel guests with princely flair.

The ornamentation of the traditional suites has been splendidly preserved. Hand-cut blue, red and turquoise coloured glass inlaid in intricate patterns in the walls and ceilings make a shimmering frame for these suites, which are crowned by matching crystal chandeliers. The polished teakwood doors are inlaid with ivory.

Having passed from princely palace to luxury hotel, Shiv Niwas remains in both setting and service the epitome of oriental swank and a reminder of the bygone days of splendour.

LAXMI VILAS PALACE

The rulers of Udaipur never fully resigned themselves to British paramountcy and made every effort to keep at arm's length the succession of colonial officers thrust upon their kingdom. This attitude was betrayed by the original location chosen for the British Political Agent's residence. The Residency was a garden house outside the city walls to the east in an area called Dabok, where Udaipur's airport now stands. Built by the Rawat of Begun, one of the noblemen of Mewar, the property was purchased by Maharana Jawan Singh (1828-38) for the sum of 10,000 rupees and converted into a palace under the supervision of a Mr Kak.

Until 1861 the British had played an intentionally peripheral role in the affairs of Udaipur from the time Colonel Tod had served as the British East India Company's agent in Mewar after the treaty between the Native State and the Paramount Power was signed in 1817. This was to change,

however, with the minority accession of Maharana Shambhu Singh (1861-74) to the Udaipur Gadi, which led to the direct involvement of the Political Agent in the governance of the state. In 1871, then, the garden palace at Dabok was converted into a permanent official residence for the British Political Agent in Udaipur.

In 1865 Louis Rousselet lived in the Residency for over two months during his visit to Udaipur and described it as 'a huge palace, surmounted by domes and extensive terraces which cover the whole summit of a hillock within a short distance of the ramparts'. A 'short distance from the ramparts' makes it seem as if the Political Agent's quarters were something of a hop, skip and jump to the City Palace, but this is misleading. While the Residency was undoubtedly pleasant and commodious, it necessitated a time-consuming journey through what David Walker described as late as 1921 as 'the usual agglomeration of miserable houses and narrow streets, the air reeking with the mingled smells of koporous fuel and joss sticks'.

For a traveller like Rousselet, on an unhurried oriental holiday, the journeys from Residency to Palace may have been a pleasant adventure. Possibly even for early political agents with a more desultory schedule the hillock palace was in a desirable location but, with British involvement in Udaipur affairs inexorably increasing as the century wore on and turned, the hapless politicals trying to keep a pulse on the City Palace must have found all the to-ing and fro-ing fantastically tedious.

In 1911 Maharana Fateh Singh finally made a slight concession to his British guests by constructing a small two-room bungalow marginally closer to the City Palace on a hill overlooking Fateh Sagar Lake for the use of Mr Wingate, the then Political Agent. Laxmi Vilas, as the bungalow was called, was hardly next door to the palace; it stood well outside the city walls to the north – still at arm's length. But the location was more convenient than the Residency in that the route to the City Palace was uncluttered and comparatively direct along the waterways connecting Fateh Sagar with the Pichola and relieved the Resident of a tortuous journey through twisting inner-city streets when his presence was required at the palace for an extended period or he was detained into the night.

For the next three decades the little bungalow remained a rest house for political agents in Udaipur until Fateh Singh's successor, Maharana Bhopal Singh, built a new residency just outside Hathi Pol Gate and converted Laxmi Vilas into a palace guest house. In 1945 Bhopal Singh completely reconstructed Laxmi Vilas, transforming it into a genuine royal guest palace for visiting princes and dignitaries. The Maharana even resided in the palace periodically, supervising renovations.

Laxmi Vilas Palace continued to be used as a guest palace after Independence until 1962, when it was acquired by the Government of India and converted into a hotel under licence to a private hotelier. In 1965 the management of the palace hotel was given over to Indian Tourism Hotel Corporation Ltd, a government company which was merged the following year with the Indian Tourist Development Corporation (ITDC). Laxmi Vilas Palace Hotel is now owned and operated as part of the ITDC-Ashok chain which in 1973 expanded the fourteen-room capacity to thirty-four rooms and added a conference hall and swimming pool.

JAIPUR

PINK CITY

But to return to Jeypore – a pink city set on the border of a blue lake, and surrounded by the low, red spurs of Aravalis – a city to see and to puzzle over. There was once a ruler of the State, called Jey Singh, who lived in the days of Aurungzeb, and did him service with foot and horse ... Knowing his own worth, he deserted the city of Amber ... and, six miles further, in the open plain, bade one Vedyadhar, his architect, build a new city, as seldom Indian city was built before – with huge streets straight as an arrow, sixty yards broad, and cross-streets broad and straight. Many years afterward the good people of America builded their towns after this pattern, but knowing nothing of Jey Singh, they took all the credit themselves.

He built himself everything that pleased him, palaces and gardens and temples, and then died...
Rudyard Kipling, *Letters of Marque*, 1887-9

Jai Singh's legacy – first named Jai Nagar in honour of himself, and only later known as Jaipur – became in many European minds the quintessential Indian city and, despite any such American plagiary, those 'cross-streets broad and straight' emanated from an ancient Indian treatise on city planning. It was an inspiration to visitors like Kipling not only for its indigenous peculiarities but for the progressive and romantic vision that was expressed within its remarkable precincts.

The House of Amber had been the first of warrior tribes to make alliance with the Mighty Mughal and thus became his leading Satrap in Rajputana and richest Imperial vassal. Aurangzeb's death and the weakening of Mughal supremacy led the formerly faithful Jai Singh to cut loose and succumb to hubris. In 1727 he ventured forth from his mountain stronghold and, flaunting independence from his declining overlords, transferred the capital to an unprotected plain. Jaipur was a dream city and its creator did indeed spin out his landscaped fantasies in stone and mortar.

By Kipling's day Jai Singh's city had developed into 'a big, bewildering, practical joke' perpetrated by his descendant Ram Singh, who painted its once-white walls pink and, 'lightened by all the lamps of British Progress', kitted out his capital with gasworks and lampposts, tramways and water pipes, carriage drives and cricket pitches, a School of Art and even a Museum – so that an Anglicized gentility had settled down against the wild, visionary formulations of her Rajput architecture and the fervid, riotous Hinduism of her people.

With Residents standing crisply in the background, the Maharajas continued in their processional splendour while colonial administrators worked fervently to re-invent the Indian city. The princely rulers of Jaipur learned well how to smoothly mix their new-found European ways with the deep dynastic traditions of their race. This strange yet graceful reconciliation of two diametrically different civilizations made Jaipur among the most exotic and irresistible of cities in the Raj.

Later, when we reached the city, and glanced down the chief avenue, smouldering in its crushed-strawberry tint, whose splendid effects were repeated; for every balcony, and every fanciful bird-cage of a snuggery countersunk in the house-fronts, and all the long lines of roofs, were crowded with people, and each crowd was an explosion of brilliant color.

Then the wide street itself, away down and down and down into the distance, was alive with gorgeously-clothed people – not still, but moving, swaying, drifting, eddying, a delirious display of all colors and all shades of color, delicate, lovely, pale, soft, strong, stunning, vivid, brilliant, a sort of storm of sweet-pea blossoms passing on the wings of a hurricane; and presently, through this storm of color, came swaying and swinging the majestic elephants, clothed in their Sunday best of gaudinesses, and the long procession of fanciful trucks freighted with their groups of curious and costly images, and then the long rear-guard of stately camels, with their picturesque riders.

For color and picturesqueness and novelty and outlandishness and sustained interest and fascination, it was the most satisfying show I had ever seen, and I suppose I shall not have the privilege of looking upon its like again.
Mark Twain, *Following the Equator*, 1897

RAM BAGH PALACE

The sprawling, lavishly appointed Ram Bagh Palace had its beginnings in the early nineteenth century as a modest garden outside the walls of the city belonging to Kesar Badaran, the chief handmaiden of Chandravatji and governess to her son, Sawai Ram Singh, the heir-apparent to the rulership of Jaipur State. Her garden was known simply by her name: Kesar Badaran-ka-Bagh – The Garden of Kesar Badaran.

When Ram Singh's father, Maharaja Sawai Jai Singh III died in 1835 under mysterious circumstances at the age of sixteen, his successor to the Gadi was only fifteen months old. There was a Rajput court tradition that until a child Maharaja passed out of minority he would not be permitted to venture outside the zenana. The British East India Company relentlessly resisted this practice in all the Native States throughout the nineteenth century for obvious reasons; some sane and some self-serving.

Clearly, the effeminate, hot-house ambience of the zenana, with its eunuchs, gossip, intrigues and treachery (Ram Singh's own adolescent father was believed to have been poisoned in his palace) was not a healthy environment for a ruler to be raised in.

At the same time, the Paramount Power realized that its paramountcy could be strengthened and maintained only by co-opting the Native chiefs and inculcating into them 'progressive' – that is, British – values. This process of indoctrination could only be carried out on a young, impressionable mind, disentangled from the conservative influences of the court. The zenana, with its matriarchal pull, its purdah system and its traditionalism (some would say backwardness), was the greatest obstacle to its implementation.

Thus the zenana became the enemy of the East India Company's representatives in the struggle over young princely hearts and minds in Indian India. One of the British strategies in this struggle was to suggest or insist that a young ruler have a palace built for himself away from the zenana.

In 1835, however, the Company's grip on Jaipur was not so firm and its policies were still unformed, so in Ram Singh's case the Political Agent simply insisted that the boy be taken away frequently from the zenana. He wanted the young prince to be brought up with discipline and the virtues of a gentleman, and to be allowed to exercize and learn the games that were so central to the British colonial concept of manliness and breeding. The Resident prevailed over the protests of conservatives at court and saw to it that Ram Singh was taken regularly to Kesar Badaran-ka-Bagh.

It is believed that the first formal structures – an enclosure and a four-room pavilion – were built on the grounds during this period, probably in 1836. Ram Singh spent much of his youth in that garden and never forgot its fragrant serenity and the freedom it afforded him. When Kesar Badaran died without issue in 1856 the property became *khalsa* – that is, it automatically reverted to the state. In this way Maharaja Sawai Ram Singh II (1835-80) acquired the garden, which became thereafter Ram Bagh – The Garden of Ram – and served increasingly as Ram Singh's favourite retreat. Ram Bagh was used variously as the Maharaja's rest house outside the city walls, a hunting lodge and an official guest house.

If anything, the importance of Ram Bagh increased in the reign of Ram Singh's adopted successor, Madho Singh (1880-1922). More rooms were built in 1887 to accommodate the Maharaja's guests and Ram Bagh was transformed into a luxurious twenty-six-room mansion. The mansion was further expanded into a ranging palatial country guest house to plans drawn up by the extraordinary Sir Samuel Swinton Jacob, who served the Jaipur State government as Chief Engineer and Director of the Public Works Department from 1867 until he retired from service in 1902. Throughout that period he distinguished himself – largely outside Jaipur, it must be said – for his attempts to revive local architectural styles and thus became known as a leading exponent of what has come to be called, slightly inaccurately, the Indo-Saracenic style. Jacob was particularly attached to Rajput architecture and had completed a comprehensive study of the architectural details of the city's traditional buildings.

After Jacob's retirement Madho Singh asked him to stay on as a superintending engineer and then, from 1905 to 1911, as his personal adviser. It was during this last period that designs were made for the extension of Ram Bagh which included ten bedroom suites, a dining room and a reading room with one spacious reception room in each of the palace's three wings and verandahs. The Indo-Saracenic aspect of Jacob's work was in the ornamental detailing and Ram Bagh was sumptuously decorated with hand-carved marble *jaalis*, sandstone balustrades and *chattris*.

Construction was carried out not under Jacob's old Public Works Department but under the Raj Imarat, which was responsible for royal construction projects and under the supervision of his protégé Lala Chiman Lal. The state Public Works *Annual Report* for 1909 written by Chiman Lal makes passing reference to the construction of a royal guest house at Ram Bagh under the supervision of the Raj Imarat. By 1911 Jacob was serving as a consultant to the Delhi Town Planning Commission assigned to create the massive new imperial capital and undoubtedly while at Delhi he kept abreast of the work going on at Ram Bagh.

In 1913 the work on Ram Bagh was still in progress as there continued to be references to it in the state public works reports. In that year Jacob had been appointed as one of a triumvirate of architects to design New Delhi, along with Herbert Baker and Edwin Lutyens. It was a doomed alliance and inevitable that he and Lutyens would clash. Lutyens refused to believe that there was such a thing as Indian architecture and considered vulgar and shoddy the Indo-Saracenic style epitomized by Jacob's work. As for Jacob, Lutyens found him 'personally a dear old gentleman' with 'no architectural ability at all' and it is not surprising that Jacob withdrew from the project only six months after signing on, retiring to England, where he died in 1917. Sir Swinton Jacob's designs for Ram Bagh Palace are among the best of his attempts at synthesizing European and Indian architecture into the Indo-Saracenic style and represent one of his last realized works in India.

In 1922 Sawai Madho Singh died, leaving the State of Jaipur to be ruled by his eleven-year-old surrogate son, Sawai Man Singh II, and in its cyclical fashion history repeated itself. Just as in Sawai Ram Singh's time, when the British resident had decided the zenana was no place for a growing ruler, Man Singh's guardian, Sir James Roberts, felt that the Prince must be given a proper education away from the women and a month after the Maharaja's death Sir James converted Ram Bagh Palace into a school for the growing Maharaja. At first there were twenty-three boys from the finest families of Jaipur but when the lads became too boisterous under Roberts' rough-and-ready tutelage, a Mr Mayne from Rajkot College was sent for, the class was cut to six students and Man Singh's subsequent studies were carried out with more decorum.

Just as Ram Singh developed a great attachment to Ram Bagh dating from his youthful years on its open premises, so did Man Singh; so much so that even before he reached majority he made Ram Bagh his official residence and on 20 January 1925 the garden-cum-country-manor-cum-guest-house-cum-school finally became a royal palace. Forty lakhs of rupees were spent on preparing the property for the young Maharaja's permanent presence. A modern cooling plant was installed to replace the ancient system of spraying screens of *khas*, or vetiver root, with water to cool the warm breezes circulating throughout the palace.

By this time Man Singh had already been married two years and although the Maharani, a sister of the Maharaja of Jodhpur, lived separately in quarters at the City Palace, it was thought that Ram Bagh, which had until that time lacked a zenana, should now have its own wing for the women of Man Singh's court. It was during this period that the U-shaped wing which looks out over the wide expanse of gardens was constructed for this purpose. Over the next decade Man Singh continued to expand his palace, further enlarging it with a new dining hall which he had had designed in London. With each succeeding year Ram Bagh became ever more luxurious, evolving into a vortex for European and princely society, enhanced by the Maharaja's dashing and athletic reputation as one of India's premier polo-players. Thus Ram Bagh Palace served as the chic and festive

official residence of the last ruling Maharaja of Jaipur, who was known to intimates as Jai. The City Palace remained the centre for ceremonial functions but Ram Bagh was the ruler's real home.

When Man Singh took the ravishing and relatively liberated Princess Gayatri Devi from Cooch Behar as his third wife in 1940, Ram Bagh became an even more glamorous princely palace on the pleasure circuit of the Raj. Her Highness Gayatri Devi, today known as Rajmata, or Queen Mother, of Jaipur, was the only one of Man Singh's wives to have been raised without the restrictions of purdah. Sensitive to his young wife's background and tacitly hoping by her presence to bring the women of his court and society out of purdah altogether, the Maharaja set up his bride in apartments in Ram Bagh outside the traditional zenana where the Maharani's co-wives lived.

For the young Maharani, 'Ram Bagh meant a pleasantly informal life where I was not expected to be in purdah although, as a married woman, I had to cover my head when I wore a sari.' Until a recent renovation, Ram Bagh remained almost exactly as the Princess remembered it and well-heeled guests could, at a price, approximate the luxury in which she lived.

Gayatri Devi and Man Singh were married on the eve of war and as Jaipur's only 'liberated princess', the twenty-one-year-old bride was plunged into wartime activities and, with the blessing of her absent husband stationed away with his troops, the administration of Ram Bagh's household affairs. In her autobiography, *A Princess Remembers*, she has provided a vivid picture of the way in which a palace was run and why many of the later palaces of the Raj were so easily adapted for use as hotels:

There were something over four hundred servants at Rambagh, and while Jai wanted to eliminate unnecessary extravagance, he had a military eye for detail and expected everything to be perfectly run. The guards at the nine gates, for example, were inspected at regular intervals. All the gardens had to be impecccably maintained. At various points throughout the palace, groups of boys were posted to prevent the many pigeons from settling or causing damage to the buildings.

The household and its running fell into two general departments. It was the function of the Comptroller to order the stores and maintain the store-rooms, make the menus, and issue the supplies to fulfil the day's needs. He was also in charge of the linen, including the uniforms of the staff. He acted as a sort of super-housekeeper, seeing to the general running of the palace. He had several people under him to handle such duties as attending to the laundry or collecting the vegetables, milk, and eggs from the farm that supplied the needs of Rambagh.

The other branch of the household was headed by the Military Secretary. It was his job to keep the building itself in perfect condition, see to any repairs that might be needed, and supervise the grounds and gardens, which had to be maintained in as flawless a condition as the building. He was in charge of cars for the constant flow of guests that we used to have in Rambagh, though he had an assistant to supervise the care of the garages and cars, just as another assistant was in charge of the day-to-day work in the gardens. Whenever we entertained – as we did a great deal – the Military Secretary would have to coordinate plans with the Comptroller in assigning rooms to the guests, seeing to meals and seating arrangements, and organizing activities for them. The ADCs also took their orders from the Military Secretary as to when they were on duty or which of them was assigned to attend a visiting nobleman or some other guest. Jai himself always had three ADCs on duty with him. Jo Didi [Man Singh's second wife] and I each had one for the day and one at night. All these timings were worked out by the Military Secretary.

Finally, apart from the household itself, there were the people in charge of the shoots, who arranged for such things as providing bait for the tigers and getting beaters ready.

Throughout the 1940s, the royal routine of Ram Bagh continued more or less as it always had, until, following India's independence in 1947, the state of Jaipur was merged with Jodhpur, Jaisalmer and Bikaner to become the Greater Rajasthan Union in 1949. As ruler of the largest, richest and most powerful of Rajput states, Man Singh was given the compensatory and largely ceremonial honour of acting as Rajpramukh or Head of State of the Union, with Jaipur as Rajasthan's state capital. Ram Bagh Palace thus became the official government residence of the Rajpramukh, which, through the early years of the 1950s, remained a centre for the state's official entertainment.

Although Man Singh had been appointed Rajpramukh for life, in 1956 his office was abruptly eliminated. The gradual erosion of the princes' prerogatives was accelerating and Man Singh, a seasoned pragmatist, made moves to reduce his expenses and prepare his family for the inevitable loss of wealth and privilege that was in store for all the princely dynasties of India.

The year after his dismissal as governor of Rajasthan, Man Singh set about converting his beloved home into the state's first luxury hotel. At first he did so surreptitiously for fear of upsetting his family. When they found out, they were indeed thunderstruck. 'We were speechless,' wrote Gayatri Devi:

Jai patiently went on explaining that times had changed and that it was no longer possible to keep Rambagh in the way that it had always been, and deserved to be, maintained. He also felt that now he was no longer Rajpramukh, or even the ruler of Jaipur, it was unnecessary for us to live in our previous style. If Rambagh was to be kept up in a proper way, it would have to be given up for a public cause. Jaipur badly needed a good hotel.

I was wretched, and so was Jo Didi when she heard the news. We had both come to Rambagh as brides. For nearly half my life – longer for Jo Didi – Rambagh had been the center of my activities and of my allegiance. It was my home. We both pleaded with Jai to change his mind, but he remained determined. Other Maharajas were critical of Jai when they heard of the project. It seemed like such a concrete symbol of our vanishing way of life.

On 8 December 1957 the Ram Bagh Palace Hotel was formally opened and the Maharaja of Jaipur became the first active princely hotelier in India, setting a trend which has continued down to the present day. Still, the Maharani had a difficult time accepting the fact that her beloved former home was now open to the public:

For a long time I could not accustom myself to the idea that people could come and go as they pleased in our old home, and Jai used to complain, half amused and half irritated, that I treated the hotel guests as interlopers. On one occasion, before our swimming pool at Rajmahal was ready, he came along to the Rambagh pool to discover one of my maids posted outside to keep the hotel guests away while I took my morning swim. After that, he

insisted that I really had to come to terms with the fact that, as long as the hotel guests paid their bills, they had as much right to be in the palace as I had.

Ram Bagh Palace was expanded in 1968, from twenty-six rooms to eighty and, in 1972, came under the management of the Taj Group of Hotels.

MAJI-KA-BAGH
Raj Mahal Palace Hotel

In 1729 a small palace was constructed in a walled garden set on the outskirts of Sawai Jai Singh's new city. The garden palace was for Jai Singh's wife of twenty years, Maji Shree Ranawatji Sahiba, a princess from Udaipur known in Jaipur history as the Sisodia Rani, after the name of her Rajput clan. This palace was subsequently known as Maji-ka-Bagh – the Queen Mother's Garden – but the Sisodia Rani's first sojourn there was cut short for, suspecting that her unborn child would be put to death, she sought safe haven in her homeland from the treacheries of the Jaipur court. She returned to live within her garden palace but not before two decades had elapsed and fratricidal war and intrigue had brought the proud kingdom that Jai Singh had so skilfully consolidated to the brink of prostration.

There had never been any traditions of marriage between the Sisodias of Udaipur and the Kachhwahas of Amber. Indeed, relations between the rival Rajput kingdoms had been venomous since 1576 when Man Singh I of Amber rode out with Akbar's armies against the Sisodia Rana Pratap Singh. The Sisodias despised the Amber dynasty for collaborating with the hated Mughal and held them in even greater contempt for having given up their daughters in marriage to Muslim kings. However, in the aftermath of the emperor Aurangzeb's death in 1707 a series of events led to a rapprochement between the rulers which culminated in the marriage of Jai Singh to the Sisodia Rani.

A battle for succession to the Mughal throne had erupted between Aurangzeb's two sons and in this Sawai Jai Singh backed the wrong man. Bahadur Shah defeated his brother Azam Shah at Agra and, although

Jai Singh had judiciously shifted his support to the winning side while combat was still raging, the ascendant emperor, who assumed the name of Shah Alam, never fully trusted his Rajput general again. By way of punishment and to halt a rising Rajput defiance to Mughal authority, Shah Alam confiscated Jai Singh's capital at Amber, renaming it Mu'minabad.

In consequence, Sawai Jai Singh entered into collusion with Ajit Singh of Jodhpur, whose father had suffered similar forfeiture during Aurangzeb's reign. Both disenfranchized rulers set out together toward Udaipur to seek a tripartite alliance with Rana Amar Singh II to recover their lost dominions. The Sisodia Rana welcomed the prodigal Rajput chiefs and sealed their alliance by giving his sister in marriage to Ajit Singh of Jodhpur and his daughter to Sawai Jai Singh.

With the upper hand in this affiliation, Amar Singh stipulated five conditions within the marriage contracts which were drawn up:
1 The Rajas had to agree to accept whatever their brides would say to them.
2 They had to demonstrate greater respect toward the Udaipur princesses than toward their other wives.
3 They had to pass all festival nights with their new brides.
4 Upon return from every battle they had to proceed straight to their Sisodia ranis and reside with them.
5 The palanquins of these honoured brides would precede in every ceremonial procession.

These marks of honour were innocuous enough but there was one other implicit and more costly catch to this arrangement: the male children from these marriages would take preference in succession to the thrones of both kingdoms over any older sons from senior wives. It was a measure of their desperation that the rulers acquiesced to this condition and it was a decision which would have devastating consequences for Jaipur.

Sawai Jai Singh's marriage was duly celebrated (fortunately for Ajit Singh and Jodhpur, his nuptials were postponed and never performed) and in 1708 the combined Rajput forces from Jaipur, Jodhpur and Udaipur marched out to retake by force of arms first Jodhpur and then Amber. Entangled as he was with a more serious insurgency in the south, Shah Alam was not in a position to move against his rebellious Rajput vassals. They seized their capitals back and the emperor could do nothing but validate the *fait accompli*.

From that time the disintegration of the Mughal empire accelerated and Sawai Jai Singh began to build up his kingdom from its random fragments, expanding his territories to cover over 50,000 square miles. He consolidated his dominions, created his new capital and built a garden palace outside its walls for his princess from Udaipur.

It is probable that the Sisodia Rani insisted upon living at a distance from the other Jaipur queens as a natural precaution against the endemic treachery of the zenana. This may even have been an additional implicit condition in her marriage arrangement; the fact that none of Jai Singh's other ranis received a similar consideration seems to confirm this but nothing is recorded to the effect. What is certain is that when the Udaipur princess conceived a child she had good reason to suspect that it would not be allowed to live and that she removed to Udaipur because of this.

In the two decades between the marital alliance of the two Rajput houses and the building of Jaipur, it had become clear that Sawai Jai Singh had set his sights on his second son, Ishwari, becoming his successor. This preference took on an altogether more sinister cast when Jai Singh's oldest son, Shiv, died mysteriously in 1724, either poisoned or thrown from the tower of Jaigarh above the Amber Fort, according to which rumour one believed. Whether the son's murder had been instigated by Jai Singh himself or by Ishwari was irrelevant, for Ishwari Singh was now in place as heir-apparent to the Jaipur Gadi and seemed certain to succeed his father. Then in 1730, after over twenty years of marriage, the Sisodia Rani conceived a child and the issue of succession became a threatening reality.

In 1731 Madho Singh was born, some say in Maji-ka-Bagh but it is more likely that the birth took place in Udaipur under the protection and care of the Sisodia Rani's brother Rana Sangram Singh II (1710-34). Madho Singh was raised in Udaipur.

Sawai Jai Singh died in 1743, leaving the throne to Sawai Ishwari Singh (1743-50). Before he passed away he tried to appease Madho Singh, his mother and her clan by offering to divide his kingdom between his two sons, but this gesture was rejected and his chosen successor was destined to spend the entirety of his reign fending off attacks by the Sisodias and their allies.

After seven years of war, his treasury exhausted, his nobility secretly in sympathy with his enemy and refusing to mobilize their military forces, Sawai Ishwari Singh found his undefended city surrounded by Maratha armies in alliance with Madho Singh and committed suicide by swallowing poison and offering himself to the fangs of a cobra.

Thus in 1750 the Sisodia Rani returned to Jaipur in triumph, the mother of its ruler, to live out her remaining years in her garden palace which was thereafter known as Maji-ka-Bagh. It was a hollow victory, for the kingdom she had returned to was no longer what it had been in her husband's time. Civil war had drained the state and made it vulnerable to successive Maratha aggressions, ultimately driving Jaipur kingdom into the British fold.

Maji-ka-Bagh was used as a garden palace for various members of the ruling family until 1821, when the British East India Company first installed a permanent Resident in Jaipur, at which time the property was given over for the residence of Captain Stewart, Jaipur's first Political Agent.

Although the palace was subsequently referred to as the 'Residency' or the 'Residency Bungalow', the original name remained. The nineteenth-century French traveller Louis Rousselet, visiting Jaipur in the 1860s, recorded that:

Independently of the Court, we had a charming little society round the residence of Ma-je-ka-Baugh, which comprises three gentlemen, as many ladies, and lots of children . . . and the king's excellent band, led by a worthy German, M. Bocker, played in the delightful gardens of the Political Agent when a select party assembled on the lawn.

Aside from their role in the official history of the Raj, the delightful gardens of Maji-ka-Bagh have had the additional distinction of serving as the site of the first cricket match ever played in northern India, under the personal supervision of the Resident.

In 1904 a Mr G.A. Mathews took his wife on an autumnal Indian tour and in his diary recorded his impressions of the Residency at Maji-ka-Bagh:

October 4th – We found a letter awaiting us from the Resident inviting us to call on him next morning, so after chota haziri *[early-morning tea] and a late breakfast, to say nothing of our first experience of an Indian bath, we started off in a carriage to the Residency.*

It was only a few minutes' drive when we found ourselves opposite a strikingly handsome gateway copied from the Ganesh Pole at Amber, and having passed through into a beautiful garden we were soon at a standstill outside the Residency itself. As we drove through the lovely grounds and caught our first glimpse of the palatial Eastern structure in front we experienced an unaccountable feeling of awe at the sight of such inconceivable grandeur, and a doubt as to whether we should demean ourselves with sufficient decorum amid such surroundings caused us considerable uneasiness.

With Independence, the Residency was vacated by its British lodgers and became briefly the residence of the third and last Indian Dewan, or Prime Minister, of twentieth-century Jaipur, Sir Venkatachari, who moved from Jai Mahal in 1948 and lived in Maji-ka-Bagh until 1949, when his office was disbanded with the merging of Jaipur State into the Greater Rajasthan Union.

The property remained empty and unused until Sawai Man Singh II (1922-49) decided to convert his own residential palace, Ram Bagh, into a luxury hotel and move into the smaller Maji-ka-Bagh. Between 1956 and 1959 the Maharaja's new residence was completely renovated and redubbed Raj Mahal Palace. From 1959 until his death in 1970 this palace was the domicile of the last hereditary ruler of Jaipur.

Throughout that period Raj Mahal accommodated aristocracy of the old order and the new, from Queen Elizabeth II when she visited Jaipur in 1960 to Mrs Jacqueline Kennedy. America's First Lady stayed as the private guest of the Maharaja and

Maharani despite the protests of the US Ambassador John Kenneth Galbraith, who was afraid to offend the Congress government by allowing the Maharaja, whose wife was a popular opposition MP, to make what he considered to be political capital out of the visit.

Raj Mahal remained a royal palace until 1976 when it was converted into a hotel, at first operated directly by the royal family. In 1984 management was handed over to the Taj Group, which has made plans for a major reconstruction of the property. Until this takes place the palace, with its eleven large suites, remains unretouched and fading – an ageing memory wherein one can perhaps sense the resonance of what royal hospitality must have been like in those last evaporating days of princely protocol in India.

NATANI-KA-BAGH
Jai Mahal Palace Hotel

The property presently known as Jai Mahal Palace was probably first developed in around 1745, during the reign of Sawai Ishwari Singh (1743-50), by the Raja's Military Commander and Prime Minister Hargovind Natani, and has since then always been referred to as Natani-ka-Bagh, the Garden of Natani.

Hargovind Natani is a complex figure in Jaipur history. He was undeniably an outstanding military commander and an accomplished administrator who served Sawai Ishwari Singh with distinction in both capacities throughout most of his reign, but he is also known as something of a traitor. Natani was not from the warrior caste of Kshatriya Rajputs but emerged from the lower trading castes and proved himself to be, in the words of one eighteenth-century chronicler, 'an exceptionally brave and able general'. It was Natani who in 1747 led the Jaipur armies to victory at Rajmahal in the district of Tonk against the onslaught of Madho Singh's powerful coalition of forces from Udaipur, Kota, Bundi and the Marathas of Holkar. It was one of the only triumphs in the beleaguered and tragic raj of Sawai Ishwari Singh and was commemorated accordingly with a victory tower called Ishwar Lat which overlooked Natani's town house in Chhoti Chopar.

According to a contemporary report, the battle of Rajmahal

began at noon on Sunday the 1st of March and ended at sunset the next day. The allies were completely defeated, though both sides suffered heavily. Each contingent of this ill-knit army had been attacked and routed in succession through the skilful planning and personal leadership of Hargovind.

In consequence of this and other heroic services to the Gadi, Hargovind Natani was elevated to the position of Dewan, or Prime Minister, of Jaipur. Within three years, however, the tide had turned against Ishwari Singh, and Natani, along with most of the nobility of the Jaipur durbar, had secretly cast his lot with the enemy and betrayed his sovereign. It is said that Natani persuaded the Raja to deploy his entire army to crush a non-existent insurgency in the Sheikhawati region, leaving Jaipur undefended. He then passed word of this diversion to Madho Singh, who set loose his Maratha allies to surround Jaipur City, leading to its ruler's suicide.

When Sawai Madho Singh marched into Jaipur upon Ishwari's death, it was Hargovind Natani who supervised the peaceful transference of power and he remained in place as the new Raja's Dewan.

Subsequent to this event, quite possibly long after Natani had passed away, his hereditary properties, including Natani-ka-Bagh, became *khalsa* – that is, they reverted to the state. In Jaipur a property only became *khalsa* for one of two reasons: either the owner died without issue or was disgraced in some way and had his property seized as a punishment or part of a punishment which often included exile. Since descendants of Hargovind Natani exist, we know he did not die without issue. This has led local historians to speculate that Natani's properties were seized by the state because of some very serious offence and since nothing is recorded concerning this event it has been mooted that the properties were taken posthumously in retaliation for Natani's part in the betrayal of Ishwari Singh. Whatever the case, Natani-ka-Bagh became a princely property and remains so to the present day.

How it was used once it reverted to the state is unknown until sometime in the 1860s when it was given over for use as the Residency Surgeon's house. One of the occupants was Dr Thomas Holbein Hendley, a physician dedicated to bringing 'every man in the State within twenty miles of a dispensary – and I've nearly done it'. Hendley also acted as the Political Agent for a time but he has left his mark on Indian history not as a doctor or as a government official but as Jaipur's pre-eminent art historian. He organized the first Jaipur Exhibition in 1883 and became curator of the Jaipur City Museum, which was much appreciated by Rudyard Kipling on his visit to Jaipur.

During Hendley's tenancy, in January 1881, a meteorological observatory was established adjacent to Natani-ka-Bagh which measured rainfall, the temperature of the soil, and the velocity, force and direction of the wind. This observatory was eventually incorporated into the gardens of the palace and there is still a dilapidated tower at the bottom of the garden which formed a part of the installation.

After Sawai Man Singh II (1922-47) became ruler of Jaipur State, Natani-ka-Bagh became the official residence of the Prime Ministers of Jaipur including Sir Beauchamp St John (1933-39), Raja Gyan Nath (1939-42) and Sir Mirza Ismail (1942-47). The palace continued to be used in this capacity until 1948 when Jaipur's last Dewan, Sir Venkatachari, decided that he would rather live in the abandoned Residency at Maji-ka-Bagh.

At some point during this period Maharaja Sawai Man Singh invested Natani-ka-Bagh with a new name, Jai Mahal. It is unclear whether the name was given in honour of his second son, Jai (nicknamed Joey), his great ancestor, Sawai Jai Singh II, or simply named after the city itself.

Between 1948 and 1955 Jai Mahal Palace remained uninhabited but in 1950 a chance meeting in New York City led to its conversion into one of India's earliest palace hotels. Laxmi Kumar Kasliwal, proprietor of the Gem Palace, one of Jaipur's leading jewellery houses, was passing through Manhattan and learned that Sawai Man Singh was also visiting the city and residing at Hotel Hampshire House. The jeweller dropped by to pay a courtesy call on the Maharaja and in the course of conversation the subject of hotels came up. Kasliwal remembers that he mentioned to Man Singh that there was not a decent hotel in Jaipur City with which to accommodate the growing tourist traffic:

Up to that time there was only a makeshift hotel for tourists called Khasa Kothi which had formerly been one of the Maharaja's guest houses. I suggested that we badly needed a good hotel in the city. He said, 'But who will invest that kind of money to build a new hotel in Jaipur?' So I suggested that if he allowed me to use one of his empty palaces I would take up the venture. My idea was that a good hotel in Jaipur would attract tourists and that the tourists would then patronize my business.

After the office of the Dewan had been abolished Jai Mahal Palace was designated by the government as personal property of the Maharaja and was at that time lying vacant, so he agreed to let me convert it into a hotel. Back in Jaipur we discussed the matter again and he asked for Rs. 12,000 per year which was about Rs. 2,000 more than his budget for maintaining the property.

But he set one condition: that I retain his staff working there. Some of these men were eighty years old but I was happy to keep them because they were really faithful. They were a legacy of the feudal times and never complained about how many hours they had been working – they were an asset. The gardener, for example, had served five Prime Ministers in Jai Mahal.

In fact, there was no written contract or agreement between us for a long time. He asked me once, 'What happens if my family needs the property?' I said, 'It will be returned.' And I kept my word. Legally they couldn't have evicted me because in post-Independence India there is a Rent Control Act and the tenant has a greater right than the owner does.

So I took it over and made extensions to the property. When the remodelling was going on I had instructions to be available at eight o'clock every morning to meet the Maharaja who came every day to see that nothing was built which did not harmonize with the original structure. The Maharaja would arrive in the company of his personal architect Durga Lal Nandiwal, who had designed the extensions.

Nandiwal had been a disciple of one of the proteges of the late Colonel Sir Swinton Jacob. [see

Left Wrote Colonel Tod of Jag Niwas and its princely proprietors c. 1829: 'Here they listened to the tale of the bard and slept off their noonday opiate amidst the cool breezes of the lake.

Below Sajjan Vilas was a relatively late addition to Jag Niwas, built as a pavilion between 1874 and 1884 by Maharana Sajjan Singh with hand-painted scenes from mythology and nature traditional to Rajput ornamentation.

Left The curve of Shiv Niwas reflects the rising European influence in Udaipur at the turn of the century.

Above and below Rambagh Palace. Special rooms featuring various cultural styles of the day were high Raj fashion. Chinoiserie was a favourite.

Above Natani Kabagh evolved from 18th century pleasure garden to residence for British officials and Jaipur's prime ministers. In the 1940s Maharaja Man Singh II renamed it Jai Mahal Palace.

Left Narain Niwas was originally developed in the 1880s as a suburban garden house for the Kanota family. The palace was constructed between 1928 and 1934 replete with Rajput flourishes, Raj furnishings and traditional Jaipur painted wall decor.

Right The original
Samode Palace was
built as a fortress in the
16th century but
reached its glory
during the 19th
century when the
Nathawat clan
virtually ruled the
Jaipur durbar. Today
it is one of the most
beautiful and
successful palace hotels
in India.

Below The Sheesh
Mahal, or glass palace,
was one of the
additions made by
Thakur Sheo Singh
during his tenure as
Prime Minister of
Jaipur in the mid-19th
century.

page 21] and he was a master in designing domes. He was very old even then and he lived all the way into the 1970s. The Maharaja was very fond of him. Now, I have seen both periods, before and after Independence and this old man, he was a real product of the feudal period. He used to call the Maharaja 'Huzoor Sahib' which was the old way of addressing the ruler and he was very devoted to him. One day we were out on the site of Jai Mahal and Nandiwal made a suggestion to build a tower or something like that and the Maharaja just looked at him and said in the local dialect 'Bewuqouf!', which means basically, 'You are an idiot!' It's very insulting. The Maharaja then walked on a little further; he had a limp from a riding accident while he was playing polo, so he limped ahead of us. And then Durga Lal came up to me and whispered, full of pride, 'You see how much he loves me?' It was a sign of affection. That was considered a special treatment, you see?

Alterations to Jai Mahal were made between 1952 and 1955. The Maharaja was preoccupied during this period as Rajpramukh (Governor) of the Rajasthan Union and with extensive travelling and took decisions on Jai Mahal very slowly. Finally, in December 1955, the palace opened its doors as a hotel. Its first guests were the entourage of Nikita Khrushchev and Nikolai Bulganin. Until 1957, when Ram Bagh Palace opened as a luxury hotel, Jai Mahal Palace was Jaipur's leading hotel.

In 1962 a formal contract for twenty years was finally signed between the royal family of Jaipur and the Kasliwals naming Jagat Singh, the Maharaja's youngest son by Maharani Gayatri Devi, as owner of Jai Mahal Palace. This was the first time the Kasliwals knew who actually owned the property.

In 1967 Didi Contractor, an American artist who had designed the interiors of the Lake Palace Hotel in Udaipur (see page 15), was called in to consult on some renovations Mr Kasliwal had in mind. Ms Contractor remembers that even in 1967 almost all the architectural features of the building had been covered over.

Only really had this feeling that the building had been used as a government office or something. You could see that it was a beautiful old building a character and that the character had been obscured.

In Udaipur I used to sit with the hereditary palace carpenter and learn how to diagram space – you know, how to determine various different curves and the width and height of pillars. When I saw an arch in Jai Mahal that had previously been exposed *[in what is now the Rang Mahal bar]*, I knew immediately that its structure was based on a system of eight and that the columns had to be four pedestals and moving in a colonnade. So I had them break the wall open. It was very exciting, the moment when the colonnade emerged. It was very beautiful! Hidden in there was a beautiful building with lots and lots of overlaying construction. Periods and layers.

In 1976 Rajmata Gayatri Devi asked the Kasliwals to vacate Jai Mahal Palace so that it could be used as a private residence and the jeweller, true to his word to her late husband, complied. For one reason or another the property was never used and lay empty and unattended for nearly a decade until in 1984 it was turned over to the Taj Hotel group to totally renovate and manage.

Surjit Dhillon, who was brought in to supervise the development and to take over as general manager when the luxury hotel opened, remembers that the building 'was in a shambles. All the doors, chandeliers, curtain rails, fixtures were all taken away. Only one room was locked with some dining furniture remaining.'

In 1985 construction commenced and was finished in May 1986. Forty rooms had been completed at that time and within six months another sixty rooms were added. Aside from the unfortunate use of square picture windows in the new wing, the construction is admirably harmonious with and almost indistinguishable from the original building. The structural integrity of the older buildings has been retained and the palatial character restored in the renovation. Jai Mahal Palace is probably the most successful palace adaptation undertaken by the Taj Group.

More impressive than the structure itself are the newly landscaped gardens of the palace. In 1988 Elizabeth Moynihan, wife of the US Senator (and former Ambassador to India) Daniel Patrick Moynihan and the author of an exceptional study of Persian and Mughal landscaping, *Paradise as a*

Garden, designed a terraced Mughal garden to be landscaped on the extensive grounds of Jai Mahal Palace, inspired by and using elements from Babur's Lotus Garden of Dholpur.

The Jai Mahal garden features a tiered watercourse cascading past stone pavilions into fountained pools and interlinked by red stone steps and walkways. It is the most elaborate and expensive recreation of a traditional Mughal garden made in modern times and is one of the most charming adornments of any restoration and commercial development among India's princely palaces.

NAHAR GARH

The siting of Jaipur City reflected Sawai Jai Singh's refined command of military strategy for although it was indeed set out on the open flatlands, the city was surrounded on the north, south and east by stony hills perfect for defensive fortifications. In 1734, seven years after his new capital was constructed, Jai Singh began to build a massive fort upon the northern eminence, the highest and nearest of these surrounding hills, which he named Sudarshahnagadh in remembrance of Lord Vishnu's protective ring which concealed a powerful weapon.

Rajput history is infused with tales of the unseen – an effluvium of devas, demons, avatars and ghosts interacting with ordinary mortals who have left behind them fortresses, folklore and glory. One such legend has attached itself to these ramparts. There are five martyred warriors from the Amber dynasty who are believed to haunt Jaipur and are known as Bhomias. One of these ancestral wraiths was Naharsingh Bhomia. He was said to have been long settled upon the rugged precipice which Sawai Jai Singh suddenly expropriated to build his fortifications. Naharsingh Bhomia was understandably put out by this encroachment on his terrain and launched a campaign of ectoplasmic sabotage to drive the trespassers away. Whatever was constructed during the day would be dismantled by the ghost at night. This irritating cycle continued until the baffled ruler beseeched Pondrik Mahabhag, the

Mahaswami of Jaipur, to intercede for him with Naharsingh Bhomia.

The holy man ascended the mountain in the dead of night carrying oblations for the disgruntled spirit. Upon meeting Naharsingh Bhomia the swami made his offerings and asked if he could tie a sacred thread to the ghostly wrist. Once the thread was tied the Brahmin priest delicately ventured to request Naharsingh to vacate his home for the sake of Jai Singh's ramparts, promising in exchange to have the ruler construct a temple upon the ridge in his memory and to make another dwelling for him. Naharsingh Bhomia was apparently mollified, for he moved his home to a site the ruler constructed for him along the road to Agra. The fortress was completed and renamed Nahar Garh, in honour of the ghost.

The main crenellated parapet extending across the ridge was built in Sawai Jai Singh's time and used throughout the long turbulent period that followed the ruler's death for fending off successive attacks from the Sisodias and Marathas. Nahargarh was also used as the repository for the treasures of Jaipur kingdom and even the highest state officials could only approach the fortification blindfolded.

With the cessation of hostilities in the Pax Brittania, the importance of the fort diminished and in the 1880s Maharaja Sawai Madho Singh decided to transform Nahar Garh into a retreat for the monsoon season. He ordered the Raj Imarat in charge of constructing all royal properties to draw up plans to design a pleasure palace within the fortress walls. Two-storey apartments for each of the Maharaja's nine wives were set around three sides of a rectangular courtyard. The ruler's personal living quarters formed the fourth side. The architecture was fundamentally of the traditional style with interpolations of European elements like rectangular windows, and utilities like Western-style toilets. There was also a European sense of order in the arrangement of the apartments around the court, with the name of each Rani inscribed above her door. The designs were created by an engineer in the Raj Imarat by the name of Thakur Fateh Singh and their construction cost two and a half lakhs of rupees.

Madho Singh's successor, Sawai Man

Singh, had only three wives, lived a more thoroughly European lifestyle revolving around Ram Bagh Palace and found little use for the lovely but inconveniently placed palace apartments in Nahar Garh. The fort continued to retain some ceremonial importance and legends continued to circulate as to the riches concealed within its walls but only the Maharajas of Jaipur were privy to the secrets of their wealth.

With Independence, Nahar Garh was mooted for a number of civil and military usages but was left more or less to crumble. The deterioration has hardly been arrested by its opening as one of Jaipur's tourist attractions and one of the city's most popular rendezvous for young lovers. It is preserved, in a manner of speaking, under the authority of the Archaeological Survey, and the Rajasthan Tourism Development Corporation runs a snack-bar concession and one room for overnight guests in the fort, commanding a superb view of the city below.

There has been a proposal to turn Madho Singh's nineteenth-century zenana within the ancient ruin into a luxury hotel but this has inevitably met with fierce resistance from conservationists who want the state to develop the property as a parkland area. The controversy may well arrest any sort of development scheme for quite some time. Nahar Garh is most likely to remain in bureaucratic oblivion, inexorably deteriorating as tourists tramp across its desiccated remains, admire the views and conjure images of marching armies and departed ghosts.

A THAKUR AT HOME

He lives amid a curious pile that towers/Above the mud-built dwellings of the herd./Whose friend he is and chief of earthly powers./The sorcerer's spell, the Brahman's blighting word/Maintain their sway beside his easy rule,/And no one seems to feel the Thakur's thrall,/For, save our modern thing, the Government School,/Time-honoured custom is the lord of all./The sun goes down on droves of goats and kine/Streaming within the village gates: the moon/Looks on the Thakur boosing o'er his wine/And lulled by beat of drum in endless tune./Contentment holds the village and its chief:/The scene is one of dirt, but not of grief.

Col. G.H. Trevor, *Rhymes of Rajputana*, 1894

The *thakur* was, approximately, the Indian equivalent of a medieval feudal baron, living as lord and master of his estate, but owing tribute and allegiance to a sovereign overlord, usually but not always the chief of his clan. This landed aristocracy, commanding a patchwork of agrarian territories within a princely state, formed the bulwark of Indian India and the backbone of its traditional structure.

In the days of war-lords and fortifications the thakur wielded a sword in service of his liege lord, laying down his life for the sake of martial glory. From the blood and agony of the battlefield, many a ferocious and heroic soldier snatched his fortune, winning his fiefdom from an appreciative master and raising a fortress 'above the mud-built dwellings of the herd'. The thakur was a titled nobleman in the ruler's durbar, presiding over his estate, or fiefdom, called a *thikana*, comprising so many villages and so much farm land; an inalienable grant, conditional only upon fealty and feudatory tribute. Some thikanas encompassed hundreds of villages, others but a few acres and a horse or two.

Not every thakur owed his fiefdom to the ruler's magnanimity. Before the Mughals held sway in northern India many adventurous secondary sons of ruling Rajput princes, blocked by primogeniture from any hope of inherited sovereignty, set out to conquer kingdoms for themselves. The stronger of these conquests became independent realms but many of the less resilient principalities reverted to a tributary status within the ancestral state.

When the Mughals came they codified this feudal system, calling all Rajput noblemen *jagirdars* and their landholdings *jagirs*. Jagirdars by definition were holders of land grants (jagirs), received from a ruler as a reward for services rendered, most commonly but not always, in combat. Those thakurs whose ancestors had conquered their own estates resented the implication that they were grantees and continued to reject its legitimacy down to the bitter end of the British Raj.

As the Mughals began to lose their grip on India in the eighteenth century a number of aggressive Rajput thakurs liberated their lands and set up independent states. The

British displaced the Mughals in this feudal system and stratified the aristocratic hierarchy, sometimes legitimating these parvenu rulers while relegating once-autonomous rajas to a feudatory position in perpetuity.

By the time Colonel Trevor wrote his doggerel tribute, war had long since ceased to preoccupy the thakur and, deprived of chivalry, it was not unusual to find him 'boosing o'er his wine' in reveries of some long-ago ancestral geste. Just as often, however, the thakur could be found officiating in his master's capital: as judge, police chief, magistrate, minister. His sons were acculturated in Princes' Colleges. His fort was now little more than a holiday retreat. But in his village the thakur was still a symbol to his peasant populace, his curious pile a proud reminder of the majesty of his clan. Apart from the government school, the medical dispensary, some metalled roads and a scattering of municipal amenities, his fiefdom remained much the same as it always had been – contented, tradition-bound, dusty and peaceful – of dirt but not of grief.

KANOTA GARH & NARAIN NIWAS

In 1872 Maharaja Sawai Ram Singh II granted the *thikana*, or fiefdom, of Kanota, comprising seven villages, to Zorawar Singh Champawat (1827-1908), one of three brothers who had followed their father from his small and relatively impoverished hereditary thikana of Peelva in Jodhpur State to render service to the Jaipur Maharajas. Zorawar Singh was now *thakur* (feudal lord) of Kanota, and he marked out land in the village of that name in the flatlands some ten miles from Jaipur, and began to build himself a fort.

Rajput rulers frequently preferred the service of 'foreigners' – that is, members of alien Rajput clans from other princely states – to that of members of their own clan in order to counteract a coalition of subversive forces from within. As Robert W. Stern wrote in *The Cat and the Lion*: 'Armed hostilities between clan factions and vendettas between branch families were pursued indefatigably and interminably. While his clan was an ostensible source of

pride to a Rajput aristocrat, his clansmen were sources of real anxiety.'

The fealty of feudal barons toward their own particular sub-clan or family branch ultimately prevailed over that toward their hereditary ruler of the state. When given too much executive power within the durbar, a thakur of the same clan as the Maharaja could easily form a network of his own sub-clansmen within the government bureaucracy which would become entrenched and self-interested and work in opposition to the interests of the ruler and other factions within the state, as was the case with the Nathawats of Samode and Chomu during the minorities of Sawai Ram Singh II and his father, Sawai Jai Singh III.

Therefore the Maharajas of Jaipur were inclined to take on outsiders to run their government machinery. They were expendable in the sense that their services could be terminated for one reason or another without igniting a civil war within the clan and they were also, theoretically at least, more faithful to the ruler inasmuch as their position in the state was by his command and not due to their hereditary status within the clan.

Thakur Zorawar Singh and his two brothers, Shambhu Singh and Fateh Singh, were Champawats, a sub-clan of Rathor Rajputs from Jodhpur State. They came to Jaipur to seek their fortunes and found favour with Maharaja Ram Singh II. Zorawar Singh was the last of the brothers to migrate to Jaipur, having been adopted to another fiefdom in Jodhpur, where he resided for some years cultivating the land. He used the profits from his crops to start up what developed into a lucrative money-lending business which he maintained after he moved to Jaipur in 1861.

The three brothers proved exemplary civil servants and courtiers, swiftly rising through the bureaucratic ranks to reach the administrative summit as members of Ram Singh's council of advisers. Fateh Singh rose further still, attaining the rank of Prime Minister of Jaipur State (see page 33). All three were given their own *jagirs*, or feudal estates – Shambhu Singh became Thakur of Gondher and Fateh Singh became Thakur of Naila – and in 1873, the year after Zorawar Singh received his thikana, the three brothers were confirmed as *Tazimi*

Sardars, nobility of the highest rank in the Jaipur durbar, distinguished by a gold anklet and honoured by special marks of ceremonial deference from the Maharaja.

Construction of a single-storey town house with a courtyard began at Kanota as soon as the jagir was granted. On completion of this *haveli*, a larger two-storey mansion set upon a plinth was constructed over a period of several years. In the beginning the main residence was divided into two sections: the *mardana*, or men's section, was on the ground floor; the *zenana*, or women's section, was on the upper floor. In later years the zenana was shifted to the original house at the centre of the compound. At the same time as these constructions were built, a fortress battlement was erected with soft earthen walls wide enough for a horseman to patrol upon, and was completed in 1915.

Kanota Fort was not used as a permanent residence for Zorawar Singh or his descendants. The Champawat brothers and their children lived in a family compound of three *havelis* in a district within the city walls of Jaipur and their administrative activities in the capital precluded any extended residence in their estates. The forts they built were the headquarters of their feudal establishments. The stables at Kanota Garh contained fifty horses, two hundred camels, and several elephants. A permanent staff of fifty retainers lived within the fort to maintain its operations.

When the thakur retired from state service after the turn of the century he went to live in Kanota Garh and died there in 1908.

Zorawar Singh was succeeded by his eldest son Kunwar Narain Singh (1850-1924), who had taken up service in Jaipur at thirteen, only two years after his father had arrived, quickly becoming one of Maharaja Ram Singh's most trusted retainers. He commanded the ruler's bodyguard, trained his horses, supervised the preparation of his meat and the lighting of his water-pipe. Narain Singh remained in Ram Singh's service for seventeen years and was deeply devoted to his master. Following the death of Sawai Ram Singh in 1880, he was elevated to the post of Inspector General of Jaipur Police and liaison to the rebellious Sheikhawati region, serving with distinction in both capacities until 1897.

One of the most fashionable marks of upward mobility among Jaipur courtiers of the late nineteenth century was the acquisition of a *bagh*, or pleasure garden, outside the city walls. Sawai Ram Singh had developed his own, Ram Bagh, and members of his court eagerly sought precious grants of land in proximity to the Maharaja's garden. In about 1880 Narain Singh had successfully solicited the Maharaja's approval for a tract of land near to Ram Bagh to make his own garden but was thwarted by his own uncle, Fateh Singh, who as Prime Minister of Jaipur obstructed his nephew's acquisition of the land. Narain Singh's son, Amar Singh wrote that:

At that time, the Ram Niwas garden was just ready and my father one day said that he too wanted to make a Narain Niwas. The durbar [Maharaja Ram Singh] was pleased and said that he could have land of the bagar *[a grazing area for livestock] where his cattle were and to tell his uncle Fateh Singh jee to give him a* putta *[a title-deed] for the land. Fateh Singh jee was absolutely against this idea and though the durbar gave the order several times he would not do the job until at last he was put aside from his post of prime ministership. It was Babu Kanti Chander [the new prime minister] who made the* putta *of it and had it signed by the present durbar [Maharaja Madho Singh, Ram Singh's successor] . . . My father did the policy of putting up a mud wall all around the unoccupied place in the vicinity of the* bagar. *Thus, we are indebted to the foe of our family for this land.*

It is not clear whether Fateh Singh was obstructive out of some personal antagonism toward his nephew or as a conscientious check on nepotism and the misuse of his powerful office, but in 1881 Narain Singh's uncle was dismissed from his position by the new Maharaja and the application for Narain Niwas Bagh was accepted by Sawai Madho Singh. The development of Narain Niwas Bagh began as soon as the land was formally granted. A wall was constructed and a small garden house was built amidst surrounding orchards, but Narain Singh's enjoyment of his country garden was to be short-lived, due, ironically, to the man who had facilitated its acquisition, the 'foe' of the Champawat family mentioned by Amar Singh; the new prime minister who was to become Narain Singh's personal nemesis.

Babu Kanti Chander Mukherji was another 'foreigner' who had become part of the Jaipur bureaucracy, in this case a non-Rajput foreigner, a Bengali. Bengalis had long served the Jaipur durbar. Indeed, the illustrious Vidhyadhar, architect of Jaipur City and later chief minister, was Bengali. In the late nineteenth century Bengalis were especially popular bureaucrats because of their facility with English. Kanti Chander Mukherji exercised a powerful influence over the new Maharaja, Madho Singh, and conceived of a partisan enmity against the Champawats, who had been influential in the court of Ram Singh. Narain Singh clashed repeatedly with the new prime minister and despite his outstanding service record, Mukherji eventually managed to poison the mind of Madho Singh against his General Superintendent of Police, paving the way for his dismissal in 1897.

Narain Singh was a popular and highly respected figure in Rajputana, not only among the Rajput nobility but among the British as well, and was one of the rare Jaipur State officials who had ever managed to develop good relations with the refractory Sheikhawats (see page 37). Upon his dismissal the British arranged to have him appointed as a guardian of Maharaja Sawai Jay Singh Bahadur of Alwar (see page 45), who was still a minor. This posting evolved into a position on the durbar council of Alwar and a professional exile from Jaipur that would last for over two decades. During this period Narain Singh rarely visited Narain Niwas Bagh but as he was still the Thakur of Kanota he would spend his annual service leave at his fort there. Finally, in 1921, during the very last year of Madho Singh's reign, Narain Singh was called back and reinstated as General Superintendent of Police. He died in 1924.

Narain Singh's oldest son and successor was Thakur Amar Singh, a distinguished and much-decorated officer in the Indian Army who has left one of the most extraordinary documents in the history of letters. From 1898 to 1942 – forty-four years — Amar Singh kept a detailed diary in English, never missing a single day's entry. When he died in 1942 this journal comprised eighty-seven volumes of 800 pages each. The diary of Thakur Amar Singh of Kanota, which can be seen in Kanota Fort, provides a unique record of an extraordinary period in history.

With his family under a cloud, Amar Singh spent many years abroad in active military service and assumed a place in the Jaipur government only after Sawai Madho Singh's death, when in 1923 he was appointed Commandant of the Jaipur Lancers and put in command of the Cavalry and Artillery Corps of Jaipur. In 1931 Sawai Man Singh appointed Amar Singh Commander of the entire Jaipur State Forces.

Having returned to Jaipur, Amar Singh settled in the garden house in Narain Niwas Bagh and made plans to build a palace there to live in. He supervised designs and in 1928 work began on the structure, which was completed in 1934. The Kanota family settled permanently in Narain Niwas Palace toward the end of the 1930s, having moved from the older palaces in the more congested areas of the inner city.

On the death of Amar Singh in 1942 his son Sheo Nath Singh became Thakur of Kanota until 1954 when the feudal estates were abolished and re-distributed by the Government of India, for which the thakurs were remunerated. All that remained of their landholdings were small parcels of agricultural land, their not so very old fort and their homes in Jaipur.

Narain Niwas Palace remained the private residence of the Kanota family until 1978, the year after Thakur Sheo Nath Singh died, when his son and heir Mohan Singh converted the garden palace into a hotel in order to be able to maintain the building. Once a remote country palace surrounded by wild animals, Narain Niwas Palace had become one of the most conveniently located residences in Jaipur and was immediately successful as a hotel.

Mohan Singh and his family continued living in part of the palace until the early 1980s, when he moved permanently to Kanota Garh. Whenever his hotel became over-booked he would accommodate his guests at Kanota Garh and gradually the fort has become part of the thriving Kanota family tourist business.

SAMODE PALACE &
SAMODE HAVELI

The rulers of Samode (situated some twenty-four miles north of Jaipur) which, according to the *Rajputana Gazetteer* of 1879, was a 'large and flourishing town, the principal place of the zamandari [a private landholding] of that name held by one of the principal thakurs of the State . . .' were the Nathawat clan from Chomu. This clan was a branch of the House of Amber, tracing its affiliation back some 600 years to the fabled Prithviraj Singh, the seventeenth prince of the house of Kachhwaha, whose ancestors are said to be descended from the god Rama.

One of the sons of Prithviraj was Gopal Singh, whose father made him Thakur of Samode, which at the time was among the wealthiest territories in the Amber kingdom. The *zamandari* eventually passed within the clan to the hands of Behari Das, a Rajput warrior in Mughal service. After six generations in the hands of his descendants, Samode was relinquished to the Raj. In 1757 the territory was returned to the Nathawat. One Hamir Singh, the eldest son of Thakur Jodh Singh of Chomu became the Rawal of Samode and his descendants maintained this hereditary title as rulers of their large thikana, or feudal estate.

The Rawals of Samode commanded total allegiance within their small dominions and arbitrated absolutely the fates of their subjects. At the same time these palatines were feudatories of the Maharaja of Jaipur and distinguished themselves in a multiplicity of services to the Durbar. Rawal Ram Singh, for instance, is remembered for his valour when, at sixteen, he defended the fort of Ranthambor against the Marathas, fighting fiercely and triumphing in combat even, according to legend, after his head had been severed from his body.

No documents exist which trace the history of Samode Palace but the estimated age of the hereditary home of the Nathawat is 400 years. For the first half of its existence, however, it was little more than a fortified stronghold in the rugged Rajput tradition. Not until the early nineteenth century under Rawal Bairi Sal Singh and his son and successor Rawal Sheo Singh did the feudal castle begin to take on the sumptuous decorative aspect it is now known for.

Rawal Bairi Sal was a leading courtier in Jaipur who first reached distinction as the principal signatory (on behalf of the Maharaja) of the historic treaty of 1818 that made Jaipur a protectorate of the British East India Company. He was as a result heavily favoured by the Company and became in effect their front man in Jaipur.

Through British influence Bairi Sal was installed as Dewan, or Prime Minister, of Jaipur during the minority of Maharaja Sawai Jai Singh III. It was not an enviable post, for he found himself caught in crossfire between the Regent Maharani and the British East India Company, which was trying to wrest control of the Jaipur administration from her incompetent and corrupt zenana faction led by the Maharani's sinister paramour, Jhota Ram. In such circumstances Bairi Sal's position as Dewan rapidly became untenable and the Regent Maharani replaced him in 1823 with Jhota Ram.

The Rawal then became a pawn in the power struggle between the zenana and the British East India Company which lasted until the Maharani died in 1834. With the sudden and mysterious death of her unfortunate sixteen-year-old son, Sawai Jai Singh III, the following year, the British made their move against the zenana faction and, invoking their paramount authority, summarily dismissed Jhota Ram, who had been suspected of engineering the child Maharaja's murder, from his position as Dewan. The Company then reinstated Rawal Bairi Sal as Dewan as well as appointing him to head a Council of Regency to govern on behalf of Sawai Ram Singh, without consulting the child Maharaja's mother, the new Regent Maharani.

The Jhota Ram clique within Jaipur was finally overthrown and extirpated from the Durbar when a British political officer called Blake was murdered by a mob inside the city walls and the former Dewan was indicted as an instigator, tried, convicted and imprisoned for life.

From this point until his death in 1838 Rawal Bairi Sal Singh of Samode wielded almost absolute power over the government of Jaipur. There are conflicting reports as to the character of the man. The *Jaipur*

Handbook, published in 1935, states that Bairi Sal was:

a very wise and judicious administrator and a perfect model of a statesman . . . He was . . . at the helm of the entire administration of the State which he controlled with great credit. He was fully alive to the responsibilities of his high office . . . and earned universal gratitude by restoring perfect peace and order throughout the State . . .

But other narrators tell a different story about the Dewan and his successor.

When Bairi Sal died the British installed his son Rawal Sheo Singh as Dewan of Jaipur and head of the Council of Regency (in Sawai Ram Singh's minority), as well as appointing Sheo Singh's brother Thakur Lachman Singh, the adopted Rawal of Chomu, as Army Minister and Regency Council member, thus perpetuating the Nathawat domination of Jaipur for a second generation.

From 1835 to 1862 Bairi Sal and his sons served British interests in Jaipur very well indeed, and evidently served their own interests even better. According to Robert W. Stern:

In the early years of the regency, the resident discovered that the Nathawats, father and sons, had, under cover of two decades of British patronage, expropriated crown lands and the lands of their political opponents with a 'rapacity' unexcelled even by the notorious zenana party at its most rapacious.

Nevertheless, the brothers were by this time too entrenched in power to unseat and British interests were in any case so completely intertwined with the Nathawat administration that they were stuck with it.

The Nathawats remained at least nominally in power long after Maharaja Sawai Ram Singh reached his majority in 1851. By 1854, however, their grip on the administration of Jaipur was beginning to loosen as Maharaja Ram Singh gained confidence in governing his state and cleverly set about consolidating his own authority over the Durbar through a showdown with Sheo Singh which forced the Dewan's resignation. In this he had the support of the East India Company, which was fed up with the peculation of Sheo Singh and his clannish network, which had driven the state deeply into debt. Ram Singh realized, however, that the Nathawat influence had become so pervasive in the state that a sudden purge would have disastrous consequences. Therefore he appointed Lachman Singh to take his brother's place.

Rawal Sheo Singh's position in Jaipur politics was further weakened three years later when he joined the rebellious factions during the Mutiny of 1857. The Nathawats were tainted and Maharaja Ram Singh used the Mutiny as an excuse to finally purge his administration of their partisans. So, although Rawal Lachman Singh served as Dewan until his death in 1862, his appointment was the beginning of the end of the clan's supremacy in Jaipur affairs and through most of his ministerial tenure he was without real authority.

By the time of his dismissal, Sheo Singh had used his expropriated revenues to adorn Samode Palace with ornamentation that is, according to the writer Aman Nath, 'considered as good, if not superior to that of Jaipur's City Palace'. Sheo Singh is credited with the palace's most fabulous addition: the extravagantly florid, hand-painted durbar hall with an overlooking zenana gallery which forms the breathtaking Sheesh Mahal, or Hall of Mirrors.

Early in the nineteenth century Rawal Bairi Sal had also constructed a large *haveli* (town house) within the old city of Jaipur which over the years was similarly elaborated, featuring a reception hall with painting almost as dazzling as that in Samode Palace, a beautiful courtyard verandah and a lovely back garden. An elephant ramp was added in the 1940s for the wedding of the thakur's sister.

Although the thakurs of Samode never again achieved positions of influence within the Jaipur Durbar they had sufficiently enriched their estates to live in comfort until 1954 when the Jagir Abolition Act eradicated feudalism in India and stripped all feudal barons of their territories. Samode Palace remained the private residence of the Nathawat family, but without income from their estates their fantastically decorated castle had become a colossal millstone and at the beginning of the 1970s the thakur put his hereditary property on the market for one lakh of rupees. They could not find a buyer. Fortunately.

In the early 1980s the late thakur's youngest son Yaduvender Singh had just passed out of Mayo College at Ajmer, and was burning to get into the hotel business. His uncle Vikram Singh, the hereditary Rawal of Chomu, was a veteran hotelier and General Manager of Ram Bagh Palace Hotel in Jaipur. Yaduvender was planning to follow in his uncle's footsteps and work for a big hotel chain. His older brother, Raghuvender, was already a working capitalist and proposed that they join forces and convert their hulking hereditary home into a hotel. The Nathawat brothers contacted a travel agency, which looked over the property and advised them to begin by offering luncheons and dinners to test the market.

In 1984 Samode was still very much off the beaten track for travellers but the palace was so spectacular that success was inevitable. Almost immediately Samode Palace was used as a principal location for the lavish television mini-series *The Far Pavilions*. The film company restored some of the ornamental painting in the palace and the brothers began to invest their revenues from the rental into further renovations. This fortuitous prelude was followed by a privately arranged visit from that great patron of royal India, Mrs Jacqueline Kennedy Onassis, who had been told about the palace by her friend Rajmata Gayatri Devi of Jaipur. Mrs Onassis brought along a team from *House and Garden* who did a feature for the magazine and gave Samode Palace a strong international launch. In October 1985 Yaduvender and Raghuvender Singh opened their impressive home to the public as a hotel.

Encouraged by the success of their first venture the Nathawat brothers launched the second of their hotels in Jaipur City itself when they opened Samode Haveli, their family's private Jaipur town house, in October 1987. Both properties are among the most delightfully evocative palace hotels in India.

SHEIKHAWATI

NO MAN'S LAND

Sheikhawati was a loose, belligerent confederation of principalities in the desolate region to the north of Jaipur, first carved out and cobbled together in the fifteenth century by descendants of Raja Udai Karan, the Kachhwaha king of Amber and named for his great-grandson Rao Sheikha whose forename has an unusual Muslim derivation. Sheikha's father had been childless for many years and made pilgrimage to the holy village of Brindaban to seek some sort of thaumaturgic intercession that would yield him an heir. A guru advised the supplicant to lead his cow into the forest where the grazing was better and once there the Hindu Rajput ran into a Muslim saint called Sheikh Burhan who asked Allah on his behalf for the birth of a son. The Sheikh's prayers were answered when in 1433 a boy was born to the Rajput chief and the child was named Sheikha, in honour of the Muslim Sheikh.

Rao Sheikha extended the conquests of his forefathers and consolidated these territories into an independent entity. The Sheikhawat lineage was further strengthened when the Rao's descendants ingratiated themselves with the Mughal emperors, attaining influential positions within the Delhi Durbar.

The Jaipur kings never really accepted the independence of Sheikhawati and tried repeatedly to subdue their prodigal clansmen, but it was a fierce, inhospitable desert these war-lords lived on – what Sir Arthur Lothian called 'a no man's land' – and while the region came to represent one third of the territory of Jaipur State, its treeless wastelands were something of a disincentive to concentrated campaigning. Moreover, the chieftains who controlled them were skilled desert fighters and repulsed Jaipur forces over and over again. But the Mughals were a different matter, and it was the threat of an invasion from Delhi that drove the Sheikhawats into the protective arms of Sawai Jai Singh II, who made Sheikhawati a protectorate of Jaipur in the early eighteenth century. This, however, was only

a temporary expedient as far as the Sheikhawats were concerned and in the chaotic, internecine aftermath of Jai Singh's death these recusant war-lords managed to extricate themselves from their feudal bonds once again and return to virtual autonomy.

The greatest threat to Sheikhawat territorial integrity was not Jaipur or even Delhi but the Sheikhawats themselves, who divided and subdivided their territories through a succession of lethal domestic treacheries, clan wars, raiding and brigandage. This fragmentation was aggravated when, after an heir-apparent was poisoned by his younger brothers, the patriarch of one major branch of the Sheikhawat renounced the practice of primogeniture, setting the precedent of equal division of territory between all his male offspring. As noble as this initiative was, it effectively partitioned many of these principalities into oblivion, further weakening the desert federation.

The obstreperous spirit of the Sheikhawats remained very much alive, however. Feudatories though they were in name, tribute was rarely forthcoming and never on time. Brigandage increased and turbulence prevailed. When the British East India Company established its primacy in Jaipur during the 1830s, it organized a military force called the Sheikhawati Brigade to subdue the rebellious chieftains once and for all and although this campaign finally succeeded, many of the Sheikhawati barons still held on to their sense of sovereignty. If a tribute called for the delivery of 5,000 camels and horses to the Jaipur Durbar, the chieftain would send 5,000 of the weakest and most disease-ridden from his herds. The Sheikhawats remained troublesome and untrusted to the very end of the Raj. Until the reign of Maharaja Man Singh II (1922-47) they were not permitted to carry swords into the durbar, they were never allowed to own property inside the walls of Jaipur and their land was always known as Ilaka Gher – 'Foreign Territory'.

MANDAWA GARH
Castle Mandawa

Thakur Sadhul Singh (1685-1739), founder of the Sadhani branch of Sheikhawats, had rejected his father's patrimony and set out to usurp and conquer of his own accord the entire territory of Jhunjhunu, comprising over 1,000 villages in northern Sheikhawati. At the end of his life the feudal lord apportioned his expanded principality in equal parts among his five sons, according to the practice of his forefathers.

Thakur Nawal Singh (1715-79) was the fourth son of Sadhul Singh and received a territorial share including the village of Rohil, which he made his capital and renamed Nawalgarh (see page 00), and the land upon which the village of Mandawa was soon to be situated. In 1755 Nawal Singh constructed a fortress on this site. For thirty-five years Mandawa Garh was never used as more than a frontier outpost to guard the borders of this Sheikhawati *thikana*. No one among the Sadhanis lived within its walls, but gradually a village grew up around it.

Upon the death of Nawal Singh in 1779 Mandawa village and its fortress were bequeathed to his eldest son, Narsingh Dass (1779-92), along with his share of the estate. The rest of his territory, including Nawalgarh, was divided between the thakur's nine other sons, but Narsingh Dass attacked Nawalgarh to wrest it from his younger brother and seized the entirety of the feudal estate in an attempt to re-establish primogeniture within his line. Before this usurpation erupted into a full-scale clan war the case was taken to the Jaipur Durbar and Narsingh Dass was forced to yield part of the estate. He did, however, manage to retain both Nawalgarh and Mandawa, which together comprised over twice as much land area as all his brothers held collectively. He ruled his territories from Nawalgarh.

Narsingh Dass had four sons. Udai Singh and Mohabat Singh remained at Nawalgarh and Padam Singh and Gyan Singh moved permanently to Mandawa in 1790. Up to this time Mandawa was used simply as a defensive fortress. After 1790, however, the brothers settled in Mandawa and began

to construct living quarters within the walls of the fort, including sleeping rooms, public rooms and a durbar hall. Rooms and *mahals* were added according to need and inclination from generation to generation. Thakur Baghwat Singh built a number of large suites in the late nineteenth century.

The thikana of Mandawa remained interrelated and interactive with Nawalgarh until 1954 when feudalism was banished from democratic India and the area was redistricted in the newly formed state of Rajasthan. By this time Sheikhawati had long since ceased to occupy even a contentious place in the modern scheme of things. The district was remote, desolate, and undeveloped. Scions of the Marwari business families indigenous to the region had long ago scattered to commercial centres of India to make their mega-fortunes and their hometown connections had become attenuated. Sheikhawati was still very much a no man's land and would have remained quite unknown but for a strange and arresting decorative feature which has made the region famous and attracted travellers from throughout the world.

The Marwaris of Sheikhawati are the most prosperous trading community in India; great mercantile dynasties – the Goenkas, the Birlas – were born in this desolate region. The Marwaris had first amassed their fortunes in service of the Mughals. With the ascendancy of the British in India they shifted their mercantile activities to the seaports of Bombay and Calcutta to profit from the new imperial masters. All the while they continued to contribute to their ancestral communities through traditional philanthropic activities like the building of temples, schools, *dharamsalas* (pilgrims' lodges) and wells. At the same time the Marwaris constructed *havelis*, grand town houses with courtyards, for their relations who had remained in Sheikhawati and to stay in on visits to their home villages.

In the nineteenth and early twentieth centuries the most fashionable status symbol among these Marwari merchants was to have flamboyant, often outlandishly kitsch, frescoes covering the interiors and exteriors of their havelis from floor to (and including) ceiling. The more affluent the merchant, the more intricate and extensive the painting would be. These frescoes depicted anything from mythology to technology, including crowded martial sagas, genealogical portraiture, theogonic tableaux, and such up-to-the minute images as steam trains replete with top-hatted or hoop-skirted Victorian passengers, grand viceregal visits, and the maiden flight of Orville and Wilbur Wright at Kittyhawk. One hundred and twenty of these painted havelis were built in Mandawa alone.

After Independence these extraordinary properties were mostly left to moulder, tenanted by poor relations who encamped in the florid, glorious town houses as if they were fetid slum tenements, which they soon came to resemble. Wind, dust, rain, leaking water pipes, makeshift electrification, desert floods, vandalism and neglect were ravaging this unique and colourful artistic legacy.

Mandawa was incorporated into the district of Jhunjhunu after the feudal estates were abolished in 1954, and was subjected to the usual infrastructural priorities like road-building, electrification and well-digging. The preservation of these eccentric town houses was not even at the bottom of a bureaucratic list. With the loss of their land revenues and administrative powers there was little the former feudal lords of Mandawa could do, even if they were aware that something needed doing.

Thakur Jai Singh (1903-) remained resident in Mandawa but his oldest son Devi Singh (1922-) was an active politician based in Jaipur, where his children were being educated. It was difficult enough for the Mandawa family to keep up their own massive, dilapidating fort, much less do anything about semi-vacant surrounding houses with absentee owners.

In 1977 Sheikhawati was 'discovered' by Francis Wacziarg, a French businessman, Indophile and long-time resident of Delhi, and his partner, the Indian writer and graphic designer Aman Nath. In their peregrinations through India the two young men had stumbled upon the Sheikhawati frescoes and decided to expose them in a photographic essay.

Mandawa is particularly rich in examples of this extraordinary art. Their first journey to the town brought them into contact with Devi Singh's youngest son, who had returned to his hereditary village to try his hand at farming there. His father and other

brothers were living and working in Jaipur. The young man suggested that they contact his father in Jaipur, and a fast friendship was formed with the family. Within a few months, during the monsoon season of 1977, Aman and Francis visited Jaipur to put on a slide show of their photography of the Sheikhawati frescoes for the Mandawa family. Francis remembers that:

We said, 'Look you have these extraordinary frescoes.' They said that first of all they didn't know what frescoes were and secondly, they didn't know there were any wall paintings in Mandawa. When we showed them slides they said, 'That isn't in Mandawa.' We said, 'Yes it is. That is the house on the left side as you come out of the fort and you walk this way, etc.'

Then the two men had a brainwave: why not turn Mandawa Fort into a resort? But of course! Today this seems such an obvious move. At that time, however, it seemed positively wacky. Mandawa was a remote, unknown village completely off the beaten tourist track, out in the middle of a bleak sand desert, and approachable only by dirt roads. Foreigners were unheard of out there. True, the village had a fortress and these wall paintings, but its location and anonymity defied all the traditional wisdom about tourism. Travel people in Delhi thought the pair had been pixilated by some desert *jinni*. In January 1978 the two men managed to persuade a reluctant French travel agent from Nouvelle Frontière to accompany them to their new discovery. They drove out in driving rain that almost drowned the car.

It was a real adventure because in those days nobody ever went to Sheikhawati. It was unheard of. The roads were just mud tracks. There was no bathroom. There was just one room that was built in the early years of this century that had a kind of bathroom with a washbasin and a WC with a bucket.

The travel agent was enthralled with both the property and the painted havelis and advised the Mandawa family to open the place for lunches to begin with, until they could determine whether the idea would work. She began to promote Mandawa in France and little groups began to turn up from time to time. Word circulated rapidly about this amazing painted village with its ancient fortress out in no-man's land and Castle Mandawa, as it is now called, has been developed into a fifty-room hotel.

ROOP NIWAS KOTHI

Although Nawalgarh and Mandawa formed separate estates, they have remained closely affiliated down to the present day and whenever a ruler of one of the thikanas had no issue, an heir would be adopted from the other.

Thakur Roop Singh (1877-1926) of Nawalgarh was the second son of Thakur Ajit Singh of Mandawa and was adopted to succeed Thakur Durjan Sal of Nawalgarh (1868-95), whose own son and heir had predeceased him. Roop Singh ruled over Nawalgarh from 1899 until his death. As he had no issue his young cousin Madan Singh of Mandawa was adopted to succeed him.

Madan Singh (1907-) was the second son of Thakur Hari Singh of Mandawa and younger brother of Mandawa's present thakur Jai Singh (1903-). Madan Singh was still a student at Mayo College, Ajmer, when his obese cousin Roop Singh died suddenly from heart failure. The young man was permitted to complete his studies before assuming control over Nawalgarh in 1928.

Thakur Madan Singh was a thoroughly modern ruler and he felt the need for a thoroughly modern residence removed from the archaic interiors of Nawalgarh town. He settled down in a small three-room farmhouse built about ten years earlier by Thakur Roop Singh in the middle of a grazing area outside the town walls. In 1930 Madan Singh began to expand his house and continued building year by year until he had transformed the property into a large, rambling colonial-style country-palace complex, with an ornamental entry gate, numerous outbuildings and wide, landscaped grounds with fountains and watercourses. He named his residence Roop Niwas Kothi, in honour of his predecessor.

Madan Singh ruled his thikana with such exceptional skill that he was invested with the title of Rawal by Maharaja Man Singh II of Jaipur. His intelligence and strength

of personality naturally propelled him into the leadership of the Kshatriya Mahasabha, an organization of Rajput nobility which represented the special interests of *jagirdars,* or feudal lords, in the years leading up to the introduction of land reform and the abolition of feudal estates. As vice-president of this organization Madan Singh became chief spokesman for the feudal lords in the negotiation of terms of compensation with the Congress government.

Rawal Madan Singh is an unusual Rajput. Unlike his warlike ancestors and many of his contemporaries, he is a quiet, ascetic gentleman who has always preferred chess to hunting, lemonade to wine, and vegetables to venison. His estates were governed with cool efficiency and he saw to it that both his sons were educated in professions long before this was fashionable among feudal nobility. Kunwar Sangram Singh (1927-) is a leading art historian and collector and Kunwar Sumer Singh (1928-) is an engineer.

During the feudal period commerce was deemed beneath the station of a thakur but Madan Singh harboured no such prejudice and formed business alliances with his Marwari neighbours which have served him well since Independence. Even today Madan Singh is a director of several corporations and although in his eighties he commutes regularly to Bombay for board meetings.

It is this business acumen which prompted him to open Roop Niwas Kothi to tourists in 1980. Two years earlier his brother, Jai Singh of Mandawa, had allowed his son and grandsons to open their hereditary fort as a hotel (see page 38) and foreign travellers attracted to the extraordinary painted houses of Sheikhawat were beginning to explore this desert district. Nawalgarh was on the road to Mandawa and, as in any case Roop Niwas Kothi was only partially occupied, the property was opened first for lunches and later for overnight guests.

DUNDLOD QILA

Dundlod Qila was built in 1750 by Thakur Kesri Singh (1729-62), the fifth and youngest surviving son of Thakur Sadul Singh of Jhunjhunu (1685-1742). It was one of four small defensive fortresses Kesri Singh constructed in the villages of Dundlod, Bissau, Tamkore and Nuwa to protect his patrimony – a subdivision of Sadhul Singh's vast estate. Dundlod was a small desert settlement originally known as Shivgarh. In the early nineteenth century the name was changed to Dund Lodra in honour of a local deity called Dundpal (the fact is substantiated in a temple on the outskirts of the village) and was eventually abbreviated to Dundlod – the Abode of Dundpal.

Dundlod Qila was manned by soldiers from Kesri Singh's private army but it was not used as a residence until the early nineteenth century, for the war-lord and his sons continued to rule from their family *mahal,* or palace, in the village of Jhunjhunu.

Thakur Kesri Singh left two sons, Hanuat Singh (d.1784) and Surajmal (1755-87), who divided their territory equally between them but presided over their estates from the same fortified palace in Jhunjhunu. The principal village in Surajmal's estate was Bissau while Dundlod was the centre of Hanuat Singh's domain. Both warriors served the Mughal durbar and were honoured by the emperor for their bravery on the battlefield. Hanuat Singh was perpetually engaged in military campaigns until he died from old battle wounds in 1784, leaving his territory *in toto* to his only son, Ranjit Singh (d. 1808). Thakur Surajmal died on the battlefield three years later, devising all of his estate to his only son Shyam Singh (1771-1833).

These two cousins continued to live together in apparent harmony for twenty-four years, each ruling his independent estate from their hereditary palace in Jhunjhunu, until a streak of treachery and greed that so often seems to have crossed the hearts of Sheikhawats twisted one to intrigue, villainy and parricide.

The cold-blooded double murder of Thakur Ranjit Singh and his son Pertab Singh by Shyam Singh and his accomplices might well have remained simply one more

murderous episode lost in the anonymous and ruthless history of Sheikhawati but for a riveting eyewitness account narrated by Ranjit Singh's youngest son and heir, Sheoji Singh (1795-1850), who narrowly escaped his uncle's sword. Sheoji Singh fled from Jhunjhunu and was given refuge by Raja Abhey Singh of Khetri who mobilized an army of over 6,000 soldiers, horse and foot, from among his allies and stormed the fort of Dundlod, seizing it from Shyam Singh's partisans. The Khetri forces, further fortified with 3,000 men from Bikaner, laid seige for twenty-eight days to the fort of Buggur, where Shyam Singh had retreated. The prolonged length of the siege was due in no small part to the fact that all the combatants were relatives and frequently resisted firing upon one another for fear they would hurt a kinsman. Harnath Singh, the last thakur of Dundlod, wrote that 'Buggur might have been taken by a company of Sepoys in ten minutes'.

The siege was lifted when an unscrupulously negotiated settlement highly favourable to Shyam Singh restored less than half of the usurped territory to the thirteen-year-old surviving son of Ranjit Singh. Sheoji Singh tried for many years to retrieve his birthright through the intercession of the Jaipur durbar but Shyam Singh of Bissau had allied himself with the sinister and powerful Jotha Ram, who ruled Jaipur during the Regency of Maharaja Sawai Jai Singh III, and managed to block Sheoji Singh's demands for justice. The lost territories of Dundlod were never restored.

With no home to return to, Sheoji Singh took up residence in his small fort at Dundlod in 1809. It was during this period that both the village and its fort began to flourish. Sheoji Singh established a strategy of attracting merchants and craftsmen to his tiny settlement which was carried on by his descendants throughout the nineteenth century. He would travel to neighbouring villages like Nawalgarh and offer incentives and concessions to those artisans or traders who would pull up stakes and move to Dundlod.

At the same time the thakur rebuilt and expanded his fort. For most feudal nobility in India the early nineteenth century was a time when war was receding and defences were let down, but in the light, or rather darkness, of Sheoji Singh's childhood experience it is easy to understand why he constructed heavy parapets around his fort, surrounded by a deep moat. A *Diwan Khana* (an open audience hall which could be entered on elephant back) was also added along with a *rawala* (ladies' apartments on the second floor) and a double-roofed hall called the *Duo Chatta,* with a false ceiling which kept the room cool in the summer and warm in the winter.

After Sheoji Singh died in 1850, his son Jai Singh (1836-75) did little to extend Dundlod fort but his grandson Paney Singh (1855-97) constructed Angoori Mahal as well as private rooms for each of his three wives. His younger brother and successor Chander Singh (1858-1901) also erected rooms for his three wives. As each of these thakuranis passed away their apartments were converted to storage rooms.

The adopted successor of Thakur Chander Singh was Harnath Singh (1905-54), the last Thakur of Dundlod. Born in the village of Malsisar, Harnath Singh assumed control by force of arms after Bissau, still a bitter enemy, tried to block his accession. After assuming control of his thikana he made extensive improvements to the fort, including the enclosure and the painted ornamentation of the Diwan Khana, for which he brought in artisans from Jaipur. There were further renovations in 1932 for the wedding of Harnath Singh's daughter to Rawat Karan Singh of Kanaur in Udaipur.

The thakur also built a bridge across a courtyard to allow his wife direct access to the rawal from her apartments. Lieutenant-Colonel Raghuvir Singh, Harnath Singh's second son, remembers that his mother:

got really fat when she got older. She said to my father, 'Can't you make a shortcut or something so that I can come across without going up and down the stairs?' So the bridge was made. At the opening ceremony she said, 'If I walk across, suppose it falls down?' My father said, 'You just walk slowly and we'll see how it holds up.' Of course, it didn't fall down and I remember my father and I standing to the side as she walked very slowly across the bridge.

There was no electricity in those days and Raghuvir Singh recalls that:

the farrash would accompany guests to their rooms with a lantern and place it in a niche. When my father would arrive, he would have a torch lit at the main gate and walk across the courtyard. We would stop whatever we were doing to pay our respects to our father as he crossed the courtyard in torchlight. In winters pots of charcoal would be placed in each room to provide heat.

Dundlod Qila was the centre of the community. According to Raghuvir Singh:

There was no question of getting a pass or special permission to come into the fort. The village and the fort lived together as one family. The villagers could come at any time provided that they behaved well. They were proud that they had a castle in their village. The whole system of the village was based on a mutual respect. Whoever would come to us, we would have to help them. There have even been cases of murderers taking refuge in the fort. And the police didn't dare to try to capture them within these walls. We would definitely hand them over to the police for trial, but first we would talk to them to get at the truth of the incident. So the villagers knew they had someone to look after their interests. When a conch was blown to announce a death in the community, if we were about to have lunch, my father would send the food away saying, 'There is a death in the village, please take the lunch away.' Look at the empathy there was then. And it was a custom in the thikana that there was not supposed to be cooking in a bereaved household so my father or grandfather would order grain and other ingredients from the local shop and have food cooked in the fort to send to the house.

In 1943 Harnath Singh moved his family to Jaipur in order to educate his children in better schools and, as with so many provincial fortresses, Dundlod Qila became a secondary residence.

Recently the sons and grandsons of Harnath Singh have opened sixteen rooms in their moated fort to travellers.

ALWAR

ALWAR

The machinations of Rao Raja Pratap Singh (1740-91) turned his insignificant little landholding of Machari, comprising two and a half villages inside the eastern borders of Jaipur State, into the independent kingdom of Alwar. Through predacious ambition and a machiavellian grasp of *realpolitik*, this ruthless and remarkable *thakur* (feudal lord) from the Naruka clan of Kachhwaha Rajputs played both ends of empire against the middle in his quest for sovereignty, swiftly shifting alliances from Jaipur to the Jats of Bharatpur and back again, then turning on his erstwhile allies in armed collusion with the Mughal forces of Najaf Khan to win imperial sanction for his usurpation and official independence from Jaipur. In 1775 he seized the fort of Alwar from the Jats of Bharatpur and established himself as ruler over his newly forged dominion. His successor, Bakhtawar Singh (1791-1815), collaborated with Lord Lake against the Marathas, establishing Alwar as a British protectorate in 1803, and subsequent East India Company treaties ensured the mutual integrity of all the princely states of India.

Once a province called Mewat, populated by a community of Muslim freebooters known as Mewatis, or Meos, Alwar was an exceptionally beautiful and fecund land, set around the eastern outreaches of the Aravalli mountains. It was a country of uncommon serenity and loveliness – a land of jagged, undulating peaks, of green and fertile valleys, of proliferating gardens, of exquisite temples, palaces, cenotaphs, and tanks, of keen air, peaceful villages, teeming wildlife and ageless nature. It was, in the words of the French traveller Louis Rousselet, 'a happy corner of the earth'.

SILISERH PALACE

In 1815 Maharao Raja Sawai Viney Singh (1815-57) ascended the Gadi of Alwar, a princely state cut away from the Jaipur kingdom by his predecessor Pratap Singh less than forty years before. Sawai Viney Singh was characterized by Major Powlett as:

Jealous of power, fond of state and ceremony, anxious to be just without sacrificing what he considered his interest at the shrine of justice; at times generous to excess, at others, niggardly; kindly dispositioned, but occasionally cruel, he was, on the whole, an excellent type of a good Native Chief of the past generation. His good deeds are remembered and his bad ones forgotten by the people, though some of the bad were bad enough.

Historical consensus has it that the best of Viney Singh's good deeds was the construction of a dam in 1844 some ten miles south-west of his capital, which formed a lovely reservoir about a mile in length and 400 yards in width. The waters from this artificial lake were brought to Alwar by a masonry aqueduct, transfusing life into its barren, rocky landscape which was soon to bloom with luxuriant gardens.

He named this new-formed reservoir Siliserh in honour of his Rani Seela and built for her a small white palace set high upon a rise overlooking the waters. The reservoir of Siliserh and its pleasure palace thus became a favoured resort for the Alwar rulers, most particularly for Sawai Mangal Singh (1874-92).

Maharao Mangal Singh was educated in the modern way at Mayo College, Ajmer, and judged 'progressive' by his contempories. His progressiveness was much appreciated by his British superiors, who promoted him to Maharaja and presented him with a KGCSI (Knight Grand Commander of the Most Exalted Order of the Star of India) and other princely honours in commendation of his multifarious services to the empire. His progressiveness also included the vice of alcohol abuse, which killed him at the age of thirty-four.

It was on *shikar* at Siliserh that Maharaja Mangal Singh had a brief encounter which has invested the little lake palace with a sad, romantic legend. On one of the prince's frequent hunting expeditions into the jungles surrounding Siliserh, Mangal Singh had pitched the royal tents in a clearing on the far side of the artificial lake. From his encampment the ruler rode out early one morning, crossing through the village of Kishanpur. As he passed beside the fortress of Thakur Bidada Singh, the feudal lord who ruled the village, he was struck suddenly by the sight of a young woman of spectacular beauty standing unguarded out upon the fortress wall in the morning air, combing her long black silken hair. The Maharaja impetuously entered into the compound of the Thakur and into the *rawala*, or ladies' quarters, to gaze upon this unknown beauty. Her name was Silika and she assumed that the man who had so casually entered into her apartment must have been her father's guest. She treated him hospitably, without the slightest notion that he was, in fact, her Maharaja.

When Thakur Bidada Singh returned to his fortress and entered into his family *rawala* he was outraged to find the ruler in intimate and uninvited conversation with his daughter. The Thakur insisted as a matter of honour that the Maharaja marry Silika to save her from disgrace. The ruler protested that he only wished to gaze upon her exquisite face; that he was on shikar, not in search of marriage. But Bidada Singh threatened that he would kill his daughter if the Maharaja refused to marry her.

Aside from the purely humanitarian consideration of saving a beautiful and innocent young girl's life, there were other factors which forced the ruler's hand in this matter. Alwar had a traditionally turbulent populace with a history of uprising and the Maharaja was in no position to inflame his Rajput subjects. Besides, Silika clearly made a stunning bride and Mangal Singh consented to marry her.

The marriage took place in the village of Kishanpur and was conducted by the court priest of Alwar. Rani Silika accompanied her husband to the capital and lived within the City Palace for between nine and fifteen months. She bore the Maharaja's child but the infant died at birth, casting Silika into a deep and inconsolable sadness. She asked permission of her husband to return to her family in Kishanpur. The Maharaja prepared the palace at Siliserh for Silika to

live in proximity to her parents. Silika lived in Siliserh Palace for nine months and then she died, it is said, of a broken heart.

After the early death of Mangal Singh in 1892 and the accession of his son, Sawai Jay Singh, shikar became even more central among princely recreations at Alwar but the use of Siliserh as a hunting lodge diminished with the construction of Jay Singh's own palatial 'shooting box' amidst the tiger-infested jungles of Sariska. After Independence, when control of the reservoir of Siliserh was assumed by the State Government, the beautiful little palace was converted into a tourist guest house, and is presently, and most unfortunately, under the feckless management of Rajasthan Tourism Development Corporation (RTDC).

SARISKA PALACE

Maharaja Sawai Jay Singh Bahadur of Alwar (1892-1937), the son and successor of Sawai Mangal Singh, was regarded by the British and many of his fellow princes as one of the most perverse and disturbing figures on the horizon of the twentieth-century Raj. He was reputedly a pederast and sadist rumoured to have been responsible for a number of really macabre sex-related deaths. He also claimed to be an incarnation of the god Rama, demonstrated an absolutely pathological revulsion to leather, wore gloves to protect himself from the contaminating touch of Europeans and other untouchables, and bankrupted his state treasury with bizarre and extravagant expenditures like buying up a fleet of Rolls-Royces and using them as garbage disposal units in retaliation for an imagined snub in one of the company's London showrooms. Sir Arthur Lothian, who briefly served in Alwar during an uprising of the ruler's Muslim subjects over excessive taxation and harsh oppression, described the atmosphere of the state under Jay Singh as 'sinister beyond description'.

So how ever on earth did this flagitious despot stay on the Gadi for forty years? For a start, Jay Singh happened also to be a man of overwhelming charm and scintillating intelligence who very shrewdly culti-vated key people in high places, particularly Sir Edwin Montague, Secretary of State for India. The Maharaja was a Sanskrit scholar, brilliant orator, a fantastically charismatic raconteur fluent in several languages, who never failed to beguile his listeners with a smoothly flowing blend of Hindu mysticism and wit. At the beginning of his reign he demonstrated a gift for administration and did much to modernize and develop his state. He was a great patron of education and Indian art and culture. There were even those who saw in Jay Singh's malicious, *outré* behaviour toward various members of British officialdom, including several Vicerenes, a frustrated princely form of Hindu nationalism.

The Maharaja was also a superb sportsman, a crack marksman and a generous host who put on a first-rate *shikar* out in the tiger-infested jungles of Alwar State, using highly trained beaters conscripted from his armed forces (and, it is said, peasant children conscripted from his villages as tiger bait) and was never wanting for eager colonial guests to partake of his hospitality. Although he had inherited the lovely Siliserh Palace near the capital, Jay Singh built his own 'shooting box' further into the jungles where the hunting was better. At the turn of the century, while still a minor, the Maharaja initiated the construction of a hunting lodge which was finished in 1902, the year before Jay Singh was invested with full ruling powers.

It was an enormous forty-room structure which, including staff quarters within the compound, could accommodate up to one thousand people. Seen from a distance with its four domed towers rising up in stunning isolation from the ragged wilderness, Sariska Palace appeared like some sudden oriental hallucination, a white *non sequitur* in the deciduous jungle. Closer up it became clear that, aside from its mock minarets, this was an oversized European colonial bungalow with verandahs, a semicircular bay entrance and wide, manicured gardens with fountains and walkways.

Yvonne Fitzroy visited Alwar as secretary to Lady Reading during a viceregal visit and penned a vivid vignette of an evening in this place which betrays a creepy sense of how Sariska was used and a trace of the ruler's notorious cruelty:

In March of 1922 we arrived at the elaborate white palace that at Alwar adorns the humble name of shooting-lodge, but although startling in effect it has ceased to have any terrors for the jungle which reaches to its doors and permits panther to stroll in its garden. In this they are encouraged, for on the front lawn is placed a table, above it a powerful electric light, upon it an unhappy baby goat. After dinner the guests are invited to gather on the veranda, the goat is encouraged to wail (and indeed, poor little wretch, needs no such encouragement) and the panther is expected to kill. I am glad to say that on the occasion of our visit the goat drew blank and was finally removed by special request, but this, like the iron cage supplied in the jungle for the same purpose, is an aspect of Oriental 'sport' few Englishmen will be found to appreciate.

Miss Fitzroy went on to describe one of the Maharaja's impressively organized tiger shoots:

The country round Seriska, as the palace is called, is barren and dusty, broken by those sudden, peculiar hills of Rajputana that lift untidy heads above the plain. The morning after our arrival news of three tigers – a mother and two full-grown cubs – was received and immediately after luncheon the entire party set forth. We were to meet the elephants four miles away and then take up our stands within view of the beat. The elephants at Alwar are famous as the staunchest and best trained in India, and to eliminate risk they are all female, since the male is often a dangerous beast at this season of the year. . . . The Maharaja has worked on the theory that a brave mahout makes a staunch elephant, for they are as sensitive to their rider's nerve as a horse, and so it is of the mahout that he asks courage first and foremost. The system certainly produces remarkable results.

The Maharaja's Military Secretary accompanied His Excellency, and he and the Maharaja climbed each to their elephants, we to our own, and though the howdahs were exceptionally comfortable nothing can really assuage the pangs caused by the admirable creature's walk . . .

Reflect what it means in experience, judgement and skill to bring a tiger over six miles of mountainous country and make him break cover within fifty yards of a given point – and it is done.

On the first beat the tigers escaped as it were with a warning, and while the Maharaja and His Excellency proceeded by elephant to the next stand, the rest of us motored for some distance, did a mile's stiff walking and reached the top of a low

hill, covered with thick scrub and dropping steeply to a valley below. The ridge of rock and scrub with a clearing on our right reaching from the summit to base. At the foot of this clearing stood His Excellency's elephant, while the Maharaja rode up and down the valley directing the beat. A row of elephants stood in the valley to prevent the tiger breaking in our direction.

For the first three decades of the twentieth century Maharaja Jay Singh presided over shoots like this. In spite of his peccant reputation and malevolent misdemeanours he managed to hang on to his throne, ever skirting the edge of the outer limits of official respectability. He got away with it all until finally in 1933 he lost control altogether and, more importantly, in public.

After losing a polo match the Maharaja flew into an uncontrollable rage directed at a pony he blamed for his bad showing. Out on the field between chukkers, in front of a horror-stricken crowd including a number of English ladies and gentlemen, Jay Singh had the pony doused with kerosene, personally lit a match to the animal and watched the bonfire with grim satisfaction. Needless to say, that sadistic little set-piece got him the sack. He was deposed and exiled to Paris, where he died from alcoholism and other excesses four years later.

As Jay Singh had no issue, the British Government had to find a suitable successor and went, as per custom, to the lineage that had traditionally been drawn on for adoption. They turned to Tej Singh, the adopted son of the Thakur of Thana. Jay Singh had earlier conceived an intense hatred for the thakur, stripped him of his feudal estates and driven him into exile in Jaipur. Twenty-six-year-old Tej Singh (1937-47) returned to Alwar and ascended the Gadi to rule until Independence.

The new Maharaja was not an avid *shikari* and had little use for his predecessor's hunting lodge. Sariska Palace was left alone and uninhabited in its wild isolation until after Independence, when the government scramble for empty properties produced a succession of tenants. During the time of Pandit Nehru Sariska Palace was used as a management-training institute and for a number of years as the military training centre for the Central Reserve Police (CRP) which produced a battalion of law enforcers

on its premises. Sariska had formally become a wildlife sanctuary in 1955. In consequence the government of Mrs Indira Gandhi decided that animal conservation and gunfire were incompatible and the CRP training centre was removed from Sariska Palace.

After a decade of disuse followed by the depredations of official occupation, the building had badly deteriorated. In 1979 the animal sanctuary at Sariska was greatly expanded and by this time Maharaja Tej Singh was eager to sell off his worn-out white elephant at even a concessionary price. The Rajasthan State government was interested in acquiring the property, as were the Birla family, India's leading industrialist dynasty, for one of their cultural or education institutions, but the building's isolation, its state of degradation and the spectre of heavy maintenance costs discouraged prospective purchasers until Ranjit Singh, a businessman from Bikaner, bought the property in the name of his company Siva-Wheels, completely renovated the building, re-landscaped the grounds and opened Sariska Palace as a hotel in 1983.

NEEMRANA FORT

Neemrana was the principal township of a feudal territory of the same name within the princely state of Alwar. Set back from the Delhi-Jaipur highway, it is a small, rundown farming hamlet of stone and rubble houses with narrow, rutted, leaking roads cluttered with chickens and domestic pigs. These dwellings are clustered at the base of a rocky hill beneath the acclivous ruins of a massive fortress – a strange anomaly in this humble place – reflecting wasted majesty and lost dominion. Indeed, Neemrana Fort was the final hereditary stronghold of the Chauhan dynasty of Rajputs, tracing their lineage from the fabled Prithvi Raj Chauhan III, the last Hindu king of India, whose life has been immortalized in thousands of songs. *Prithvi Raj Raso*, a single epic ballad glorifying the exploits of this legendary king, is composed of 125,000 verses.

Prithvi Raj III reigned over Ajmer and Delhi until 1192 when he was routed on the battlefield and killed by the invading armies of Sultan Muhammad Ghori. His descendants were driven into exile and took refuge in eastern Rajasthan in the region known as Rath which came to be synonymous with the Chauhans, inspiring the proverb: '*Kath nave par Rath nave na*' – 'The plough handle may bend but not the Rath.'

Madan Singh Chauhan, known as Rao Made, established a new dynastic capital with the foundation of the village of Madanpur, today known as Mandawar. In the early fifteenth century Rao Jhama of Mandawar was put to the sword by Muslim iconoclasts for refusing to convert to Islam but in 1442 his son Rao Chand, either through coercion or genuine belief, shed his idolatry to embrace the religion of Muhammad, continuing to rule as a Muslim under the name of Raoji. In protest against his nephew's apostasy, Chand's uncle Rajdeo abandoned Mandawar and established himself in the province of Neemrana.

In 1464 construction began of a square *giri durg*, or hill fort, and a magnificent palace on a natural plateau halfway up the slopes of Neemrana. Although much reduced in size and power this new Chauhan territory was still a rich principality and there was said to have been much treasure buried within the fortress of Neemrana. In the late eighteenth century the Chauhan capital was further ornamented when Raja Maha Singh constructed the temple of Siddhi Nath and a magnificent *baoli*, or step-well, which cost the ruler 856,000 rupees. This astonishing structure, excavated on the lowlands below the hill fort, is a wide, exposed chasm extending hundreds of feet at the surface, with a broad stone stairway at its opening which descends directly seven storeys into the depths of the earth. At each level landings lead to a surrounding gallery supported by a series of pillars constituted in stone and lime plaster mixed with jaggery. These galleries contain elegant apartments, constructed of stone, for the ruler and his entourage to savour the subterranean cool in the heat of summer. The stairway leads down into a large rectangular reservoir, fed by a deep circular well. The French traveller Louis Rousselet visited a similar baoli in the 1860s and wrote: 'I know of few monuments that strike the traveller more, when, entering them for the first time, he penetrates gradually into these mysterious galleries.'

Neemrana may have been half a kingdom but it was still a kingdom – independent and sovereign – until the beginning of the nineteenth century when the Raja of Neemrana made the mistake of siding with the Marathas against the British. In consequence of this unfortunate alliance, his territories were seized and distributed between Alwar, Jaipur, Patiala, Nabha and British India. The core of the raja's truncated province was subsumed into Alwar and reduced to the station of a tiny *jagir*, or feudal estate, owing tribute to the Maharaja of Alwar. The Rath refused to bend to this humiliation for over half a century as a protracted dispute between Alwar and Neemrana continued until 1868 when a negotiated settlement gave the Raja of Neemrana civil and judicial authority within his estate in exchange for Neemrana's formal acceptance of its tributary status.

The palace within Neemrana Fort remained the hereditary home of the Chauhans until 1947 (new wings were built as late as the 1920s) when the last ruler of Neemrana abandoned the family castle. Raja Rajinder Singh ruled in name for the two years preceding Independence but delegated his authority to officials because, as he explained, 'My views were somewhat different. I didn't like the aristocracy; I *wanted* to live as a commoner.' This unusual attitude was the outcome of an incident in the raja's youth. Rajinder Singh had been offered a commission to serve as an officer in the Indian army. Full of enthusiasm, he approached his father for permission to take it up but the Raja swore that he would commit suicide if his son disgraced the Chauhans by submitting to British service.

Rajinder Singh obeyed his father but lost all love for the way of life that had deprived him of a military career. With the approach of Independence he closed down his family fortress to save the enormous cost of maintenance and moved into Vijay Bagh, a more modest house in the lowlands below the fort, eager to be done with the feudal life once and for all. On 10 August 1947, four days before Independence and seven years before the abolition of feudal estates, Raja Rajinder Singh voluntarily handed the government

of his thikana over to its citizens.

Already Neemrana Fort had begun to crumble. In 1946 an entire wing collapsed. Gradually other walls began to give way, roofs caved in and the entire property became an empty, bat-infested carcass.

In the late 1970s the Indian writer-graphic designer Aman Nath and the French businessman Francis Wacziarg (see page 40), two of India's most dedicated cultural explorers, turned off the Delhi-Jaipur road on an impulse to see what they could see of Neemrana village. What they saw utterly captivated them and drew them back time and again. Aman eventually met Raja Rajinder Singh, who had moved to Alwar, and learned that he wanted in the worst way to rid himself of his tumbledown fort.

Aman formed a partnership with two like-minded friends from Delhi, businessman O. P. Jain and Lekha Poddar (née Birla), to purchase Neemrana Fort from its owner with the intention of making the property habitable. Rajinder Singh agreed with alacrity but before he signed a deed of conveyance he raked through the ruins of the fort, digging holes in every room to see if he could find the treasures said to have been buried there. This was not entirely wishful thinking, for the Raja remembered as a boy watching his family, who had by then fallen on hard times, dig into the centre of a courtyard in the sixteenth-century *haveli* at the back of the fort and pull out a silver urn filled with gold coins. After riddling the fortress with holes, the Raja gave up and sold his property without a trace of sentimentality or regret. All he says is that he is 'very pleased the palace is in good hands'.

The new owners spent a year clearing rubble from the interiors and another year rebuilding the collapsed wing. The partners have proceeded slowly, renovating the property room by room, visiting the site every Sunday, conferring with the contractor and masons and making decisions as to each successive phase of the work.

Each room is of a different motif representing a specific part of India – Kerala, Rajasthan, Gujarat, etc. – using the indigenous arts and crafts of each region, ultimately covering the traditional styles found in thirty contemporary Indian states and territories.

Instead of bringing in an interior decorator to impose a uniform design upon the palace, the partners, who are all avid collectors of traditional Indian art, have decided to make their fort-hotel a work-in-progress, using the talents of some of India's finest contemporary artists. At the end of 1989 Aman Nath arranged for painters to come from the art school at Maharaja Sayajirao University at Baroda to work on two frescoes – one traditional, one contemporary – on the walls of the palace. He explained how this came about:

Some of our best contemporary painters come from M.S. University. I'd gone there to interview painters for a major exhibition we were organizing in Delhi and saw that they had a whole department for fresco painting. Now students love to do frescoes on wet plaster and they don't really have walls so they have to work on tablets. They learn these techniques and then have nowhere to practise them so they end up painting on canvas and that's usually the end of it. I proposed that we could cooperate in an art project because we have lots of walls, after all. We offered to pay for everything – materials, food, transportation, etc. – except a salary for the actual work. They were delighted, really, because they rarely have a chance to do geniune fresco work on live walls. So the work was carried out very much like the Mughal atelier.

Ten students, eight from various parts of India, one from America and one from Sri Lanka, carried out the work under the direction of Ghulam muhammad Sheikh, one of India's leading contemporary painters. Two murals were designed. One, conceived by Ghulam muhammad, refers to the ancient Indian legend of Alexander the Great and the speaking tree. The other, depicting a wild boar hunt, is derived from four separate Sheikhawati frescoes and was conceived and supervised by the artist Jyoti Bhat.

Neemrana Fort is far and away the most creative and audacious conversion of a princely property into a hotel yet attempted in India.

JODHPUR

REGION OF DEATH

The Englishman came to Jodhpur at mid-day, in a hot, fierce sunshine that struck back from the sands and the ledges of red rock, as though it were May instead of December . . . In the hot weather, between ten in the morning and four in the afternoon all Jodhpur stays at home for fear of death by sunstroke, and it is possible that the habit extends far into what is officially called the 'cold weather'; or, perhaps, being brought up among sands, men do not care to tramp them for pleasure. The city is of red sandstone and dull and sombre to look at. Beyond it, where the white sand lies, the country is dotted with camels limping into the Ewigkeit or coming from the same place. Trees appear to be strictly confined to the suburbs of the city. Very good.
Rudyard Kipling, *Letters of Marque*, 1887-9

This sun-struck city of red sandstone Kipling came to visit was the capital of a kingdom five times the size of Wales; a wide, immutable wasteland called Marwar – 'Region of Death'. This harsh, encompassing desert was the final home of the Rathors, an ancient Rajput dynasty expatriated from Kanauj, their kingdom on the Gangetic plain; driven in 1194 by the same invading armies of Sultan Muhammad Ghori that had expelled the Chauhans from Delhi.

The Rathors settled in the village of Pali for two centuries before moving to Mandore in 1392. Less than a century later the reigning chieftain Rao Jodha (1455-89) followed an ascetic's oracular behest and in 1459 laid foundations for a fortress upon a high tor known as Bakurchirea – 'Bird's Nest' – some five miles to the south of Mandore. He named his newly established capital Jodhpur, in honour of himself. The majestic fort of Mehrangarh continued to ramify and spread across the ridge until Kipling could justifiably decide that it 'might have been built by Titans and coloured by the morning sun'.

From these commanding ramparts Rao Jodha and his fierce descendants swiftly regenerated the majesty of their clan in an expanding succession of conquests which culminated in the reign of Rao Maldeo

(1532-69), who was, according to the Muslim historian Farishta, 'the most potent prince in Hindustan'. Jodhpur had become by this time a flourishing entrepôt at an intersection of caravan routes from China, Central Asia and Gujarat where Marwari merchants attracted fabulous wealth to this otherwise impoverished land.

Toward the end of Maldeo's reign Jodhpur was subjugated by the armies of Akbar, concluding a golden age of Rathor ascendancy. His son Udai Singh (1584-97) sealed the disgrace by giving up his sister Jodha Bai in marriage to Akbar and his daughter Man Bai to the emperor's son Prince Salim, the future Jahanghir, becoming the first of Rajput princes to miscegenate with Mughals. This humiliating move, however, secured the restoration of Jodhpur territories and the imperial imprimatur to Rathor dominion over Marwar.

Throughout all the vicissitudes of Jodhpur's tempestuous history Marwar remained very much a region of death. In the nineteenth century alone the desert kingdom suffered seventeen calamitous famines ending in 1898-9 with the worst drought ever recorded in the history of Upper India. Driven by the unrelenting sun which, in the words of Kipling's Brahmin companion, 'Would knock you – oh yes – all to smash . . .', and the perpetual spectre of starvation and death, the Rathors and their Marwari subjects consolidated a resilient principality which even in subjection was a girded pillar of empire for the Mughals and their British successors.

Jodhpur changed in the days of compulsory peace. Impregnable battlements no longer mattered and suburban overspill with its distinguishing trees stretched out from the sandy plains beneath the craggy ridge once known as 'Bird's Nest' and renamed Jodhagir – 'Hill of Strife'. Upon those bluffs Jodhpur's astonishing fort now impressed touring Englishmen like Kipling and even the supercilious Sir Edwin Lutyens, who found it the most remarkable structural feat in his experience. The silent battlements with their cold and empty cannons offered instead of defence a supernal vantage point above the clamouring city from which they could look down aloof, lost in the awesome loveliness of the sand-swept horizon and the whitewashed honeycomb of structures below, oblivious to the bloody past and impending famines which continue to come implacably, like clockwork, upon the bleached and merciless earth.

Standing on the ramparts of the Jodhpur fort – on a level with the highest wheelings of the vultures, whose nests are on the ledges of the precipices beneath the walls – one looks down on to the roofs of the city, hundreds of feet below. And every noise from the streets and houses comes floating up, diminished but incredibly definite and clear, a multitudinous chorus, in which, however, one can distinguish all the separate component sounds – crying and laughter, articulate speech, brayings and bellowings and bleatings, the creak and rumble of wheels, the hoarse hooting of a conch, the pulsing of drums. I have stood on high places above many cities, but never on one from which the separate sounds making up the great counterpoint of a city's roaring could be so clearly heard, so precisely sifted by the listening ear. From the bastions of Jodhpur fort one hears as the gods must hear from their Olympus – the gods to whom each separate word uttered in the innumerably peopled world below comes up distinct and individual to be recorded in the books of omniscience.
Aldous Huxley, *Jesting Pilate*, 1927

UMAID BHAWAN PALACE

Legend has it that the lofty setting designated as the site of Rao Jodha's new capital and defending fortress was the hermitage of a holy man who, forced to abandon his retreat and infuriated at the disruption of his reveries, invoked a curse upon the kingdom. It was said that the *sadhu's* malediction afflicted Jodhpur with 'one lean year in three, one famine year in eight'. Whether the incident has any basis in fact, the Rathor capital has indeed suffered severe scarcity and drought every third or fourth year from the origins of the city down to the present day.

So it was that these cycles dictated the course of this desert kingdom's history and it became the custom of the rulers of Jodhpur to sustain their subjects through the severities of dearth. A tradition had developed among Rajput rulers to alleviate the sufferings of their people by creating

work for them. This work took many forms; from the building of canals to the excavation of roads, to the digging of step-wells, to the construction of temples and palaces, so that every level of labour within the country could be utilized. An extraordinary part of the richly constructed legacy of Rajasthan grew out of these seasons of adversity, through what were the feudal equivalent of social welfare or famine-relief programmes.

In 1920 the monsoons ceased and another rainless cycle began. The ruling Maharaja Umaid Singh (1911-47) sustained his people by distributing food and money to those in need. After three years of drought the people were becoming demoralized by their spiralling poverty. In 1922 they refused the alms the Maharaja offered, asking him to pay them for work rather than debase them with charity. Umaid Singh then resorted to Rajput tradition and set about creating a series of projects that would give the people of Jodhpur more than simple seasonal employment. These projects were later described by Rosita Forbes, who travelled through Jodhpur in the 1930s:

Eighteen great irrigation works have been constructed to give water to 60,000 bighas of land. The scarcity of water in the city has been remedied by the erection of a reservoir with eight pumping stations. Roads are spreading. Fine buildings are springing up on the outskirts of the lovely town . . .

The majority of the 'fine buildings springing up' was actually one single complex and the centrepiece of this famine-relief scheme, for the Maharaja had decided to build a royal palace that would distinguish his kingdom while providing a source of productivity and income for his subjects for many years in succession. It took two years for Umaid Singh to formulate his ideas for what was to become the last stupendous expression of princely architectural extravagance in the Raj: Umaid Bhawan Palace. In 1925 he went to England in search of an architect.

Umaid Singh commissioned the London firm of Lanchester and Lodge to build his palace. Henry V. Lanchester had been a protégé of Edwin Lutyens (see page 22) and was, according to Philip Davies, 'one of the most enthusiastic and inventive advocates of Baroque civic classicism in England'. In the first decade of the century he and his partner, the draughtsman Edwin Rickards, had created critically acclaimed designs for the Cardiff City Hall and Law Courts and Central Hall, Westminster. By the time the Jodhpur commission arrived, Rickards had died, leaving Lanchester on his own and, in the minds of many critics, without the creative spark their collaboration had inspired. Be that as it may, this project was to become the high-water mark of Lanches-ter's career.

Four years later the blueprints for Umaid Bhawan Palace were approved and in 1929 the foundation stone was laid upon a water-less rise called Chittar Hill – a site deemed auspicious by court astrologers – across the plain from the Jodhpur Fort. Some 2,500 to 3,000 people were constantly employed for the fifteen years it took to complete this massive sandstone palace. Because of its location the mammoth construction became commonly referred to as Chittar-ka-Bangla – Chittar Bungalow. Maharaj Swaroop Singh, the nephew of Maharaja Umaid Singh, remembers growing up around the endlessly unfinished palace: 'As little children we used to go to Umaid Bhawan and play there. It was such a massive structure that we used to take stones and mark our way while going on so that we would be able to retrace our steps and find our way out.' Finally, in 1943, Umaid Singh formally moved his residence from Rai-ka-Bagh Palace to Umaid Bhawan.

Lanchester's neo-classical palace was a colossal 347-room structure with two monumental wings separated by a central double dome soaring to a height of 185 feet which managed to incorporate the interior spatial arrangement of a traditional Indian palace within the scale, symmetry and ornamental pomp of the British imperial style.

There was a durbar hall and a billiard room, ballrooms and banquet halls and libraries panelled in Burmese teak. There were circular central reception halls, one with magnificently sweeping double staircases, the other with a soaring rotunda, 130 feet beneath the marble floors of which was a luxurious swimming pool inlaid with tiles depicting the zodiac, with quaint aquatic paintings ornamenting the subterranean walls.

The wings encompassed courtyards and included zenana apartments, staff offices and servants' quarters, and a fully equipped cinema and gigantic royal suites, finished with fashionable Art Deco interiors designed by the Polish artist and decorator S. Norblin, who also painted scenes from the Hindu epic *Mahabharata* on the walls of what is now called the Oriental Room. The Maharani's quarters were fitted with a bath tub cut from a single block of pink marble. One million square feet of the finest marble was used throughout the construction.

The Maharaja had all the furniture custom-made in England and ordered a massive air-conditioning system but these became victims of war when the warehouse holding the furniture was bombed during the Blitz and the ship which carried the royal air-conditioning system was torpedoed by the German navy and sunk. The prince simply had the same designs fabricated by local furniture-makers but had to content himself with the palace's structural cooling features and the traditional method, using *tatti* screens over door and window openings which, sprinkled with water, cool the natural air-flow. This method is still in use in many of the palace rooms and is extremely comfortable.

The ornamentation of the palace was a smooth combination of European classical elements interlaced with orientalia. Interestingly, the oriental design influences were not derived from Mughal or the so-called Indo-Saracenic models because, according to Lanchester, 'In the architectural treatment and ornamental detail, any use of "Indo-Saracenic" features was regarded as inappropiate, in view of the fact that the States of Rajasthan only came to a very limited extent under Muslim domination.' The architectural historian G.H.R. Tillotson points out in his study *The Tradition of Indian Architecture* that:

Lanchester eschewed Islamic forms . . . and looked instead to an earlier Indian, pre-Islamic heritage. Thus the dripstones or Chajjas *are ribbed, recalling those of ancient Indian temples; and the dining hall is a reinterpretation of a Buddhist* caitya *or prayer hall of the first or second century. The exterior is entirely trabeate, except for the domes, and their concentric rings echo the stepped-ring construction of the local, medieval Jain temples.*

These indigenous influences were streamlined through the prevailing architectural fashion of the day – Art Deco – creating a synthesis Tillotson calls Indo-Deco, of which he says Umaid Bhawan is 'the finest example'. He commends Lanchester for 'having set himself the more difficult task of employing an archaic architectural vocabulary', compared with the style of his Indo-Saracenic antecessors, 'but his handling of the Indian tradition is both more informed and more inventive . . .' Tillotson goes on:

He is never archaeologically scrupulous, but never illiterate either. The piers of the porte-cochère, *and the* jalis *suspended between the columns of the outer veranda, cannot be traced to specific historical models; they are new designs, but they are drawn in the spirit of the Indian originals. The planning of the palace, it is true, follows Western patterns, but Lanchester did not simply peg Indian details onto a Western frame, nor did he produce a scrapbook of Indian architecture; rather, examining that source, he designed new and powerful motifs. Among the essays in Indian styles by Englishmen, the Umaid Bhawan Palace comes closest to being a fusion of Eastern and Western traditions, prevented from being completely so only by its plan. Lanchester had progressed from toying with exotica and was approaching a new architectural logic.*

Like the grand imperial buildings of the Raj, Umaid Bhawan was made to last. Massive sandstone boulders were cut from a quarry at Sursagar, eight miles from Jodhpur, and transported on a special narrow-gauge railway directly to hangars on the construction site, where master masons would chisel the chunks into interlocking blocks of between five and seven tons which were numbered to fit in sequence. No mortar or cement was used in the construction. The blocks had been cut to form a perfect fit and chiselled vertically so that dust would not adhere to them. Each block was lifted by crane and dropped into place. The weight limit of the cranes being used was five tons so the heavier blocks had to be hoisted onto even larger blocks of ice and manipulated into position as the ice melted.

By this time the Second World War had spread to India, and Jodhpur, by virtue of its aerodrome built by Umaid Singh, an

avid amateur flyer, had become an important military base at which Allied troops from every country were stationed. At one point in the early 1940s, the temporary military barracks had been damaged and Maharaja Umaid Singh offered the Allied forces the use of his unfinished palace. Soldiers, then, were the first occupants of Umaid Bhavan.

In 1943 the Maharaja organized an elaborate sit-down Christmas dinner for the entire Allied military community in Jodhpur. Over 1,000 men were served in the palace's central rotunda. Shobha Kanwar Baiji, the granddaughter of the illustrious Regent of Jodhpur, Sir Pratap Singh, said that her father, who supervised the preparations for this royal feast, 'boasted that the soup was hot and the coffee at the end was also hot'. This spectacular Christmas banquet was repeated again in 1944. Each guest was given an elegant personal Christmas gift by the Maharaja.

At war's end, the Jodhpur family settled into the vast majesty of their new royal palace. Their repose was fleeting, however. In 1947, the year of Independence, when the princely order would irrevocably change, Maharaja Umaid Singh was stricken with appendicitis while at his hunting lodge at Mount Abu and, without adequate medical facilities in that hill station, died suddenly at the age of forty-three.

His eldest son, Hanwant Singh, was only twenty-three years old when he ascended to the Gadi and, without preparation or warning, he managed the delicate and painful transition as his domains became absorbed into greater India and the partition made his desert principality the violent, tortuous pathway for the double exodus of emigrants from India and Pakistan.

Like many Maharajas, Hanwant Singh entered into politics as a popular opposition figure. In 1952, on the day of his landslide election to the Lok Sabha and the victorious sweep to power of his party's candidates in Jodhpur, the young Maharaja was killed en route to a remote voting station when the private plane he was flying became ensnarled in power lines and crashed. His son and successor, Gaj Singh, was but four years old.

The young Maharaja's mother became regent and sent her son to England for his education. He remained there as a student through prep school, Eton and Oxford until his graduation in 1970, when he returned home to assume his ceremonial place as Maharaja of Jodhpur and head of his clan. Throughout this extended period Umaid Bhawan was maintained by a staff but rarely inhabited by the royal family since the Rajmata had taken up residence in Pune where her daughters were being educated. Travellers could on occasion find lodgings in the staff wing of the palace but, with the exception of the student prince's winter sojourns, it was a sad and empty castle.

One year after Gaj Singh's return to Jodhpur, Indira Gandhi engineered the formal de-recognition of the princes of India. Titles and privileges were withdrawn along with the privy purses which had helped the former rulers to sustain their estates and retainers. The Prime Minister's motivations were blatantly political but the move was merely the final part of an inexorable process that had begun in 1947 when a socialist state was created.

The young Maharaja had to decide what to do with himself and his estate. His mother had done the best she could to maintain the properties as they were, but she was not in a position to develop them commercially. So suddenly the young ex-ruler of a state he had barely lived in was confronted with the very real problem of what to do with his gargantuan hereditary castle.

It was clearly untenable to keep Umaid Bhawan as a private residence. The Maharaja remembers that 'At one time it was just my mother and myself in this enormous place with not enough staff even to keep it clean.' Rather than surrender Umaid Bhawan and the ancient Jodhpur Fort to bureaucratic misfeasance, Gaj Singh set up a trust to run the fort as a museum and began exploring the possibilities of turning the Umaid Bhawan into a hotel.

Baiji related that the Maharaja's 'main object was not only to give the palace over for management but also to keep his old servants employed and many hoteliers did not agree to that condition. They felt our staff was too old. So his reply was that "if you don't want my staff you can't have my palace".' Several years passed in this way until ITC-Welcomgroup agreed to these conditions and in 1977 Umaid Bhawan opened as one of India's grandest luxury hotels.

The Maharaja of Jodhpur remains resident with his family in Umaid Bhawan, having taken over the viceregal suite for his personal use, from where he monitors the development of his palace:

My wife and I do involve ourselves in anything structural or when the ambience of the palace needs to be altered. We make it a point to make certain we are consulted because otherwise, well you know how things are; it's a non-stop battle. But as I said, I'm very happy to see the palace living again which is what any building, and especially a building like this, needs. By itself, you know, it becomes rather gloomy.

These days Umaid Bhawan Palace is far from gloomy, attracting waves of strangers craning up in awe at its overwhelming scale, trying to absorb the enormity of this echoing, fantastic castle built by a serious-minded young ruler for the sake of alleviating a dearth and destined to become one of the most magnificent hotels in India, which in both its structure and atmosphere remains much as it must have been when Umaid Singh reigned supreme over his rugged desert state.

AJIT BHAWAN PALACE

. . . Surrounded by a halo of glory, Rama came out of his palace as the moon emerges from the dark blue clouds, and the chariot moved swiftly with a deep rumbling noise of a cloud . . . and Lakshmana stood by Rama with a chowri in his hand . . .
From the Valmiki *Ramayana*

Maharaj Ajit Singh (1907-78) was the younger brother of Maharaja Umaid Singh of Jodhpur. So strong was the love between these two brothers that Marwari poets of the period created songs comparing them with the mythological Lord Rama and his heroic younger brother Lakshmana, who served the avatar with intense love and constant self-sacrifice through the pages of the Hindu epic saga *Ramayana*. When Ajit Singh saved his brother from the jaws of a wild beast, these songs began to circulate, celebrating the likeness of the two brothers to their sacred ancestors, songs which are recited down to the present day. The Maharaja and his younger brother were almost inseparable; it was not unusual for them to weep upon parting company. Like Lakshmana with Rama, Ajit Singh stood staunchly beside his older brother throughout his reign, ready to serve him in any way he was needed. Like Rama with Lakshmana, Umaid Singh leaned upon his brother and looked after his welfare.

When the ruler initiated his famine-relief programme in the 1920s and made plans to construct his own magnificent palace on Chittar Hill, he also commissioned the creation of a smaller palace in close proximity to his own for his beloved younger brother. Local engineers from the Public Works Department were assigned to make preliminary designs for Ajit Singh's new palace under the initial supervision of Henry V. Lanchester when he visited Jodhpur to consult with the Maharaja on Umaid Bhawan. After Lanchester returned to England a Mr Goldstraw was appointed chief architect of Ajit Bhawan. Ground was broken at the base of Chittar Hall and the foundation stone was laid on 15 October 1927. Construction took two years and was carried out by the Jodhpur Public Works Department.

By 1929, the same year foundations were excavated for the Maharaja's own mammoth domicile, Ajit Bhawan was completed. It was a two-storey, twenty-five-room stone palace built around a rectangular open courtyard with zenana apartments upon the upper floor veiled by carved *jaali* screens. (Purdah was very much in force within the Jodhpur royal family and the zenana system was retained in Ajit Bhawan until the death of Maharaj Ajit Singh's wife in 1977.) The facade of the palace was crowned with a large central dome flanked by two smaller domes at either end of the building. Visitors would alight at an ornamental entry gate and walk to the palace itself in the traditional gesture of respect.

There were seven different types of stone quarried around Jodhpur. The finer sand-pink stone used for Umaid Bhawan came from the quarry at Sursagar. It was consi-

dered inappropriate to have the stone earmarked for the ruler's palace to be used for a secondary palace like Ajit Bhawan so blood-red sandstone from the Asler quarries was used in the structure.

In the grounds of Ajit Bhawan there were tennis courts, stables, storage areas and quarters to accommodate over one hundred servants and their families, bringing the number of people living within Ajit Singh's residential compound to around four hundred. His son, Maharaj Swaroop Singh, remembers that their palace was 'just like an institution, full of servants, horses, bullock carts, horse-drawn carriages, drivers, cooks, guards, and maid servants for the ladies'.

Shooting was a major recreation for the Jodhpur royal family, as it was for most of the princes of India, and the two Bhawans – Umaid and Ajit — were ideally situated for it outside Jodhpur City in what was still very much a wilderness teeming with panthers, antelope, gazelles, blue bulls, sambhar and spotted deer. Chittar Hill was also crawling with wild boars which invaded the compound at Ajit Bhawan, threatening its residents and regularly digging up the garden. One common diversion at the palace was shooting these snarling intruders. Swaroop Singh remembers that 'There was a big bed in one of the lower rooms which my father used to sleep on and he would lean out the window and shoot wild boars right from there.'

Maharaj Ajit Singh served his brother in a multiplicity of posts, heading secondary administrative departments such as forestry and customs before being elevated in 1940 to Prime Minister of Jodhpur, the second most powerful position in the administrative hierarchy. He retained this portfolio after assuming the supreme post of Dewan in the mid-1940s, serving in both capacities until 1947.

When Maharaja Umaid Singh died suddenly in Mount Abu in 1947, Maharaj Ajit Singh went into deep shock and refused to accept the truth; he would not believe that his beloved brother had died. When he finally recovered his senses Ajit Singh gave up alcohol, relinquished the bright colours of his turban and devoted himself to meditation for hours every day. Within one year of his brother's death, the Maharaj suffered another devastating loss along with all the aristocracy of India: Independence brought the end to his whole way of life. This he accepted with sane sobriety and forced his two young sons, Sobhag and Swaroop, to stand and fight for seats in the new Legislative Assembly of Rajasthan as a way of forcing them out of the rarified princely life they had been leading, into the hurly-burly of democratic India.

Ajit Singh was fortunate in having agricultural lands which brought in sufficient income to maintain his Jodhpur palace. As an experienced administrator he was able to run his household efficiently and within his resources. Life in Ajit Bhawan was necessarily simplified and staff was reduced but the Maharaj and his family managed to live a quiet, comfortable life free from the strains that many other Indian princes suffered in the aftermath of Independence.

It was only with the introduction of the Urban Land Ceiling laws in the late 1960s that the family began to seriously consider turning their palace to some sort of commercial use. This legislation was an extension of the Rural Land Ceiling laws instituted a decade earlier as part of a programme of land reform. It restricted the area of private properties inside cities and townships to 1,500 square metres. Most of the former aristocracy of India owned homes inside cities which exceeded this limit and were threatened with the loss of large portions of their estates. Fortunately the size of a household was taken into consideration and this helped the nobility since most of them still lived in joint families. There were also exemptions and allowances for properties which in some way served the public interest. For example, if they were used as schools, training institutes, or for some commercial purpose the limitation was lifted. One of the commercial uses allowed was for hotel accommodation. This was an ideal use for these palace properties which were in any case built for entertaining and guests. The urban land ceiling laws propelled many a princely home owner into the hotel business.

In the beginning these laws were not implemented but year by year the menace seemed to grow and the pressure to do something with property increased. Some

landowners opted to make their homes into play schools. The sons of Maharaj Ajit Singh first turned to tourism (there is now also a school on the grounds of Ajit Bhawan). Sobhag and Swaroop sought their father's blessing. Maharaj Ajit Singh said to them, 'When I die don't waste money and put a cenotaph over me. This is my cenotaph. We have made this all for you. This is a temple. Anybody coming into this temple, you should receive him with love and affection.'

It was a gradual process beginning in 1971. Maharaja Gaj Singh of Jodhpur had a friend from West Germany who came to visit and asked Swaroop to look after him. He enjoyed his stay and suggested that the family open up their palace as a guest house. Their German friend then arranged for the Lufthansa flight crews to spend a few days at Ajit Bhawan, which became a regular practice throughout the 1970s. This informal set-up gradually shaped the character of Ajit Bhawan when it finally opened as a fully fledged hotel. Swaroop Singh pioneered the village tour, taking his guests to the rural communities over which his family still had vestiges of influence. Guests would also take long walks and camel safaris into the desert. Today a number of Rajput landowners follow the same practice but this creative interaction with travellers originated at Ajit Bhawan.

Maharaj Ajit Singh died in 1978, in the midst of the most turbulent period in India's post-Independence history, Indira Gandhi's State of Emergency. It was during Mrs Gandhi's virtual dictatorship that the urban land ceiling laws were brandished like a vindictive sword. The threat of politically motivated eminent domain moved Sobhag and Swaroop Singh to officially convert Ajit Bhawan into a hotel. In 1980 twelve rooms of their palace were opened for paying guests and construction was started on a complex of traditional huts within the gardens. Ajit Bhawan is now a thriving tourist resort personally presided over by Maharaj Swaroop and Maharaj Sobhag Singh who receive their guests with love and affection.

JAISALMER

GOLDEN FORTRESS

If you look long enough across the sands, while a voice in your ear is telling you of half-buried cities, old as old Time, and wholly unvisited by Sahibs, of districts where the white man is unknown, and of the wonders of far-away Jeysulmir ruled by a half-distraught king, sand-locked and now smitten by a terrible food and water famine, you will, if it happen that you are of a sedentary and civilised nature, experience a new emotion – will be conscious of a great desire to take one of the lobbing camels and get away into the desert, away from the last touch of Today, to meet the Past face to face.
Rudyard Kipling, *Letters of Marque*, 1887-9

The kingdom of Jaisalmer was founded in 1156 by Rawal Jaisal, ruler of the Bhatti clan, descendants of the moon-born Yadu kings who reigned supreme in India three thousand years before, from the Yamuna to 'the world's end'. The Bhatti kings of Jaisalmer ruled through every form of adversity from siege to famine to internal tyranny, protected by or trapped in their golden lime-stone fortress that rose dream-like upon the horizon.

The sand-locked isolation of Jaisalmer was for many centuries its greatest asset, attracting rich Marwari traders to build baronial refuges of golden stone to which they could escape with their treasures from the cities of Upper India in times of upheaval and war. Not until the British arrived with their peace-keeping treaties and railroad trains (which bypassed Jaisalmer) did the fortunes of this fortified town decline, but in one respect far-away Jaisalmer benefited from this colonial neglect: its ancient wonders were left unretouched, burnished in the desert sun.

JAWAHAR NIWAS PALACE

In 1897 Thomas Holbein Hendley described Jaisalmer as 'almost wholly desert' and 'very inaccessible' (meaning, among other things, that the desert city was still over one hundred miles from a railhead, approachable only by

camel tracks); two very good reasons why it took Her Imperial Majesty's Government until the 1880s to send a permanent Political Agent to the picturesque but barren principality.

The change may possibly have been encouraged by the reigning prince's competence and 'progressiveness', for Maharawal Bairi Sal Singh (1865-91), an adopted heir to the Gadi of Jaisalmer, was characterized by one historian as 'a man of taste and culture, and also a philanthropist'. Taste, culture and philanthropy rarely being ascribed to 'old-fashioned' rulers, it might be assumed that these were marks of a 'modern' – that is, 'European' – outlook, certainly an attribute that would have elicited British approbation. Bairi Sal, to give him credit, was evidently a good ruler who tried to improve the conditions of his people.

Whether for this or other reasons, the Maharawal found himself faced with the honour of accommodating a representative of the Viceroy in his remote, relatively poor, and still exceedingly medieval state. Thus in 1884 Bairi Sal built for his newly appointed Political Agent a small European-style palace (with the usual Indo-Saracenic flourishes) outside the walls of the city in the distinctive yellow sandstone of Jaisalmer. This new residency was called at the time Ishal Bungalow.

In almost any other context, Ishal Bungalow's European design would have been an unremarkable addition to a late-nineteenth-century Native State and perfectly in keeping with princely building trends of the day but, for Jaisalmer, which had retained its design traditions virtually unadulterated by any European influences at all, it was a sudden and discordant architectural departure. G.H.R. Tillotson presents the building as an example of the subversion of traditional Rajput architecture in Jaisalmer, calling Ishal Bungalow 'scarcely more Indian than Sezincote or Elveden'.

Later palaces built by Bairi Sal and his successors continued to reflect European influences but seem to revert much closer to their Rajput roots, leading some scholars in search of an evolutionary place for this palace to attribute a later date – around 1900 – to its construction. What is more

likely is that Bairi Sal simply went out of his way to build a structure he thought would please his European guest and that the European design elements introduced in this construction were infiltrated to a lesser degree into subsequent Jaisalmer royal palaces made for inhabitants still very much entrenched in Indian traditions.

Ishal Bungalow remained the Political Agent's residence for several years and subsequently became an official guest palace for distinguished visitors to Jaisalmer. After Maharawal Jawahar Singh (1914-47) ascended the Gadi he renamed Ishal Bungalow Jawahar Niwas in honour of himself. Jawahar Niwas remained a royal guest palace until Independence when it reverted to the private use of the royal family of Jaisalmer, but it was never used as a permanent royal residence. It was instead reserved for weddings, parties and family gatherings for which it was used with decreasing frequency until, by the late 1970s, it had fallen into complete disuse and was lying deserted. The present hereditary Maharawal, Brij Raj Singh, fearing that his abandoned guest palace would be seized by the government of Rajasthan, converted Jawahar Niwas palace into a hotel in 1982.

BIKANER

A STRANGE PLACE

This is a strange place indeed . . . The accepted description of Bikanir by the globe-trotter is an 'oasis'. This is a wrong use of the word. There is no visible water. There is nothing to justify, or even make possible, the presence of a town in the centre of this vast waste of gravel and sand . . .
Perceval Landon, *Under the Sun* (early twentieth century)

Fearlessly conquered and fiercely defended by its Rathor overlords, Bikaner was for most of its history a scorched and waterless wasteland, adjacent to and geophysically no different from the 'no man's land' of Sheikhawati, with nothing but its martial heritage to recommend it. Yet in the twilight of empire this vast waste of gravel and sand came to be regarded as a sort of Indian utopia of exoticism and progress – its thriving capital a drawing card – and travellers never ceased to be startled by the stark dichotomy of primeval desert and modern development in this strange, extraordinary place.

With scant hope of inheriting the kingdom of his father and too much pride to be bound in tribute with a compensatory *jagir*, Rao Bika, the second son of Jodhpur's founder, set out from his father's capital in 1465 to magnify the glory of his clan and capture a country of his own. The young chieftain marched east across the wilderness with an army of one hundred horse and five hundred foot soldiers, settled down in the heart of an undefended desert and began to storm surrounding kingdoms and appropriate their lands.

Twenty-four years passed before Rao Bika raised the capital of his hard-won kingdom in 1486. Ironically, by this time his elder brother had died and the ruler of Bikaner had become heir-apparent to the Jodhpur Gadi. As Bika already was a king, his ageing father Rao Jodha asked him to stand aside in favour of his younger brother Surajmal and in return promised that the hereditary emblems of Rathor sovereignty – Throne, Umbrella, Yak's Tail, Sword, Drum, Cooking Pots and other totemic

tokens – would be passed to Bika. When Jodha died, however, Surajmal refused to surrender these symbols of seniority and several clan wars were fought before the trappings of Rathor supremacy finally found their way to Bika's kingdom.

But all the regalia on the earth could not alter the bleak reality of Bikaner. 'Endless distances', wrote K.M. Pannikar, 'vast stretches of unrelieved sand, deceptive mirages which created a sense of human helplessness – these were the physical characteristics of the country which Bikaji conquered for himself and his successors.' Through incessant campaigning, a wise compliance with Mughal power and constant service to the emperors of Delhi these iron Rajput warlords retained their territory with fiery tribal pride, as if their desiccated kingdom was some kind of Elysian oasis.

In 1829 Colonel James Tod wrote that Bikaner 'is but little known to Europeans, by whom it has hitherto been supposed to be a perfect desert, unworthy of examination'. Even late in the century Bikaner remained to English eyes an arid Indian outland; slightly better known perhaps, but still an endless, undeveloped void. In the 1880s Rudyard Kipling wrote, bemused and unconvinced:

There are Englishmen in these wastes, who say gravely that there is nothing so fascinating as the sand of Bikaner . . . 'You see,' explained an enthusiast of the Hat-marked caste, 'you are not shut in by roads, and you can go just as you please. And somehow, it grows upon you as you get used to it; and you end, y'know, by falling in love with the place.'

And so it was when suddenly, as the century turned, this inveterate perception was reversed. Bikaner was no longer simply a sandy, lapideous desert 'unworthy of examination'. It was a model to be studied, a prototype to be followed; its ruler the *ne plus ultra* of Indian princes.

Maharaja Ganga Singh (1887-1943) was a progressive visionary who, through the singular alchemy of Indian colonialism, transfigured his wasteland state with electrification and libraries, relief workers and railways, public parks and palaces, farm cooperatives and free hospitals, life

insurance and scholarships, girls' schools and men's colleges, coal mines and canals, monuments and memorial gates, a cigarette factory and the Boy Scout Movement. Impressive though this reformation was, Bikaner's setting in a primordial sea of sand and gravel made all these marks of progress seem all the more improbable and disorienting, and globe-trotters who traversed this forbidding, dehydrated sea could be forgiven for misdescribing their unexpectedly civilized destination as an 'oasis'.

LALLGARH PALACE

There is a strange prejudice here which is so often found at Rajputana. The Maharaja, by tradition and by preference, has built himself a new palace. In old days, a new chief contented himself with adding a few rooms for his own personal use to the great palace of his ancestors in the town. The present ruler has elected to build himself an entirely new residence, a mile outside the walls. This, in a way, affords a more striking contrast than anything else in Bikaner. If Jaipur is the town that Solomon transplanted, this house is nothing less than the palace which Aladdin's wicked uncle deported into the desert by the rub of the lamp – the same palace which Aladdin had at a similar insignificant outlay of trouble built for his bride in a single night. This, believe me, is the very palace. The story that Aladdin moved it back again must be untrue. They say here that it was built from the designs by Sir Swinton Jacob, but everyone will agree with my version who has once seen the rose-coloured walls, terraces, cupolas, and without an interposition of even so much grass or herbage as a Brixton villa can boast of, straight out of the gaunt emptiness and still moving sand of the Great Indian Desert.
Perceval Landon, *Under the Sun*

I t was definitely not lamp-rubbing that conjured Lallgarh Palace, but Maharaja Ganga Singh's brand-new, hand-made oriental residence, outfitted with every available mod-con of the period and standing right in the middle of nowhere, did have a mesmerizing impact upon unsuspecting visitors to the remote, sand-blown Rajput kingdom of Bikaner. At the same time Lallgarh served to symbolize its princely occupant's impressive success at integrating English efficiency and organization with Indian empathy and

tradition in the governance of his progressive State.

After the better part of a century of effort, the British experiment with the ruling chiefs of India finally produced a paradigm. Maharaja Ganga Singh was the very model of an English-educated Indian monarch; a fierce Anglophile and Imperialist, combining all the Victorian virtues with a conscientious sense of Rajput chivalry and conservatism. Nowhere was this synthesis more dramatically evinced than by the Aladdin's castle outside his capital.

Yet although Lallgarh Palace ultimately evolved into a genuine projection of Ganga Singh's own powerful Anglo-Indian personality, he had much less to do with its original creation that many assumed, as revealed by the following document:

File No. 210 of 1896
Note
Building of a house for H.H. the Maharaja at a distance from the Fort
1. In 1894, the ladies of the Zanana asked for the withdrawal of H.H. the Maharaja Ganga Singh from the Mayo College at Ajmere–
2. The Council decided with the approval of the Political Agent and the A.G.G., that the Maharaja should be with-drawn from the College – One of the conditions, on which his withdrawal was sanctioned was that during his minority – he should have his residence at a distance from the female palace and that every precaution should be taken to keep him away from the bad influence of an Indian zanana and from bad company, advice, & temptations.
3. With this view Rs.100,000 were provided in the current year's budget to build a new house for the Maharaja at a distance from the female palace.
4. I think it is most necessary to build a house for the Maharaja at a cost not exceeding Rs.100,000 – the minimum cost being fixed at 50,000 Rs.
S. Hakim
V.P. (Regency Council)

This internal memorandum, scrawled out in fading ink on brittle, yellowing paper and stashed among the dusty stacks of files in the Bikaner State Public Works Department at Lallgarh Palace, exposes as explicitly as was ever officially communicated the perpetual tug-of-war between the Political Department of the Indian Government and the cloistered female forces manipulating

power in the Native States from deep within the labyrinthine old traditional forts and palaces of India.

Lallgarh was but one of many modern palaces constructed during the last half of the nineteenth century expressly to keep impressionable young princes away from the matriarchal clutches of multifarious maharanis, concubines and maid-servants left behind by previous regimes who invariably opposed attempts to liberalize the administration of the state and exercized all the ancient palace arts of persuasion to retain power over a ruling prince. It was not, as Perceval Landon and many casual travellers presumed, by tradition and preference that late nineteenth century princes abandoned their ancestral castles in favour of suburban palaces. It was the long-range struggle initiated by and directed from 'the white core of India' to keep teenage Maharajas away from 'the bad influence of an Indian Zanana', which animated this palace-building spree. The British Political Department privately detested the zenana and evolved a policy towards the Indian princes calculated to minimize its influence.

After decades of experimentation the Indian Government devised a two-pronged strategy which proved eminently successful at segregating growing young rulers, both physically and intellectually, from the reactionary female forces of the Indian court. First and foremost the Government established elite Princes' Colleges, modelled on the British public school system, to educate the princes along English lines, instilling in them loyalty to the Empire and a modern, progressive and European outlook. These institutions were probably the single most effective westernizing instrument developed by the British Government in Indian India.

Secondly, to perpetuate the separation of the princes from the zenana, British Political Agents, who usually headed a Regency Council during the Maharaja's minority, would either encourage or command the Council to remove the Maharaja from the City Palace to a garden house or a newly built suburban residence.

Maharaja Ganga Singh (1887-1943) was the younger half-brother and heir-apparent of Maharaja Dungar Singh (1872-87) who died at the young age of thirty-three, leaving the throne of Bikaner to his seven-year-old sibling. Ganga Singh had thus to endure an unusually long minority of over eleven years while a Council of Regency, presided over by the Political Agent, controlled the state. The Council of Regency saw to it that the child Maharaja was entered into Mayo College at Ajmer in 1890 at the age of nine and remained a boarding student there for five years until 1895 when he was withdrawn.

According to K. M. Pannikar, Ganga Singh's official biographer, he was called back to receive his training in the army and to 'gain knowledge of administrative affairs and experience of official business'. This may have been the rationale which motivated the Regency Council to agree to the prince's withdrawal from Mayo College but we can see from File No. 210 of 1896 that the initial overtures were made by 'the ladies of the Zanana'.

Therefore upon the Maharaja's permanent return to Bikaner the building of a new residence for the young ruler became a priority and Colonel Sir Samuel Swinton Jacob, Chief Engineer of Jaipur State (see page 21), was commissioned by the Regency Council early in 1896 to design the structure. On 25 March of that year Jacob wrote to the Political Agent that 'all the plans connected with the design for the proposed Residence for H.H. the Maharaja of Bikanir are well advanced but are not quite ready yet, but I hope they will be ready in about 3 weeks.'

The architect had gone over these plans with Mr Gabbett, the Executive Engineer of Bikaner State, who wrote to the Political Agent that:

Colonel Jacob remarked to me that the cost of the bungalow would largely depend on the amount of the carved work in it – that he had taken the dimensions of the principal rooms from my rough drawings and that the cost would probably be considerably over a lac [lakh] of rupees – that however if thought advisable reductions might be made by taking the plan on a smaller scale and that in places stucco might be substituted for carved stone.

From this and other correspondence, it seems unlikely that the fifteen-year-old

Samode Haveli was built in the early 19th century by Rawal Bairi Sal as his Jaipur residence. Behind the verandah seen here, is an exquisitely hand-painted dining room. Samode Haveli also features an elephant ramp and a beautiful garden.

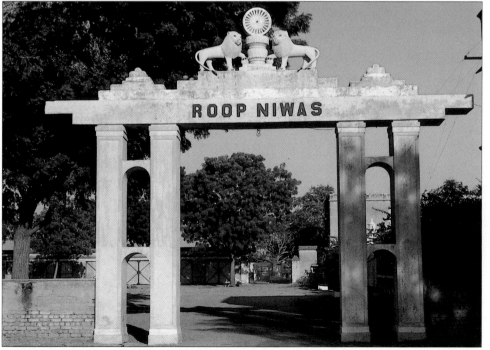

Roop Niwas Kothi began as a three-room farmhouse outside the town wall of Nawalgarh. In 1930 Thakur Madan Singh began expanding his residence until he had transformed the property into a country palace with this ornamental entry gate, fountains and water courses.

Right Dundlod Qila
was built in 1750 by
Thakur Kesri Singh
and remained a small
defensive fortress
manned by soldiers
until 1809 when
Thakur Sheoji Singh
occupied it.

Below The *Diwan
Khanna*, constructed by
Sheoji Singh sometime
after 1809, was open
onto the fort's interior
courtyard and could be
entered on elephant
back. The gallery
above is a *Rawala*, or
women's apartments.

Above In the 1880s the Marchioness of Dufferin described Siliserh lake and its palace: 'It is about four miles long, a most calm and peaceful sheet of water nearly surrounded by hills, and with a picturesque little castle on its banks, where we breakfasted.'

Left When finished in 1902 Sariska Palace could accommodate up to 1000 people for Maharaja Jay Singh's popular tiger shoots.

Above For Umaid Bhawan, the architect Henry V. Lanchester synthesized Hindu, Jain and Buddhist design elements with the Art Deco style of the day, thus inventing a style that has been called Indo-Deco.

Right Neemrana Fort was first built in 1464, as a *giri durg*, or hill fort. By the end of the Raj, Neemrana was reduced to feudatory status and its fort was crumbling.

Above Maharaja Umaid Singh had the 25 room Ajit Bhawan palace built for his younger brother, Ajit Singh, at the same time his gargantuan Umaid Bhawan was under construction.

Left Jawahar Niwas was built in 1884 for Jaisalmer's first British resident. Despite the use of local sandstone, it represented a stark departure from local building tradition.

Above Lallgarh Palace was, according to one early 20th century visitor, 'nothing less than the palace which Aladdin's wicked uncle deported into the desert by the rub of a lamp'. In fact, it was the result of successful moves on the part of the British Resident to get young Ganga Singh away from the clutches of the zenana.

Right Raja Charanjit Singh outfitted Chapslee with furnishings from his other Simla residences when he renovated his newly purchased home in 1939.

Left Maharaja Jari Singh built Gulab Bhavan in 1925 on a site overlooking Dal Lake, more isolated than the City Palace on the River Jhelum and without the rococo decor fashionable in princely buildings of the era.

Below During the 19th century Woodville was the official summer residence of the Commanders-in-Chief of India. The property was acquired by the Maharaja of Gondal in 1926 who gifted the house to his daughter, the Rani of Jubbal.

Above Sir Arthur Ker purchased Chapslee in 1896 and totally renovated the property from 1907 to 1911, adding Burmese teakwood procured from the same shipment imported for the Viceregal Lodge.

Right Al Hilal Palace was built by the Nawab of Bahawalpur in 1931 to escape the summer heat of his home state. In 1950 Maharani Tara Devi of Kashmir bought the palace from the state government and renamed it Taragarh.

Maharaja was very much involved in the selection of Jacob as architect for his residence or in the initial planning stages, although he was undoubtedly consulted and certainly approved the designs and location 'a distance from the female palace'. Soon, however, Ganga Singh began to take an increasingly active and ultimately commanding role in the construction and design of his new domicile with the result that penny-, or rather, rupee-pinching was banished, along with any suggestion of a reduction in scale, along with the substitution of stucco for stone-carving, along with the original budget of 'not more than Rs. 100,000', transforming the 'bungalow' into a certifiable Aladdin's castle. When Lakshmi Vilas, the first quadrant of the Lallgarh Palace complex, was completed in 1902 costs had escalated to approximately ten lakhs (one million) of rupees and the ornamental stone-carving had become the most intricate and extensive of any modern palace in India.

In retrospect, architecture and building seems so much a part of Maharaja Ganga Singh's gestalt (he became one of the most famous and prolific princely builders of the twentieth century Raj) that it is difficult to imagine some incipient cause for his active involvement in the design and construction of Lallgarh Palace, but he may initially have been driven to it by circumstances very much beyond his control.

During this final phase of the Maharaja's minority, the Regency Council running his state had split into factions, rendering the government largely ineffectual and opening the way to numerous feudal abuses. This was a particularly difficult and exasperating period for the precocious and energetic young prince and may explain the intensity with which he participated in the construction of his new residence and how this participation rapidly developed into a consuming passion for Indo-Saracenic architecture and building in general. The Maharaja was shackled to a passive role in the management of Bikaner and forced to watch a divided caretaker government bickering and manoeuvring while the administration of his state floundered. It is easy to see how he could have used the construction of his palace as an outlet for his frustrated energies and enthusiasms.

Construction of Lallgarh Palace, which Ganga Singh named in honour of his father Maharaj Lall Singh (who was also father of Maharaja Dungar Singh) began sometime in late 1896 and continued for the next six years. The palace was built with a roseate sandstone extracted from a quarry in the village of Dulmera which, apparently, had been discovered following a search instigated in the early 1890s by the young Maharaja, who had been so impressed with Jodhpur's red stone that he sent out prospectors to find something similar for his own buildings. By mid-1899, however, only months after Ganga Singh had reached majority and received his administrative powers (on 16 December 1898), his interest in the building of Lallgarh was eclipsed by a full-scale catastrophe.

In that year the whole of northern India was ravaged by a terrible famine. Bikaner, positioned in the heart of the Great Thar Desert, was particularly hard hit. Bikaner State had never really recovered from a drought in 1897. Its granaries were empty, its water storage tanks were dry and when the monsoons failed again, livestock rapidly began to perish in the barren, waterless wastelands and entire villages in the worst-afflicted districts began to emigrate *en masse* to the Punjab. The eighteen-year-old ruler worked tirelessly throughout the calamity, touring on horseback to every nook and cranny of his domain and striving ceaselessly to alleviate the sufferings of his people until he contracted cholera from exhaustion and exposure to the epidemic which was spreading rapidly among the debilitated populace. In recognition of his genuinely heroic efforts the Maharaja was awarded the Kaiser-i-Hind medal for humanitarian work by the Queen-Empress.

The drought finally broke at the end of July 1900, and within a month Ganga Singh was on his way to China at the head of his Camel Corps to assist in suppressing the insurgency in Peking as the first Indian prince to fight abroad under the British flag, returning in triumph at twenty-two, a paragon of Indian princes – soldier, reformer, war hero, faithful servant of Empire – with a spectacular Aladdin's cave to further enhance his status. In his absence construction on Lallgarh Palace stalled under the supervision of Mr Clarke, the new

State Executive Engineer. Workers at the Dulmera quarries began walking off the job, evidently because the contractor's wages were below those offered for similar work in the city and this crisis was exacerbated by another epidemic which had spread through the state.

No matter how the exteriors of Lallgarh Palace invoke Junagadh, the Rajput fortress of the Maharaja'a forefathers, with its profusions of carved *jaali* screens, mock battlements with ornamental *chattris* and decorative crenellations, its purpose and interior plan were almost purely European. According to architectural historian Thomas R. Metcalfe, the elaborately traditional facade of Lallgarh was 'to enable the maharaja, not so much to play at being a Rajput warrior, as to make manifest – to himself, to the British, to his subjects – his warrior descent'. It was, in fact, this self-conscious re-creation of the image rather than the reality of a Rajput castle that elicited comparisons with the Arabian Nights and lent an air of theatrical enchantment to the place.

The interiors of Lallgarh ostensibly reiterated the traditional Rajput fortress pattern, including a durbar hall, courtyards, zenana, mardana, and so on, but the usage, dimensions, spatial arrangement and furnishing of the rooms were in every other way completely European. The floor plan was rigidly ordered, with large guest suites ranged in numerical order around the courtyards, and included all the usual elements of a European colonial residence: billiard hall, card room, drawing room, smoking room, dining room, administrative offices and a study for the Maharaja which, according to palace records, featured a dancing floor. All fixtures and furnishings were of the European style from the Belgian crystal chandeliers throughout to the plush furniture and the concert piano in the drawing room.

A driveway led up to a *porte-cochère*, a roofed extension of the entrance to the palace beneath which carriages could stop, allowing European guests to alight at the door without making the traditional walk from the palace gates. Indeed, with the later construction of the northern wing of Lallgarh, the Maharaja's European guests could go straight from one of these covered porches into an outer reception room for drinks, proceed directly to the colossal banquet hall for supper and leave, never actually entering the palace proper.

All these interpolations were what Indo-Saracenic architecture was all about and although Sir Samuel Swinton Jacob differs from many of his contemporaries in his concentration on the precise replication of traditional architectural elements and the authentic revival of indigenous Indian building crafts in the construction of his designs, his conception was inherently European in layout and function. As attuned as Jacob was to the trappings of Indian architecture, his European orientation seems to have led him into the gross error of designing the mardana, the men's public area, to overlook the zenana, or women's apartments.

Lakshmi Vilas, the first phase of Lallgarh Palace, was completed in 1902 in time for the viceregal visit of Lord Curzon, who summed up the British ideal of an Indian prince which Ganga Singh and his new palace so dramatically manifested in a speech at Bikaner. The viceroy said that with:

the advantage of the best English education, as His Highness has had, he can introduce all manner of reforms and enlightenment into the administration of his State. If he is at the same time a true Indian, by which I mean a man devoted to the interests of his own creed and caste and country, then he can obtain an almost unmeasured influence over his subjects. Thus he can combine the merits of the East and the West in a single blend; and he can be at the same time a Liberal and a Conservative, each in the best sense of the term.

Lord Curzon could not have failed to notice that the Maharaja had already accomplished this blend of opposites in his new residence.

Lallgarh Palace was the most completely integrated example of Indo-Saracenic architecture and the most perfectly realized of all the creations of Sir Samuel Swinton Jacob, undoubtedly because of the strength and clarity of his princely client. This juxtaposition of the modern and the ancient never failed to impress early visitors like Perceval Landon who described this sense of exhilarating dislocation Lallgarh induced:

It would be hard to find a greater contrast or incongruity than that one experiences in leaving the rooms of this palace luxuriously furnished with every European invention, equipped with the latest comforts of the West, served by telephones innumerable and lighted throughout by electricity – and then finding one's self obliged to allow full room for the passage of a carriage drawn by two elephants along the high road leading to the town, escorted by men in full chain armour upon camels as well drilled as any cavalry horse in Europe . . .

Maharaja Ganga Singh was already enormously popular with his British overlords and the creation of Lallgarh Palace played no small part in making his capital an equally popular stopping place in Indian India. Almost as soon as it was opened Lakshmi Vilas proved inadequate to handle the procession of state visitors he was beginning to receive. During the visits of Lord Curzon and the Prince of Wales the following year, there was an acute shortage of accommodation for the enormous number of people accompanying these great Imperialists, necessitating the fabrication of temporary tent cities.

Almost immediately thereafter Ganga Singh began to elaborate and expand his compound. The first project undertaken was a gateway and clock tower which he commissioned Sir Swinton Jacob to design in commemoration of a visit to Bikaner by the Duke of Connaught in 1903. The Maharaja specified that it was to be 'high enough for an Elephant with those Big Howdahs to pass under – Must be a *very pretty piece* of *architecture* which I have *no doubts whatever* of its being, if designed by you – At the same time we don't want to be *extravagent* [sic] in expenditure over it.'

The ruler further described what he was aiming for as 'A solid Arch something like (what I have seen photos of) the Residency Gate at Jaipur or the Marble Arch in Hyde Park would be best –? I don't mean the same Architecture or size but I meant the Massiveness – The design would of course be your celebrated oriental one.' Jacob completed drawings for Connaught Gateway by the end of 1903 and construction was immediately undertaken on this massive ornamental entrance to the palace grounds.

Ganga Singh became Jacob's greatest devotee and the most enthusiastic princely advocate of Indo-Saracenic architecture. He commissioned Jacob to design his new palace at Gajner (see page 66) and several other buildings around Bikaner and drew from Jacob's exhaustive *Portfolio of Architectural Details* for all his subsequent palace extensions.

Further additions to the Lallgarh complex were made between 1906 and 1910. In 1912 Sadul Niwas was constructed for Maharajkumar Sadul Singh, Ganga Singh's son and heir-apparent. In the 1920s a northern quadrant was added to the palace which included an indoor swimming pool and the trophy-studded Shiv Vilas banquet hall which could seat four hundred. In 1935 Karni Niwas was added to Lallgarh for the Maharaja's grandson, Karni Singh, the last Maharaja of Bikaner.

From the First World War on, the Maharaja had become one of the leading princes in India with a special relationship with King George V and his family. He became progressively preoccupied with activities more momentous than palace-building. Ganga Singh led his Camel Corps on the Egyptian front and was one of the signatories of the Treaty of Versailles. When the Chamber of Princes was convened in 1921 he became its first Chancellor by an overwhelming vote. Most dramatically, Ganga Singh spent almost two decades organizing and supervising the construction of the Gang Canal fed from the Sutlej River to give his desert state a steady source of water for the first time in its history. With this wide-ranging schedule of reforms, his direct involvement in the extension of his palace property receded and with these later phases of building, the Maharaja simply assigned his state engineers to extrapolate from the original patterns of Lakshmi Vilas in order to build the three successive extensions undertaken almost to the end of his reign.

Maharaja Ganga Singh died in 1943, much honoured for his many accomplishments and particularly celebrated for his architectural transformation of Bikaner, a process which began with the building of a bungalow to protect him from 'the bad influences of an Indian zanana'.

His son and successor Maharaja Sadul Singh ruled his state from Lallgarh Palace for the next four years and was the first and

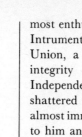

most enthusiastic Indian prince to sign the Intrument of Accession to the Indian Union, a document which promised the integrity of the princely states in Independent India. The Maharaja was shattered when the Union Government almost immediately broke all their promises to him and forced the complete merger of the states. He died only months after this breach of faith.

His son and successor Dr Karni Singh briefly entered politics but spent most of his life in scholarly, sporting and charitable pursuits. In his time Lallgarh Palace became the private residence of the royal family, maintained with income from the privy purses allotted to the former ruling families in exchange for giving up their states. When these privy purses were suddenly abolished in 1970, all the Maharajas had to drastically retrench. The de-recognized princes found various ways of coping with this loss of income, most of which had been used to sustain their properties and retainers.

In 1972 Dr Karni Singh established the Ganga Singhji Charitable Trust, endowing a part of Lallgarh Palace to be used in service of the Trust. He then converted the Sadul Niwas and Karni Niwas wings of the palace complex into a hotel with 10,000 rupees as 'seed money' to start up the business. All the income from this operation is used for academic scholarships, to help in the arrangement of marriages for girls from poverty-stricken families, for old-age pensions and for the maintenance of 8,000 ancient Sanskrit manuscripts kept on the premises in the Anup Sanskrit Library. Later the Maharaja and his daughter organized the Sadul Museum, which includes an extensive library from the family's private collection and room after room of fascinating memorabilia of the Bikaner dynasty.

When Maharaja Karni Singh died in 1988 he left the entirety of Lallgarh Palace to the Ganga Singhji Trust and there are presently plans to expend its hotel facilities into other parts of the vast complex.

GAJNER PALACE

Gajner Palace became one of the most bewitching and prestigious recreational retreats in princely India during the early twentieth century through the perspicacity and dynamism of Maharaja Ganga Singh, but the origins of this flamingo-pink hunting palace surrounded by lush gardens and set beside the green, hypnotic waters of an artificial lake, can be traced back to the middle of the eighteenth century, when Ganga Singh's ancestor set aside the site to gratify the homesick heart of an alien princess.

Shortly after Maharaja Gaj Singh (1745-87) ascended to the throne of Bikaner, he crossed the desert to marry a royal bride from Jaisalmer. He brought his rani back with him and upon the eve of their festive and ceremonial procession into the capital, the royal wedding entourage encamped some twenty miles outside the city walls at a settlement called Chandasar.

Established in the late fourteenth century by Rao Chanda, the great-grandfather of the founder of Bikaner, Chandasar became the base-camp from which Rao Bika ventured forth to forge his desert kingdom. By the side of the Chanda Sagar tank which Rao Chanda had first excavated, Maharaja Gaj Singh rested with his princess bride who dreamed wistfully of the home she had so recently relinquished.

In her intense nostalgia the rani saw Jaisalmer reflected in the terrain of Chandasar and she beseeched her husband to create a pleasure garden there as a reminder of her homeland. Among her retinue from Jaisalmer she had brought a gardener skilled in the arts of desert cultivation, who by her husband's command landscaped a low tract known as Magra, and the Maharaja made a new tank named Gaj Sagar to keep his rani's pleasure garden green.

Beside this tank the ruler built his bride a palace known as Jal Mahal with an adjacent durbar hall he called Pachis Chowk, meaning twenty-five squares. To the side of his royal resort he established a new settlement he named Gajsinghpura, in honour of himself; later to be known as Gajner.

Succeeding rulers made various improvements to the princely pleasure garden at Gajner by way of extending and improving the tanks but the garden enclave remained much as it was until Sardar Singh (1851-72) ascended the Gadi of Bikaner.

Maharaja Sardar Singh was an enthusiastic *shikari* who spent considerable time hunting in the wilderness around his capital and took to lodging at Gajner regularly. As a result he deepened and expanded Gaj Sagar into a fully fledged lake, and installed pleasure boats. He excavated yet another water-tank which he called Sugan Sagar, and he built himself a brand-new palace which in his later years he made his home.

When his nephew, Maharaja Dungar Singh, succeeded him in 1872 he extended the surrounding gardens, strengthened the banks of Gaj Sagar and Sugan Sagar with a *bund* and enclosed his compound with a fortified wall which encompassed the tomb of Pir Jetha Bhutta, a Muslim saint whose *dargah* remains a place of pilgrimage for Muslims. Indeed, such was the active interest of Dungar Singh in his hereditary pleasure garden that his younger brother and successor, Maharaja Gaj Singh, wrote that 'Gajner would probably have been a fair sized town now had it not been for the untimely and lamentable death of my brother in 1887.'

Throughout the long years of Ganga Singh's minority, little was added to Gajner with the exception of a *pukka* road between the village and the capital, constructed in 1897, one year before the Maharaja reached majority. The rainless curse on northern India in 1899 left Gaj Sagar lake totally empty and Maharaja Ganga Singh used this as an opportunity to greatly deepen the lake and widen its catchment area so that over two years' supply of water could be held when it was properly filled in the monsoons.

At the beginning of his majority rule Ganga Singh was understandably far too taken up with matters of state and with the construction of his own massive and elaborate castle in Bikaner to give much attention to the gardens of Gajner. Gradually, though, it dawned on the Maharaja that his country palace had the potential to be a valuable diplomatic asset, for it provided a unique recreation eminently attractive to 'the white core of India', upon whom the ruler depended for the vital assistance he needed to develop his isolated and waterless desert state. The four or five acres of Gaj Sagar and its connecting tanks was the only large body of water for many miles in every direction and, on winter mornings, attracted thousands of migratory birds including demoiselle cranes and the particularly rare and delectable imperial sand grouse which would descend in susurrant, sky-blackening clouds to slake their thirst at Gajner.

Sir Arthur Lothian described Ganga Singh as 'perhaps the finest stage manager in India' and the imperial sand grouse shoots at Gajner were among the Maharaja's most expertly staged productions. Before a shoot village boys from throughout the region would be stationed at every open tank to drive away the sand grouse, preventing them from having so much as a sip of water for two or three days. By the morning of the shoot, the birds would power-dive toward Gajner lake in a craze of thirst, oblivious to the barrage of fire that would bring down thousands of them in the space of three hours. It was calculated that when the Prince of Wales visited Gajner in 1905 over 100,000 of these birds swept down upon Gaj Sagar in one morning.

Although the shoot was the main event of any stay at Gajner it was the polished hospitality and the European gentility of the resort combined with its hallucinating beauty which made the experience unforgettable and made Gajner *de rigueur* on the pleasure circuit of the Raj. In the first decade of the twentieth century Gajner had become an institution offering a sport to match Scindia's tiger hunts and a spectacle to match Mysore's *khedda*, (the traditional round-up of wild elephants) and Ganga Singh conceived a need for a more modern palace.

He turned to Sir Samuel Swinton Jacob, who had done so well by him with Lallgarh and with whom the Maharaja had developed a warm professional relationship. Jacob made designs for the palace which were realized around 1910-13.

Dignitaries would be put up in the Maharaja's new pink dulmera stone palace in spacious, deliciously painted suites overlooking the waters of the lake and

furnished with English country gentility by John Roberts & Co. of Bombay, India's most fashionable outfitters. Staff officers and lesser guests and their wives would be put up in a comfortable annexe which had a peculiar feature perfectly in keeping with the intricately organized hospitality extended by the Maharaja. Constructed on the assumption that ladies take longer to dress for *shikar* than gentlemen, each suite contained two separate bath and dressing areas so that couples could prepare themselves at their own separate paces, free from irritation and contretemps.

Ganga Singh died in 1943, leaving his kingdom and his castles to his son Sadul Singh (1943-47), who was an even better shot and a more avid hunter than his father. Sadul Singh's son, Dr Karni Singh, who died in 1988, became one of India's greatest marksmen, a trap and skeet-shooting champion who represented his country five times in the Olympic Games, but because the Maharaja's mother was a devout Hindu, a strict vegetarian who did not drink alcohol and disapproved of the *shikar*, Dr Karni Singh, also a vegetarian teetotaller, rarely ever shot anything but clay pigeons.

After Independence Gajner Palace was maintained as the private resort and hunting lodge of the royal family but desert irrigation eventually drew away most of the imperial sand grouse so that only a few thousand at a time alight upon the lustrous waters of the peaceful lake.

In 1976 the late Maharaja Dr Karni Singh opened the annexe of the palace (that with the matching bathrooms) as a hotel, keeping the main palace for his private guests. Recently the main palace at Gajner has also been inaugurated as a hotel, privately owned and operated by the late Maharaja's family.

SIMLA

CURIOUS AND CURIOUSER

Do you not see Semla on your map? A little to the north of the 31 of latitude, a little to the east of the 77 of longitude, some leagues from Sutledge. Is it not curious to dine in silk stockings at such a place, and to drink a bottle of hock and another of champagne every evening – delicious Mocha coffee – and to receive the Calcutta journals every morning?
M. Victor Jacquemont, published letters, 1828-31

It *was* curious, the incongruous gentility of life up in this rough mountain village surrounded by jungle infested with hyenas and other wild beasts, and it was to get curiouser still as the nineteenth century wore on and Simla became the summer capital of the Indian Empire. Unlike Ooty (Ootacamund), its sister hill station in the south, there was no way one could remake the vertiginous landscape into an approximation of the English countryside. Simla was unavoidably alien and the more its colonial inhabitants tried to gentrify it, shape it to English specifications, and pretend that it was a perfectly normal place to spend the summers, the more peculiar it began to appear.

The British were first exposed to the hill region around Simla through the Gurkha War of 1815. Before the Nepalese incursions Simla village and the surrounding hills had belonged to the chiefs of Keonthal and Jhind but these rulers had refused to cooperate with the British in 1815 and in the aftermath of the war most of this territory was seized as a punishment and sold off to the Raja of Patiala as a reward for his military assistance in the campaign and to help offset the costs of battle.

An anonymous British officer passing through Simla in 1816 was said to have been the first to take note of the refreshing cool of the place. However, a more permanent record of Simla was made the following year by two brothers, Patrick and James Gerard, officers assigned to make a survey of the Sutlej valley. They camped on the side of Mount Jakko and recorded in their journal

that Simla was 'a middling sized village where a fakir is situated to give water to travellers . . .'.

The cold mountain air, the lush forests, the contrast with the flat, searing monotony of the plains, never failed to impress subsequent sojourners and within a few years the word had spread about this village up in the Himalayan hills. After a journey into the area in 1821 an exhilarated Major Sir William Lloyd wrote 'It is impossible that Simla and its sublimity can ever be effaced from our minds.'

As early as 1824 the village was beginning to be used as a sanitorium, principally for invalids from the lowlands. The territory was still in the possession of Patiala and Keonthal but permission had been secured from these chiefs for Europeans to obtain rent-free land grants. Cabins began to proliferate on the landscape, beginning in 1825 with the house of Captain (later Major) Charles Kennedy, the gregarious Political Officer whose exuberant hospitality had much to do with the hill station's growing popularity. A visit by Governor-General Lord Amherst in 1827 further enhanced Simla's reputation and the next year Lord Combermere, the Commander-in-Chief of India, came up and encompassed Mount Jakko with a 'fine, broad, level road'.

Amherst's successor, Lord William Bentinck, first visited Simla the following year and in 1830 directed Major Charles Kennedy to enter into negotiations with Keonthal and Patiala for the formal acquisition of Simla. By 1831 the newly British district had sixty houses and was now 'the resort of the rich, the idle, and the invalid'.

So Simla grew and grew and in the process inexorably changed as the summer exodus from lowland to hill station became an institution. The hills were deforested and developed. Sod-roofed stone bungalows became Elizabethan manor houses, Swiss chalets, and Gothic castles. The winding roads were clogged with Himalayan rickshaws called *jampans* drawn by emaciated natives who reportedly died young from heart attacks brought on by their precipitous exertions. The simple pleasures of still hock, champagne and Calcutta journals gave way to a relentless round of tea parties, card games, cricket matches, horse racing, picnics, polo, fancy dress dances, musicales, *bals masqués*, theatricals, gaieties and frivolities which wore down all but the most maniacal socialites. Simla had become the pre-eminent hill station in India – the cynosure of Raj society – and it was only a matter of time before it would become the official summer capital of British India.

At the beginning of 1864 Sir John Lawrence was appointed Viceroy of India on the condition of his doctors that his summers would be spent in the hills. Lord Lawrence was a workaholic and insisted that his government accompany him, arguing that 'we will do more work in one day here than in five down in Calcutta'. The Viceroy proposed that the Crown formally shift the government to the hill station for the six-month summer season and threatened to resign his post if it was not. The move was, as Philip Davies points out, 'preposterous, as though the whole of Whitehall moved lock, stock and barrel to St Moritz for the summer . . .'. Yet this was India and there was logic in such extremity. The Viceroy's proposal was sanctioned.

One effect of this official investiture was to further transmogrify the still primitive and once pristine landscape into what Mr Davies has characterized as 'an eccentric suburb of Calcutta'. Another side-effect was that the hill station suddenly became the spy centre of Asia. Simla was becoming very weird indeed.

What strange scenes of fine ladies in jampans and liveried coolies!
What groups of beautiful English children with ayahs and bearers!
What endless picturesqueness of hill tribes with toga-like wrappers!
What women with nose buttons and rings, and spoons and sky blue breeches!
Verily, Simla is a queer place!
Edward Lear, *Indian Journal*, 1874

CHAPSLEE, THE SECRETARY'S LODGE

The princely manor house called Chapslee and its neighbour Auckland House occupy a hillside site on the north-eastern spur of the Simla range first subdivided in 1828 – when Simla was still a makeshift sanatorium in the hands

of hill chiefs – and granted to one Dr Blake, a surgeon in the service of the Honourable East India Company. The site had been demarcated by the Political Agent stationed at Subathu who, with arcane civil service logic, registered the contiguous plots with the numbers 13 and 54.

On plot 13 Dr Blake constructed a large one-storey, flat-roofed house which he rented out. On plot 54 the owner built a smaller house of the same style for his own use. The good doctor kept his property until 1836 when he sold plot 13 – the one with the large house – to Lord Auckland, Governor-General of India, and plot 54 to the Governor-General's nephew and Military Secretary, Captain the Honourable W.G. Osborne. The two residences were thereafter known as Government House and Secretary's Lodge.

As lodgings for the Lord Paramount of India and his adjutant, these two houses were hardly up to scratch. They were primitive, flea-infested stone cabins with packed-earth roofs that were about as impervious to the heavy Himalayan rains as a sieve. During the frequent downpours which made Simla so green, cool and otherwise congenial, staff officers at Government House and Secretary's Lodge could be found sitting down to dinner or at their writing desks underneath umbrellas held by hapless, dripping houseboys.

This was all to change, at least for Government House, with the arrival of Lord Auckland's entrancing sisters, Emily and Fanny Eden, who had such a transfiguring effect upon their rude environs that the nameless hill upon which they lived was christened 'Elysium' in tribute to the lovely ladies. The dynamic Eden sisters proceeded to redecorate what Emily called the 'poor despised house that every one abused' until it 'turned out the wonder of Simla':

We brought carpets and chandeliers and wall shades (the great staple commodity of Indian furniture) from Calcutta, and I have got a native painter into the house, and cut out patterns in paper, which he then painted in borders all round the doors and windows, and it makes up for the want of cornices and breaks the eternal white walls of these houses

Fanny and Emily also managed to do a fair amount of gardening on the grounds between the two cabins. 'We ride down into the valleys', Emily wrote, 'and make the *syces* dig up wild tulips and lilies, and they are grown so eager about it that they dash up the hill the instant they see a promising looking plant and dig it up with the best possible effect except that they invariably cut off the bulb.' By the energetic application of a woman's touch, the Governor-General's residence had become 'a jewel of a little house . . .'

. . . the views are only too lovely. Deep valleys on the drawing-room side to the west, and the snowy range on the dining-room side, where my room also is. Our sitting rooms are small, but that is all the better in this climate, and the two principal rooms are very fine. We have fires in every room and the windows open. Red rhododendron trees in bloom in every direction, and beautiful walks like English shrubberies on all sides of the hill.

All this flurry of refurbishment came none too soon, for by the summer of 1838, the year the Eden sisters arrived, Government House had become a power station of policy-making as Lord Auckland and his advisers formulated the unfortunate manifesto which led East India Company forces into the first Afghan war and its catastrophic aftermath. Already the buildings on Elysium Hill were beginning to strain at the seams with ADCs and VIPs, and Secretary's Lodge had to be converted into offices and meeting rooms for the Governor-General's Private and Military Secretaries to work from. It was from Secretary's Lodge that the historic 'Spanish Simlah Manifesto' declaring war with Afghanistan was issued on 1 October 1838.

By 1839 Elysium Hill had become a veritable command post. Two houses further down the hill, later known as 'Waverly' and 'Oakleigh', were commandeered by the Governor-General for the Military Department and Foreign Offices and Lord Auckland purchased Secretary's Lodge from his nephew, turning the building into a barracks for his platoon of ADCs.

Secretary's Lodge also became a refuge for the 'retired' ladies – wives who refused social invitations while their husbands were at the Afghan front – who 'come to console themselves with a little music and to take a little tea and coffee and talk a little'.

In 1842 at the conclusion of his term of office, Lord Auckland sold both Government House and Secretary's Lodge for 16,000 rupees to Dr J. Ransford, an assistant surgeon in the service of the East India Company who leased out the complex to the succeeding Governor-General, Lord Ellenborough. Secretary's Lodge was reinstated as the Government Secretariat and it was from here that Lord Auckland's Afghan policy was officially repudiated and reformed in the same room, on 1 October 1842, four years to the day after the war against Afghanistan had been declared.

Secretary's Lodge remained the Secretariat in the time of Lord Hardinge, the succeeding Governor-General, who spent his summer seasons in Government House from 1844 to 1848.

Elysium Hill ceased to serve as the Governor-General's estate during the tenure of the Marquis of Dalhousie who, after a season at Auckland House, removed to 'Strawberry Hill' and then to 'Kennedy House'.

In 1858 Dr Ransford sold his two properties to Colonel (later General) Peter Innes of the Bengal Army for 24,000 rupees. The officer had purchased many properties in Simla and had taken to giving them whimsical names. When he acquired Secretary's Lodge he changed the name to 'Chapslee'.

General Innes kept his Elysium Hill estates intact for a decade before selling them off in smaller parcels to different buyers. Auckland House and part of its surrounding land was sold for 8,000 rupees to the Bishop and Archdeacon of Calcutta, who were acting as trustees for the Punjab Girls' School. Chapslee and all but a parcel of its original land was sold for 5,100 rupees to Mr W. Newman, who kept the house for only two years before selling out to General W. Gordon for a heavy profit of 100 rupees. General Gordon made extensive renovations of Chapslee and resold the property for 27,000 rupees to Mr J.M. MacPherson, Secretary to the Government of India, who lived there for several years after which he leased out his house to a series of colonial gentlemen (Sir Courtney Ilbert, General Pemberton and General Sir C.E. Nairne) until Chapslee was purchased in 1888 by Mr (later Sir) John Eliot.

Mr Eliot lived there for a time before he too rented his house to another series of colonial gentlemen (Surgeon-General A.F. Bradshaw, Surgeon-General J. Cleghorn, General N. Arnott and General Sir A. Gaslee) until 1896 when he sold his property to Sir Arthur Milford Ker, manager of the Alliance Bank of Simla, the hill station's leading financial institution. Throughout this long period the house was referred to as Chapslee, the Secretary's Lodge, until memories of its former official position had sufficiently faded and 'Secretary's Lodge' was eventually dropped.

Sir Arthur Ker was either a shrewd land speculator or an avid property collector, for entries in his private diary mention numerous and regular purchases all over Simla and he was absolutely blasé about his acquisition of Chapslee. Whereas certain other purchases were registered with some enthusiasm, he wrote in passing, 'I also bought "Chapslee" from Eliot', almost as an afterthought. Obviously he must have warmed to the old house, for he decided to make the place his home. Between 1907 and 1911 the banker totally renovated his property and, according to Simla's self-appointed historian, Sir Edward J. Buck, 'improved it beyond all recognition'. The magnificent carved Burmese teak which garnishes the structure was procured from the same shipment brought in to embellish the Viceregal Lodge. Chapslee was now 'surpassed by no other Simla residence in arrangement and general advantages'. These 'general advantages' did not include plumbing or electricity.

Sir Arthur Ker and his wife lived together in their unsurpassed residence until his death on 2 October 1915, when Lady Ker inherited the property and continued living there until she died in 1928. The Kers were predeceased by their only son, who died in battle at the outset of the First World War, and so the property was left to a nephew living in England who had no personal use for the house and wanted to sell it. The Kers, however, had a plethora of relations living in India and Lady Ker's will was contested, preventing the nephew from putting Chapslee on the market. There were several other beneficiaries mentioned in the testaments of both Sir Arthur and Lady Ker who were given leave to take what furnishings they wanted, and left Chapslee an empty shell during a decade of litigation.

In 1938 some kind of settlement was reached and the nephew was free to dispense with his troublesome inheritance. The remaining furniture was auctioned off and the estate was finally put up for sale. Chapslee was still an extremely desirable property and a number of eminent buyers had been clamouring to acquire the beautiful, historic house, including the Maharaja of Gwalior, who finally gave up waiting and put his money into something else.

Raja Charanjit Singh of Kapurthala, a long-time resident of Simla, was particularly keen on making a move to Chapslee and, through a fortuitous meeting, pre-empted his competitors. The prince was out strolling on the Mall with his wife and son and stopped to have tea at Davico's, a fashionable Italian confectionery-cum-dance hall. The Raja's son went out for a walk while his parents were having their tea and happened to run into an estate agent who informed him that Chapslee had just then been put on the market. The young man rushed back to his parents with the good news and by the following day Chapslee belonged to the Kapurthala family.

Throughout 1939 Raja Charanjit Singh had his new home totally renovated. Structural changes were made according to the Himalayan vernacular technique of *dhajji*, using stone, rubble, mud and wooden cross-bracing in the three-foot-thick walls. Plumbing and electrical wiring were installed and the house was completely outfitted with furnishings from Chadwick, their previous residence on Summerhill Ridge, and various other Kapurthala palaces, as well as furniture custom-made for the new house. In 1940 Charanjit Singh and family finally occupied their new Simla residence.

Chapslee remained the summer home of the Kapurthala family until 1970 when Raja Charanjit Singh died, leaving the Simla estate to his grandson, Kumar Ratanjit Singh, who was living in Uttar Pradesh, managing the family farm. Normally such a generous bequest would be cause for celebration but the inheritance of Chapslee immediately placed the young beneficiary in a serious, life-changing dilemma. That same year the State of Himachal Pradesh was constituted from a part of Punjab State and the newly formed government was desperately looking for untenanted properties to appropriate for its bureaucracy. Ratanjit Singh had been born only months after his family moved into Chapslee. He grew up there, spent every summer of his youth in the family house and was deeply attached to it, but he had also made a life for himself in the lowlands. He had not intended to uproot his family and move up into the Himalayas, away from his farm, but the new government gave him an ultimatum: either he made Simla his permanent residence or his inheritance would be seized.

He could not allow a princely treasure like Chapslee to be reduced to some desolate accounting office or – perish the thought – a government secretariat, so he and his wife, Pronoti Deoi, and their children packed up and settled into their Simla house. Suddenly they were confronted with the two-fold problem of maintaining their large and ageing manor house and fending off persistent attempts by the state government to expropriate part of the surrounding land under the Urban Land Ceiling laws which severely limited the extent of undeveloped land around a house unless it was used in some way to benefit the community. As a brand-new state with a precipitous capital city and little developed property to draw from, Himachal Pradesh was more inclined to implement these laws than other older, flatter and land-rich states might have been. Ratanjit Singh and his wife had to find some way to preserve their property.

In 1973 Pronoti Deoi opened a small girls' school with three students. Three years later the couple registered Chapslee as a hotel for paying guests. Today the Chapslee girls' school is one of the leading educational institutions in Simla with a long waiting-list. The hotel, however, still operates with a very low profile. Ratanjit Singh and his wife run their guest house on a word-of-mouth basis, without advertising or promotion and have no intention of expanding or professionalizing their business. There is a good reason for this. The property has been kept absolutely as it was in the time of Charanjit Singh, with every stick and shred of Victoriana, every antique tapestry and

oriental carpet, every silver frame and ivory gimcrack in place. It would be impossible to commercialize such a sensitive, family-oriented operation. 'You see, this is not a business,' Ratanjit Singh told me, 'it is more an exercise in conservation.'

Against the unbridled speculative growth of the modern mountain capital with its cut-price proletarian ugliness, its reinforced-concrete angularities, its heedless urban blight beside which even the pseudo-Gothic monstrosities of the colonial past seem almost sublime, this loving act of preservation has turned out to be one of the last remaining wonders of Simla.

WOODVILLE

No records exist to indicate when the five-acre site of Woodville was first apportioned and to whom, although since Barnes Court, the neighbouring estate, is known to have been granted on 1 January 1830, one might assume that the adjacent tract of land was allocated at around the same time. The earliest existing Woodville document is a deed of conveyance dated 2 February 1866 between the seller, Major-General Arthur Milford Beecher, and the buyer, General Sir William Rose Mansfield, Commander-in-Chief of Her Majesty's Forces in India, who purchased the property for 22,000 rupees. Within this indenture there is mention of the previous owner, 'one Mr Barnes', who sold Woodville to Major-General Beecher in 1852. The dry contractual syntax does not specify whether this Mr Barnes is the same General Sir Edward Barnes, the former Adjutant-General to the Duke of Wellington at the Battle of Waterloo, who had purchased the adjacent property which, even today, bears his name, although this seems quite likely.

With Sir William Rose Mansfield's purchase of the property, Woodville became the official summer residence of the Commanders-in-Chief of India. General Mansfield resided there for five seasons and retained ownership of the property

throughout the tenancy of his successor, General Robert Cornelis, Lord Napier of Magdala, who stayed for six. In 1876 General Mansfield sold Woodville to Mrs Henrietta Ruth Maria Alexander, who continued to lease out the property to the Commanders-in-Chief of India for the next six years. General Sir Frederick Paul Haines spent five summers at Woodville, handing over to General Sir Donald Martin Stewart, who stayed but one season before removing in 1882 to Snowdon, which thereafter became the official Commander-in-Chief's residence in Simla, remaining so until the conclusion of the Raj.

The same year that General Stewart moved, Mrs Alexander sold her property to another memsahib, Mrs Eliza Maria Walker, wife of James Walker, the first manager and later Chairman of the Alliance Bank of Simla, the hill station's leading financial institution. Mrs Walker retained ownership for five years until her death. It is unclear whether the Walkers ever lived in Woodville or simply leased it out as an investment, but it is recorded that Mrs Walker died in London, at Lancaster Gate, Hyde Park, in 1892, leaving her Simla estate to her husband. Sir James Walker retained Woodville until 1919 when he sold his property to the Alliance Bank of Simla for 125,000 rupees – a considerable amount in those days.

In 1922 the Alliance Bank's headquarters moved from Simla to Calcutta, precipitating a run on the bank which led to its collapse and closure in April 1923, shortly after civil servants and army officers had deposited their salaries for the month, casting a pall over the whole of the hill station. In the subsequent liquidation of the bank's assets, Woodville was put up for sale.

In 1926 Maharaja Sri Sir Bhagwatsinh Sangram of Gondal State in Kathiawar approached the bank's liquidators with an offer to purchase Woodville. Permission had to be sought for native princes to acquire any property in British India and an urgent inquiry, dated 13 July 1926, as to whether there were any objections to the purchase, from J.M. Dunnett, Chief Secretary to the Government of Punjab to Lieutenant-Colonel J.C. Coldstream, Superintendent of Hill States, produced a revealing reply the following day:

No. 2539

Simla
14th July 1926

My dear Dunnett,
Your D.O.No.2211-S.Pol of yesterday's date.
The only objection I can see to the Thakur [sic]
of Gondal purchasing 'Woodville' is that the house
is well situated in a desirable area and close to the
main road, but I understand that the Thakur is a
man of very advanced ideas and is probably content
with a moderate entourage, I think that in his case
the objection will not be serious.

No serious objections forthcoming from the Government of India, the Maharaja of Gondal purchased Woodville for 120,000 rupees and for an additional 5,000 rupees bought the entire houseful of Victorian furniture and fittings, lock, stock and barrel.

Maharaja Bhagwatsinh kept Woodville until 1931 when he gifted the property to his daughter, Maharaj Kumari Sri Leilaba 'in consideration of the natural love and affection' he held for her. Rani Leilaba was married to the Rana of Jubbal, Sir Bhagat Chandra, who in 1938 had the original structures of the Woodville estate completely demolished and, out of funds from Jubbal State treasury, had a new manor house designed by Army and Navy Stores of London and built under the supervision of the president of the Simla Municipal Association, Muhammad Ali Shah.

The entire crew of 200 labourers, masons and carpenters were Muslim Pathans who were considered superior to the local labour force in skill and stamina. The present manager of Woodville Palace Hotel, Sri Dhian Singh, was a young boy at the time in service to the Rana of Jubbal and remembers supervising coolies who were paid exactly eight annas (about half a rupee) per day. Masons were paid one rupee and skilled carpenters one rupee two annas. In order to conserve the surrounding forest, the Rana had all the deodar wood used in the construction of Woodville hauled up to Simla from Jubbal State. Skilled Chinese workers were brought in from Bombay to lay the fashionable new Masonite flooring. The total cost of the newly built Woodville came to between four and five lakhs of rupees.

The reconstruction of Woodville was done with unusual speed so that it would be ready for the marriage of the Rana's daughter to the Maharaja of Jhalawar. Demolition was started in the winter of 1938 and the building was completely finished by May 1940, just in time for the spring wedding of the Rana's daughter.

In the frantic aftermath of Independence princely rulers found their properties under siege as leaders of the new ruling elite in India made moves to seize hereditary estates for their own use. Shortly after the establishment of Punjab State, its newly appointed Chief Minister stormed into Woodville declaring, 'These Rajas are no more! They are history. This house will be taken over by the Chief Minister of Punjab!' The Rana of Jubbal was in Delhi at the time and was informed of the Chief Minister's visit by his terrified retainers. The Raja immediately contacted an official in the central government who put a stop to the seizure. This was not an isolated instance. In the early days of the Union Government there was a free-for-all to seize princely property and it is to the credit of Prime Minister Jawaharlal Nehru that these abuses were to a very great extent curtailed.

Woodville remained the private property of the Rani Leilaba of Jubbal until 1959 when, following the generous example of her father, she gifted the estate to her two grandchildren, Rajkumar Udai Singh, aged eight, and his older sister Rajkumari Niera Devi, aged fourteen and a half.

In 1977 Udai Singh and Niera Devi opened a part of their mansion as Woodville Guest House, staffed by hereditary retainers of the Jubbal royal family, who, according to Himalayan tradition, refuse to enter the premises of their masters without first leaving their shoes outside and covering their heads. Three years later they changed the name to Woodville Palace Hotel. In 1987 Woodville Palace Resorts Pvt. Ltd. was established.

CHAIL PALACE

The Sikh rulers of Patiala earned the approbation and gratitude of the British Crown for their courageous military assistance and striking generosity throughout the nineteenth century and were rewarded accordingly with territorial gifts, elevation of titles and extraordinary privileges. One such reward was the acquisition of a mountainous tract twenty-six miles south of Simla and 7,394 feet above sea-level which came to be called Chail. This area originally belonged to the hill state of Keonthal until it was occupied in 1814 by Gurkha invaders. When British East India Company forces drove the Nepalese out of the Western Himalayas, Chail and a number of other Keonthal territories, including the village of Simla, were confiscated from the hill chief for his lack of cooperation during the Gurkha wars, and transferred to Patiala.

Maharaja Rajinder Singh of Patiala (d.1900) discovered Chail while exploring his landholdings and began to build a small resort there in the early 1890s. As a scion of the stalwart Patiala dynasty Rajinder Singh was warmly welcomed into the salons, ballrooms and banquet halls of the Anglo-Indian aristocracy, most particularly in Simla, which his ancestor had so generously turned over to the British back in 1830. The Maharaja must have been a dashing, piquant figure on the colonial social circuit: he was young, strapping, attractive, convivial and priapic; a great sportsman, fabulous dresser and illustriously (or notoriously, depending upon one's moral orientation) virile. In keeping with the tradition of his lineage, he lived hard, drank heavily and died young.

He and his voluptuous Punjabi neighbour Maharaja Jagajit Singh of Kapurthala most certainly injected a refreshing measure of oriental flash and roguery into the polite society of Simla. The wild side of mixing with these titillating potentates was that they did not necessarily understand or subscribe to Victorian proprieties and honestly did not know where to draw the line. This wild side had a down side: scandal.

Rajinder Singh reached the height of his popularity in Simla just before the turn of the century (and just before he suddenly dropped dead at twenty-eight) during the viceregency of Lord Curzon of Kedleston. He seems to have been a particular favourite of Lady Mary Curzon and during one of the Viceroy's absences he and his friend Jagajit Singh, along with the Rana of Dholpur, evidently got Lady Curzon to attend a semi-private supper at one of their residences in Simla during which, in high spirits, they enticed the Vicerene into putting on a silk sari and letting them drape her with some of their hereditary treasures: precious stones, strands of pearls and a priceless diamond tiara – irresistible!

This giddy little interlude was not particularly reprehensible in itself and might have passed unnoticed had the Maharajas not insisted on immortalizing their high-jinks with a photograph. That snap passed into the hands of some industrious Fleet Street legman and ended up in a lurid tabloid display.

Lord Curzon was understandably mortified. He summarily banned Patiala and his cohorts from the hill station for this gross breach of etiquette and made the presence of Indian princes in Simla subject to viceregal sanction. Jagajit Singh took solace in Mussoorie and set about building himself his magnificent Chateau Kapurthala there. Rajinder Singh took refuge in Chail and began to construct his palace on the piney hilltop. Chail became Patiala's summer alternative to Simla.

Maharaja Rajinder Singh died in November 1900, leaving Patiala to his nine-year-old son, Bhupinder Singh, who rapidly grew into an amplified replica of his father, becoming one of the most magnetic (and scandalous) maharajas in the twilight of the Raj. The French traveller Baron Jean Pellenc met Bhupinder Singh at the height of his powers and has left a florid description of this flamboyant princely figure:

. . . Patiala seems the living incarnation of those omnipotent sovereigns of the past whose ungovernable personalities loom large across the ages; men of the stamp of King Herod, Jenghiz Khan, or Henry VIII. None could embody more superbly the Eastern Prince of fairy-tales, the hero of our childish dreams; none more aptly illustrate the magnificence and despotic power of the last absolute monarchs.

There is much of the ideal tyrant in his physical appearance. Above a torso bulky as a wine-cask rises a huge, puissant head. Between the Sikh turban sitting well down upon his temples like a helmet, and black rolls of beard which like a chin-piece wrap his neck and jaw, a dark face peers out as from the opening of a visor. Under the heavy, drooping lids the half-shut, whiteless eyes glow darkly; but behind their veil of feigned indifference lurks something rather ominous, an elemental force emanating from a world that is not ours and may well not be heaven. The large-lipped mouth is fleshly, intrinsically carnal, but with a fine amoral beauty of its own. There is something plethoric about the whole face, inordinately proud, brazenly authoritative.

Two diamonds hung from his ears. I watched his hands as he ate, heavy hands laden with rings.

Suddenly he rose from his place at the centre of the table – now I saw him standing I judged his height a good six feet – and walked straight to the corner where we were sitting in a group. His eyes intent on us, hugely, rapidly, he bore down upon us like a river in spate. All the princes made way for him. At two paces from us he halted and, brushing aside an aide-de-camp who had darted forward to introduce us, scanned us up and down, held out his hand, shook ours and let them drop, then standing to attention gave us a stiff curt bow, punctilious as a German officer's. A brilliant conversationalist, the Maharaja quickly put us at our ease; he asked us for news of a mutual friend, and smilingly insisted that we were to stay at least a fortnight. In a few moments he had won our hearts – irresistibly.

Bhupinder Singh was even more popular in Simla than his father had been and acquired a number of residences in the hill station, including Oakover, Rockwood and the Cedars. He also developed the resort his father established during his exile at Chail. All through the 1920s he continued – irresistibly – to win hearts, conspicuously on the distaff side of Simla society. And evidently his legendary libido got the best of him, causing the Maharaja to overstep his limits – scandalously.

According to rumour (for all official records of princely proclivities and mis-behaviour were burned in June 1947 by Sir Conrad Corfield, the Viceroy's Political Secretary, to protect the rulers from future blackmail in independent India) Bhupinder Singh won the wrong heart: the daughter or wife of the Viceroy or Commander-in-Chief or a minor British officer whom he seduced or abducted or flirted with; depending upon which variation of the story one hears. The Patiala family denies any knowledge of the incident. Other supporters claim the accusation was part of a vendetta against the prince engineered by officials envious of the Maharaja's popularity in the hill station. Even in the 'Indictment of Patiala', an unofficial document of sensational charges compiled against the Maharaja in an unsuccessful campaign to have him dethroned, reference to the scandal is uncharacteristically vague (most of the rest of Bhupinder Singh's alleged crimes are graphically detailed in the report): 'At Simla the Maharaja's immoral conduct gave rise to scandals of a grave character, and for some time the British Government took steps to curtail his visits to the summer capital of India.'

If indeed there was a liaison with the daughter or wife of a British official of the eminence of a Viceroy or Commander-in-Chief, it is understandable that the scandal would have been vigorously suppressed on both sides.

Although the banning of Bhupinder Singh from Simla was evidently temporary and his disgrace short-lived (his grandson claims there was none), the incident seems to have accelerated the development of Chail into a resort to rival Simla in every respect. Such was the pride of the prince that he refused to acknowledge his punishment and instead endeavoured – with considerable success – to lure Simla society to his new alternative hill station. He had the entire top of the mountain lopped off to create the world's highest cricket pitch, featuring a concrete batting area with a matted surface and stunning views of Simla in the distance. There were swimming pools, tennis courts, stables – everything, including a palace for the Maharaja's three hundred-plus concubines. The main palace on the estate, called simply 'The Villa', accommodated Bhupinder Singh's four official wives. In 1900 Chail was a tiny settlement of about twenty souls. By the 1930s it was a booming village which, during the season, put up a population of thousands.

Chail Palace remained the summer resort

of the Patiala family after the death of Bhupinder Singh in 1938 (sans concubines, who were pensioned off and dispersed). In 1951 Maharaja Yadavindra Singh, the son and successor of Bhupinder and the last ruler of Patiala, had the palace completely razed and reconstructed on the original foundations along the same lines but with more rooms to accommodate his children. In 1972 Chail Palace was seized by the Congress government in what Raja Malvinder Singh of Patiala contends was a personal vendetta against his mother, the wife of Maharaja Yadavindra Singh:

My mother was a member of the Congress Party. Mrs Gandhi and my mother were very good friends. The Congress Party at that time had a split over who was going to be the next President of India, Mr N.S. Reddy or Mr V.V. Giri. Mrs Gandhi had given her preference for Mr Reddy and his nomination was announced. Then she withdrew her support from him and gave it to Mr Giri. On that, the party split . . .

Because of the political situation Mrs Gandhi wanted my mother to stay in her party. My mother refused because she said that it was unethical for her to have said one thing and done another. Mrs Gandhi tried to cajole and do all sorts of things and my mother didn't agree. So in 1972 [Mrs Gandhi] found the opportunity and served acquisition orders to the State Government of Himachal Pradesh to acquire this property – to take the whole damned thing. My mother was in residence at Chail then. Fortunately, the then Chief Minister of Himachal Pradesh, a very fine man in my personal view, Dr Y.S. Parmar, called my mother and said, 'These are the orders I have. Fortunately I have not received an official version so I am disappearing to make sure it doesn't catch up with me, but I have to acquire it; I don't have an option. The government acquisition orders will arrive but they are not valid until I have signed them. So I am sending XYZ to come and negotiate with you to give you some money for the property because otherwise it will just be taken over by the government.'

So the whole transaction was completed in two days. We wanted only to give the hill and main palace and to retain the cottage and the tennis courts and the surrounding hills on the other side, but in the hurry of finishing the procedures, the ADC who was detailed by my mother signed the whole damned thing away. My father was Ambassador to Holland at the time. When he found out what happened he was heartbroken. And that's how

Chail Palace eventually got into government hands and became a hotel.

Chail Palace was handed over to the Himachal Pradesh Tourism Development Corporation and converted into a hotel. Almost all the luxurious furnishings seized with the property have disappeared. Some were destroyed in a mysterious fire. Engendered by a scandal and scandalously lost, the story of Chail Palace remains shrouded in rumour and the mists of contradiction.

KASHMIR

GARDEN OF ETERNAL SPRING

Kashmir is a garden of eternal spring ... a delightful flowerbed, and a heart-expanding heritage for dervishes. Its pleasant meads and enchanting cascades are beyond description. There are running streams and fountains beyond count. Wherever the eye reaches, there are verdure and running water.
Emperor Jahanghir

The origins of this 'heart-expanding heritage' reach beyond four thousand years of recorded history to the pantheistic upheavals of Hindu mythology. Legends relate that the Himalayan valley was submerged by the deep waters of Satisar – the Lake of the Chaste Woman – named in honour of the goddess Parvati, who sailed upon its surface. But these waters were tainted by an annihilating demon called Jaldeo who lived within its depths, emerging to blast the region into an empty, devastated waste.

Lord Kashaf, grandson of Lord Brahma, came upon this dead land and resolved to defeat the fiend who had ravaged it, submitting himself to the rigours of spiritual retreat for a thousand years in preparation for his momentous clash with the devil. When the time came Jaldeo took refuge beneath the surface of Satisar. Accordingly Lord Vishnu took up his trident and struck an opening in the mountains of Baramula, releasing the waters of the lake to expose the cowering monster. Jaldeo continued to elude the gods until Parvati crushed him with the mountain known as Hari-Parbat, where the goddess is worshipped in her shrine to the present day. After the destruction of Jaldeo this peaceful valley was called Kashafmar, in honour of Lord Kashaf, and gradually simplified to Kashmir.

Much of the history of this ravishing land is as demon-ridden as its fabulous genesis. Invaders came in wave after wave, leaving viceroys to despoil the land and terrorize the simple, submissive people who lived there. For every golden age – of Ashoka, of Zain Al Abidin, of Akbar, Jahanghir and Shah Jahan – there were dark, barbaric epochs of tyranny and suffering.

After the decline of Mughal authority in the eighteenth century, Kashmir passed into the hands of Afghan kings and their merciless, extortionist governors. In 1819 the city of Srinagar and parts of the Vale of Kashmir were conquered by the Sikh armies of Ranjit Singh, led by his Dogra Hindu general Raja Gulab Singh of Jammu. With the fall of the Sikh capital of Lahore in 1846, Kashmir came under British rule and was sold to Gulab Singh for £750,000 and an annual tribute of one horse, twelve goats and six pairs of kashmiri shawls. In the Treaty of Amritsar, Gulab Singh, who had risen from a lowly soldier with a pay of three rupees per month plus rations to become a rich and privileged military commander and hill chief under the patronage of Maharaja Ranjit Singh of Lahore, was formally declared Maharaja of Jammu and Kashmir.

Maharaja Gulab Singh thus became the founder of the Dogra dynasty, which ruled the valley of Kashmir until its forced accession to the Indian Union in 1947. Throughout this period the 'Happy Valley', as it came to be called, was a favoured resort of the British, who, disallowed from owning land, built houseboats upon its lakes and set up their own separate, recreational society, insulated from the growing subterranean outrage of the Muslim populace, which was soon to explode in this garden of eternal spring.

GULAB BHAVAN

Oberoi Palace Hotel

Maharaja Hari Singh (1925-47) was a restless, compulsive builder with a modern temperament and Western tastes who began to erect Gulab Bhavan, his residential palace in palace in Srinagar overlooking Dal Lake, sometime toward the end of the 1920s on a site he had inherited from his father Raja Amar Singh (d. 1909), the younger brother of Maharaja Pratap Singh (1877-1925).

Amar Singh had purchased property in Srinagar and in Jammu as a personal investment – a necessary hedge taken by junior princes against the inequities of primogeniture. He could never have assumed that his son would one day succeed to the throne of Kashmir and that his real estate would come to contain two royal palaces.

According to Sir Arthur Lothian, who served as a political officer in Kashmir:

Raja Sir Amar Singh, the father of the present Maharaja Sir Hari Singh, had been made regent when Pertab [Pratap] Singh was deprived of his powers in 1895 for supposed intrigue with Russia. Relations between Pertab Singh and his brother were in consequence never good, and the estrangement extended to his nephew, Hari Singh, who on his father's death became heir presumptive, as the Maharaja was childless.

In fact, so strained were the relations between the Maharaja and his heir that Pratap Singh tried, unsuccessfully, to engineer an adoption simply to see his nephew disinherited.

The estrangement between the Maharaja and his successor was exacerbated by their inconsonant personalities. Pratap Singh was a tiny, gregarious, fantastically eccentric cricket buff who even in his later years played the game in gold-embroidered slippers and flowing robes. He was also an old-fashioned, religiously hide-bound ruler who was, according to Sir William Barton, 'too prone to superstition, too much under the influence of the Pundits . . .'.

His successor was a large, shy man with European tastes and secular notions. He was, according to his son, Dr Karan Singh, 'moody and aloof' and 'remained till the end of his days a virtual agnostic'. It is not surprising, therefore, that upon his ascension to the Gadi Hari Singh chose an altogether different lifestyle from that of his predecessor and to live as far away as possible from Rajgarh, Pratap Singh's ageing hereditary palace ranged along the River Jhelum. Karan Singh explained:

When my father succeeded to the throne he succeeded to the old palaces in both Jammu and Srinagar as well. He also had inherited these magnificent sites selected by his father. So he had a choice: he could continue to live in the old palaces and dispose of these lands or he could choose to give up the old palaces – to give them back to the state – and build upon the new sites. As he was a more modern man he chose to do the latter. These sites are visually more beautiful, they are more isolated and more private.

Hari Singh began to build upon the site sometime after 1925. There were, according to his son, two or three structures which first were built and subsequently torn down to make way for the Maharaja's new forty-five-room lime-and-brick palace, named Gulab Bhavan, in honour of his ancestor, Gulab Singh, who had re-established the Dogra dynasty in Jammu and Kashmir in the early nineteenth century. Karan Singh describes Gulab Bhavan as a 'handsome double-storey structure built on three sides of a rectangle' which 'commands a superb view of the Dal Lake and reflected my father's keen architectural interests. Unlike many contemporary princes, whose palaces were vast Victorian monstrosities, our residence with its clean lines and uncluttered exterior fitted well with the mountains that formed its backdrop.'

Not everyone would agree with this assessment. Pearce Gervis, for one, noticed in the 1950s 'the new palace of the Maharaja, with white walls and flattish red roofs as ugly and uninteresting as an army barracks . . .'. The absence of Gothic in Gulab Bhavan was commendable but the Maharaja's refusal to use vernacular materials (everything except the wood in the construction had to be imported) and to take into account the indigenous central Asian design motifs of Srinagar which, for all their ramshackle aspect, create an architectural charm throughout the valley, makes his palace as out of harmony with its environment as the Victorian monstrosities in other states are in theirs.

The most agreeable feature of Gulab Bhavan was its lovely, open landscaping designed by Hari Singh himself and maintained today much as it was in his time. Karan Singh recalled that the 'front lawns were carefully manicured, and beds of multi-coloured flowers shone brightly in the crisp Kashmir air . . .'. And whether one found the 'clean lines and uncluttered exteriors' appealing or 'ugly and uninteresting as an army barracks' the interiors of Gulab Bhavan were commodious and airy and captured the rich, iridescent lights of the Himalayan vale through catenations of lattice work along the back corridors and casement windows along the facade. Moreover, writes Karan Singh, the interiors were:

tastefully furnished, with exquisite European and Chinese curios, and wall-to-wall carpeting in every room and corridor. A lot of furniture came periodically from England ... Apart from the carpets, which were made in Kashmir, all the other furnishings, fabrics and fittings were European. My parents occupied inter-connecting wings on the first floor of the southern block, while I had a lovely suite on the ground floor directly overlooking the lake.

Gulab Bhavan was primarily a private residence and never used for public ceremony – Ceremonies of State continued to be carried out in the old City Palace.

Aside from family rituals and the Maharaja's normal administrative work, which he did at a desk upon the black marble verandah in the central wing out in the open air (the ruler had no formal office), leisure life in Gulab Bhavan seems to have revolved around the Maharaja's hobbies: hunting, fishing and cooking.

Hari Singh was a gourmet and, from the look of his girth, probably a gourmand. The central social activity at Gulab Bhavan seems to have been a weekly cooking party which the Maharaja and his wife, Maharani Tara Devi, both accomplished cooks, held for friends.

'We all sat down in the lawn or the black marble porch in the centre of the main block,' remembers Karan Singh, 'and then the cooking would begin.'

Liveried servants with yellow turbans brought in low asbestos stands about six inches high and five by three feet in area. On these would be placed coal stoves, and on them silver patilas, deep cooking dishes of various sizes depending on the item to be prepared. All the ingredients, carefully weighed and neatly arranged, were brought on folding tables. Three or four people cooked, including my parents, while the others watched and chatted. The chief taster was Wazir Taj Ram, a seasoned courtier a few years older than my father ...

Only two wings of the palace were ever occupied. The central wing was reserved for viceregal visits, which took place every two or three years; otherwise it was left empty.

Aside from the Viceroys, there were very few British guests invited to Gulab Bhavan. 'Unlike British India', wrote Karan Singh:

where their presence was ubiquitous, in the Indian States they were generally not too visible. This was specially so in our State, because my father genuinely distrusted them and even persuaded them to move their residency in winter to Sialkot in the Panjab rather than to Jammu. For the summer months the British Resident lived on the bund in Srinagar in the house later converted into the Government Handicrafts Emporium, but we seldom saw him and I cannot remember a single occasion on which I met him at the Palace.

It was an insular existence at Gulub Bhavan, not only segregated from the British but also from the Maharaja's own subjects, as Karan Singh recalls:

Social awareness does not come easily to a prince. I lived in a self-contained world where servants were taken for granted and the question of why some should be the rulers and others the ruled was never formulated, far less asked ...

As for Kashmiri Muslims, our contacts were mostly limited to the gardeners and the shooting and fishing guards. Once my father asked Ghulam Ahmed, a jeweller and carpet manufacturer of repute who was also his art adviser, to take me round the city. This he did, and I remember my astonishment at seeing all those dilapidated buildings on the Jhelum, looking as if they could topple any moment into the river. 'These are your people', Ahmed said somewhat dramatically. The visit had a rather disturbing effect upon me, and for days thereafter the recollection of the Jhelum dwellers would flash back upon me, their squalor in such glaring contrast to the orderly elegance of the palace as to constitute virtually a different world.

It was a world whose insularity, order and elegance were soon to disintegrate in the turbulent upheavals that were transforming India and, as if to presage the impending end of the old order, Gulab Bhavan received an unlikely visitation by the ethereal progenitor of the new order who, Karan Singh remembers, arrived in 1947, only two weeks before Independence and the changing of the guard:

[Mahatma Gandhi] visited Srinagar in August of that year. There was great excitement when we knew he was coming, and this rose dramatically when we heard that, in disregard of his normal practice, he would come to see my father at the palace. Even my father seemed thrilled, and of

course I insisted that I should meet him also. After some discussion it was agreed that my father, my mother and I would meet Gandhiji under one of the Chinar trees in the front lawn of Gulab Bhavan. Special arrangements were made for goat's milk and fruit, and we took our places under the tree an hour before he was due to arrive. At the appointed hour – five in the afternoon of 1 August, if I remember correctly – Gandhiji arrived. My father went to receive him at the porch, and they walked out in the garden to the tree where my mother and I awaited them. I will never forget how moved I was to see that frail figure walking towards us, tiny alongside the tall figure of my father. Here was a man who had become a living legend, who by sheer moral courage had shaken to its foundation the greatest empire the world had ever seen . . . . As he sat down Gandhiji turned to me and said, 'Kaise ho' ['How are you?']. Then he started a long monologue in a low lisping voice which I could not clearly follow . . . All I was able to gather from his words was that he was urging my father to ascertain the wishes of his people, to take his people into confidence, and to align himself with rather than against them in the political turmoil that was engulfing the country.

After about ninety minutes Gandhiji got up to go. My mother pressed him to partake of some milk and fruit, but he declined saying that it was not his eating time. At her insistence he agreed to have the fruit put into his car. He left, smiling at me as he said goodbye, dressed in white and with a sad smile which still lingers in my memory. Then he walked back across the lawn followed by both my parents and I was left alone under the tree . . .

Within three months of this meeting, the idyllic princely life of Gulab Bhavan was abruptly ended by the Pakistani invasion of Kashmir on 22 October 1947 which drove the Maharaja and his entourage to take flight toward Jammu in the dead of night. Two agonizing years passed before Sardar Vallabhbhai Patel, the Union Home Minister, informed the Maharaja and his wife that they must absent themselves from their state and relinquish authority in favour of their only son who was only eighteen.

Hari Singh was never to return to the kingdom he ruled and Gulab Bhavan was suddenly abandoned. Yuvraj Karan Singh, as Regent, lived in his own house of Karan Mahal a short distance from the empty palace. From 1949 to 1954 Gulab Bhavan was unoccupied but for a few retainers, and neglected. Trees began to grow on the roof and in the harsh Kashmiri winters the building began to deteriorate badly.

In 1951 Karan Singh, who as Regent of Kashmir was rapidly integrating into the new political order, suggested that an ideal use for the empty palace would be to give it over as part of the recently founded Jammu and Kashmir University:

I mentioned this to Jawaharlal [Nehru] and Gopalaswami Ayyangar, who reacted favourably. Jawaharlal wrote: 'I am very glad to learn that you intend donating Gulab Mahal Palace to the University of Jammu and Kashmir. That is the very best use you can put the building to and I am sure it will be greatly appreciated by the public.' . . .Gopalaswami Ayyangar meanwhile wrote to my father mentioning the offer and urging him to accept it. My father was furious and wrote me an angry letter. I wrote back, laying out the factors which had impelled me to suggest the gift and summed this up by saying: 'Considering all these factors – a fast deteriorating building which is ideally suited to be a University and which is lying neglected and unused, and the fact that our University greatly requires a suitable building and that education is as noble and as worthy a cause as can possibly be found – I sincerely feel that it would be a magnificent gesture on your part if you were to donate the building. The effect of such an act on the public would, I am convinced, be electrifying.'

My father, however, disagreed and in his reply angrily said that: 'The Jammu and Kashmir Government have gone out of their way to harass me personally and to humiliate the dynasty in the eyes of the public . . . I hope you will realize that the gift in the present circumstances with however lofty ideals behind it would be misconstrued as one more instance of the Ruler being proved a non-entity and of no consequence.'

Thus was Gulab Bhavan withheld from the State Government and it stood idle for three more years until Indian hotelier M.S. Oberoi approached Karan Singh, who by this time had been democratically elected to the post of Sardar-i-Riyasat, or Head of State, of Kashmir, with an offer to take over the Palace and open it as a luxury hotel. Karan Singh thought that:

this was an excellent idea, because even though the

lease money was very modest, the property would be well maintained and would provide Kashmir with its first five-star hotel. I was the first of the former princes to take this step. Jaipur and Udaipur followed a few years later, and now, of course, it is well recognized that these massive palaces dotted throughout the country can play an important role in strengthening the tourism infrastructure.

The hotelier purchased the original hand-made wall-to-wall Kashmiri carpets which had been warehoused in Jammu and reinstalled them in the Palace, which in 1955 opened for business as the Oberoi Palace Hotel, the first palace hotel in India.

HIMALAYAN HILLS

AL HILAL PALACE
Palace Motel Taragarh

In 1931 the twenty-seven-year-old Nawab Al Haj Sir Sadiq Mohammed Khan Bahadur of Bahawalpur (1907-47) built a large European-style summer residence for himself up in the cool Himalayan jungles of Kangra district, near the village of Palampur. Within the compound walls he laid out lush gardens, built a glass pleasure pavilion and a mosque, excavated a swimming tank and called his country palace Al Hilal – The Crescent Moon – to which he would retire for three months of the summer season, in refuge from the burning heat of Bahawalpur.

When India was partitioned in 1947 the Punjabi State of Bahawalpur fell within Pakistani territory and the Nawab exercised his Muslim preference, took citizenship in the newly formed Islamic republic and forfeited his Kangra retreat to the newly formed Indian Government of Punjab.

Maharani Tara Devi of Kashmir had been raised in a village in the Kangra Valley before her marriage to Maharaja Hari Singh and in the traumatic aftermath of Independence, when she and her husband were forced into exile from their state, she was overtaken by a yearning to return to her roots. Her marriage had never been a happy one in any case and after Kashmir was lost the periods of estrangement from her husband, who took up residence in Bombay, became increasingly prolonged and finally continuous until they were separated by the Maharaja's death. She therefore felt a need to make a home for herself alone, close to her family and birthplace.

The Maharani approached Prime Minister Jawaharlal Nehru for permission to acquire a residence in Kangra and he suggested that she apply to the Punjabi government to purchase Al Hilal, which had been classified as evacuee property. In 1950, then, Maharani Tara Devi acquired Al Hilal Palace from the Punjab State Government for the sum of eight lakhs of rupees. She had the glass pleasure pavilion converted into a temple in which to carry

out her Hindu rituals (*pujas*) and renamed her new home Taragarh, in honour of herself.

The Maharani moved between her Jammu palace and Taragarh until her death in 1967, when the property was passed on to her only son, Dr Karan Singh, who in 1971 opened Taragarh as a roadside motel and placed his maternal uncle in charge. The glass temple is still maintained and used for worship and every Thursday night on the eve of Jum'ua, the Muslim sabbath, a candle is lit within the mosque in the garden compound of Taragarh in memory of its Muslim builder.

NAGAR CASTLE
Castle Hotel

The rough-hewn stone and timber castle set high upon a precipice 1,000 feet above the Beas Valley floor through which the River Beas runs, was said to have been erected by the Kulu war-lord Raja Sidh Singh around 1460 when he transferred the capital of his expanding Himalayan principality south from Manali to Nagar Village. When war-lords moved in conquest so did their capitals move with them.

According to one version of the region's oral history, the excavated stones of Baragarh, a ruined fort across the Beas Valley, were hauled away to Nagar for the building of the raja's castle. Another variation relates the tale of a chain of coolies stretching more than fifteen miles from Garhdekh, a crumbling abandoned fortress once occupied by a Rana named Bhonsal, up the mountain to the precipitous construction site, passing each stone hand to hand.

The crude stone slabs were stacked in unmortared courses interrupted at intervals by horizontal bands of timber beams, connected by cross-bars. In the western Himalayan mason's indigenous craft, of which Nagar Castle is a classic specimen, the absence of mortar and the particular technique of stacking dry stones interlinked by girders of deodar or spruce together create a resilience in the structure by allowing stones to vibrate with every seismic tremor. The wisdom of this method was borne out when Nagar Castle survived a massive earthquake in 1905.

In a courtyard within the castle compound, inside a small, austere outbuilding, lies a massive, flat, triangular rock slab sanctified as Jagatipath which is believed to have been supernaturally transported from a village some fifteen miles north of Nagar. The Raja of Kulu had taken a bride in marriage from a village near the base of Rohatang Pass and moved her to his castle some fifteen miles further down the valley in Nagar. The young Rani, it is said, became homesick. So intense was her nostalgia that the *devatas* (local, as opposed to universal, deities) of the valley manifested as a swarm of bees which miraculously extracted a stone measuring five feet by eight feet by six inches from the Deotika mountain near her home and carried it aloft to Nagar to comfort the melancholy princess with a reminder of her birthplace.

The rulers of Kulu remained resident in Nagar Castle until in 1637 Raja Jagat Singh (1637-72) removed to lower down the valley to re-establish his capital in Sultanpur, which in modern times became known as Kulu. Thereafter, Nagar Castle was used by the Kulu rajas as a summer palace until in 1846, when the British took the reins of power from the Sikh invaders of Kangra and Kulu, Raja Gyan Singh sold his hereditary stone castle in exchange for a rifle to the newly appointed Assistant Commissioner of the region, Major Hay. Its new owner renovated the northern wing of Nagar Castle, installing staircases, fireplaces and chimneys, none of which exists in the traditional building of the region. Major Hay ultimately sold the castle to the Government of Punjab, which used the building as a court house and as a rest house for officials and other visitors to Nagar.

In the 1920s Nagar Castle was converted permanently into a travellers' rest house and continued to be used as such even after Independence although, when Penelope Chetwode travelled through Nagar in 1963 on a journey up the Kulu Valley, she reported that one wing of the Castle was being used as a village school. Miss Chetwode, as the daughter of India's Commander-in-Chief General Sir Philip Chetwode, had made a trek up from Simla into Kulu in 1931 with her mother, Lady

Mary Chetwode, and stayed at Nagar Castle. On her return over three decades later she spent another night in Nagar Castle 'walled in nostalgia':

That night I spread out my old green fleabag on the wide verandah which runs along the north side of the castle, and walled in nostalgia. I actually spent at least an hour simply leaning on the balustrade and contemplating the moonlit view of the Upper Beas Valley which had haunted me for so many years. There was the long white ridge at the head of the Solang Nala, and to the right of it, the twin Gyephang peaks of Lahul: no longer in my imagination at the end of a downland track, but here, in reality, in the Western Himalaya. I remembered how my mother and I and Gerald Emerson and our A.D.C., Geoffrey Kellie, had all spent the night on this very verandah by moonlight thirty-three years ago hoping to see the ghost of the poor young Rani who had thrown herself off at the far end and fallen down the steep khud-side to her death. Various versions of the story tell how some wrestlers or strolling players were performing before the royal family in the chief courtyard of the castle and at the end of their display the Raja turned to his youngest queen and asked her which man she considered the best. She singled out one whereupon the Raja had him beheaded before her on the spot, believing him to be her lover. In horror she rushed up to the verandah, ran along it and committed suicide. Her ghost has haunted it ever since, though the original wood of the verandah has been renewed several times since the tragedy. At Nagar I have always been lucky with marvellous moonlight nights, but have never seen the Rani, neither have I met anyone who has, but my old friend, the late Mr J.C. French of the I.C.S. [Indian Civil Service], wrote: 'I slept in the western room of the castle, and shortly before midnight I awoke with a sense of uneasiness and oppression. I thought the night must have turned suddenly warm (it was cold when I went to bed) and I got up to open another window. As I stood up, swift and unmistakable as a gust of cold air or a drive of sleet came the sensation of fear. I went to the west wall of the castle and opened a window, and all the time I was moving there and back the sensation of fear was with me.'

In 1978 Nagar Castle was taken over, ghosts and all, by the Himachal Pradesh Tourism Corporation and renamed Castle Hotel.

WESTERN INDIA

BHAVNAGAR

HOME OF HAPPY FORTUNE

On the western edge of India, projecting into the Arabian Sea, the Kathiawar Peninsula stretches out for 22,000 square miles between the Gulfs of Kachh and Cambay in a land the Greco-Roman traders who touched upon its shores called Saurasthrene – the Good Land – a name modified to Saurashtra and retained to this day. The Marathas renamed this fertile territory Kathiawar after their most intractable enemy in western Gujarat. The Kathis were a fierce, marauding tribe who had migrated south from Sind into Kachh, pushed by the invasions of Alexander the Great, finally settling in Saurashtra in the fifteenth century. Captain H. Wilberforce Bell describes the Kathis of Kathiawar as 'a brave and warlike race' with 'a special propensity for stealing cattle'. Apart from the name they lent, however, they were little more than a historical sideshow in this uproarious region.

Kathiawar became the locus of an agglomeration of no fewer than 282 petty principalities proliferating out of larger chiefships during the decline of Mughal domination and led by descendants of invaders, refugees, bandits, war-lords and soldiers of fortune. By the end of the eighteenth century 248 of these territories had been subdued by the Marathas. Within the first two decades of the following century the Marathas had been displaced in Kathiawar by the British, who set about trying to reform their unruly feudatories.

Far and away the most reformable estate in the region was the realm of an allegedly moon-born Rajput tribe driven by Rathor war-lords from their homeland into Saurashtra during the thirteenth century. The Gohels, or 'power of the earth', emerged as a power on the earth of Kathiawar during the reign of Bhavsinh I (1703-64), who abandoned his inland stronghold at Sihor to establish a seaside capital on the Gulf of Cambay which he called Bhavnagar, the City of Bhav, in honour of himself.

Bhavsinh was a prescient and enterprising ruler who recognized the growing profitability of maritime trade and the rising primacy of British imperialism. He developed his new capital into a thriving port city and joined forces with the British East India Company to eradicate piracy from the coastal waters of the Arabian Sea. Bhavsinh's descendants continued to rule with military skill, political acumen and flexible intelligence through the eighteenth and nineteenth centuries, pushing out the boundaries of their territory to cover 2,860 square miles. The rulers of Bhavnagar eagerly embraced the British policies of administrative reform and public works and systematically developed their prospering dominion into the wealthiest in Kathiawar and one of the most efficiently governed princely states in all of India, transforming their seaboard capital into what S.M. Edwardes, in a fulsome eulogy penned in 1909, called 'a veritable lakshmi among cities, a Mangala Vilas or Home of Happy Fortune'.

HUZOOR MAHAL AT NILAMBAG

Nilambag Palace Hotel

The original Huzoor Mahal was built around 1875 upon a site outside the city walls of Bhavnagar called Nilambag, which means the Turquoise Garden, for the adolescent prince, Raja Takhtasinh Gohel (1870-96).

Set amidst expansive gardens, the residence was designed and built by Mr Proctor Simms, who in his capacity as Chief

Engineer of Bhavnagar had designed many buildings around the city. It was an unusual, even strange, structure – a stark, low-rise rectangular stone quadrant surrounding an arcaded atrium and enveloped by verandahs with trabeated colonnades ornamented in the manner of a series of carved arches. The strong and striking smoke-grey stone, which accentuated the severity of the residence, was excavated from quarries in Rajula in the south of the Kathiawar peninsula.

During his minority period, close to the same time the garden house was under construction, Takhtasinh's senior Rani died shortly after giving birth to the ruler's first son and successor, Bhavsingh II. No matter which way one looked at it, a zenana filled with co-wives and concubines was a treacherous place for a motherless infant heir-apparent to grow up in and it was deemed safer for the Crown Prince to be reared for the first five years of his life by his maternal grandmother under the protection of his uncle, Thakur Baghwat Sinh of neighbouring Gondal State.

By the time the child returned to Bhavnagar his father had sired two more sons by other Ranis and it had become imperative for Bhavsinh to be permanently sequestered from the inevitable machinations of the zenana. The young prince was settled into the garden house at Nilambag and cared for by staff personally selected by the Maharaja. These precautions were not simply the by-product of some irrational paranoia generated by conniving British officials, for there are off-the-record stories which tell of later unsuccessful attempts on Bhavsinh's life by unnamed zenana factions.

Upon reaching his majority Takhtasinh became an excellent reform-minded ruler who did much to improve his state. He was one of the first Indian princes to travel to England as a personal guest of the Queen-Empress and was elevated to the rank of Maharaja in 1891 for his progressive administration. Nevertheless, he continued to live in traditional style with his five Maharanis in the old Motibag Palace in the city centre, having given Nilambag to his eldest son.

When Maharaja Takhtasinh died in 1896, Maharaja Bhavsinh (1896-1919) ascended the Gadi and, if anything, surpassed his exceptional predecessor in the excellence and liberality of his administration. The ruler continued his father's public works and educational programmes which transformed Bhavnagar into one of the most advanced princely states in India, and added his own twist of morality by introducing prohibition into Bhavnagar, a ban which has been upheld to the present day. Along with being a teetotaller, the Maharaja was a strict monogamist and, possibly from some unhappy early associations, pointedly did not set aside a zenana area at Nilambag.

Administrative affairs were still based in the Motibag Palace but Maharaja Bhavsinh remained in residence at Nilambag throughout his reign, adding rooms to what was now the official royal residence. Bhavsinh lived a life of exemplary simplicity and grace there. He would rise daily before the dawn, be out on the hunt by sunrise and return at around nine o'clock with the day's bag. His mornings would be spent supervising the administration at Motibag. Before noon the ruler would be back at Nilambag, relaxing in his teakwood swing out on the side verandah, which is now the banquet hall of the palace. Here the Maharaja would rest until three o'clock, sipping juices and receiving intelligence reports from a network of agents watching over the 640 villages within his domain. In the afternoon he would return to his office in the city and work there until after sunset. By seven o'clock in the evening the Maharaja was back in his swing, harmonium before him and surrounded by musicians to work out ragas that had been echoing in his imagination throughout the long official day. This is the most vivid image of Maharaja Bhavsinh remembered by an ancient retainer who survives from that period – the ruler in his teakwood swing, passionately abstracted in his musical reveries.

Bhavsinh's son and successor, Maharaja Krishna Kumarsinh (1919-47), ascended the Gadi of Bhavnagar at the age of seven and received his ruling powers eleven years later in 1930. He continued to reside in Nilambag Palace and when he took over the administration of his state, shifted his offices from Motibag to his home.

In 1933 Nilambag Palace was completely

renovated according to designs by Mr Kenoski, a German-Polish architect from Heidelberg. Further renovations were carried out in 1940, making Huzoor Mahal at Nilambag a fully fledged princely palace.

The most striking decorative addition was the intricately carved Burmese teak entry arch, elaborating the pattern reiterated in the outer colonnades. The verandah upon which Maharaja Bhavsinh would sit was enclosed to make a banquet hall. A *porte-cochère* was added to the main entrance. This construction was a clever replication of carved Rajula stone, cast with an aggregate cement as a measure of wartime frugality. The open courtyard became a wide pond surrounding a central fountain. Along the arcades were a library, billiard room-cum-office, drawing room and bedrooms. The first floor contained family quarters ranged along an arcade. In the grounds a swimming pool was excavated at some distance from the palace, concealed in a grove of trees.

In 1947 Maharaja Krishna Kumarsinh personally handed over the administration of his state to Mahatma Gandhi, becoming the first princely ruler to accede to the Indian Union in exchange for yearly compensation in the form of a privy purse which the Maharaja allowed the Mahatma to set on his behalf. For this decisive act of sacrifice Krishna Kumarsinh was rewarded (and cleverly removed from proximity to his former state), with the prestigious appointment as the first Governor of Madras State, which at the time included the future states of Andhra Pradesh, Karnataka and Tamil Nadu. The Maharaja was also appointed to the ceremonial post of Up-Rajpramukh, or Assistant Governor, of the newly formed Union of Saurashtra.

Aside from the cessation of official activities on its grounds, life at Nilambag remained more or less as it always had been, given the traditional simplicity of the Bhavnagar family. In 1952 a lift was added to the palace and in 1954 the marriage of Maharaja Krishna Kumarsinh's oldest son, Maharajkumar Virbadhrasinh, was celebrated with the addition of a second floor area to the palace for the heir-apparent's living quarters, furnished by Italian designer Pisceonari, from his Bombay showroom, The Drawing Room.

Jawaharlal Nehru stayed at Nilambag on several occasions and in 1960, when the Prime Minister attended a Congress Party convention held in Bhavnagar, he and his daughter Indira were guests at the palace for twenty-two days.

Maharaja Krishna Kumarsinh died in 1965 and his eldest son succeeded him. Without ruling responsibilities to hold him in Bhavnagar, Maharaja Dr Virbadhrasinh Gohel became increasingly involved in scholarly and commercial activities in Bombay and moved permanently there in the late 1960s. He would return to Nilambag at intervals but eventually most of the palace was shut down. His brother, Raja Shivbadhrasinh, had already moved to his own Bhav Vilas Palace and for most of the year Nilambag would stand idle and empty but for a few servants and retainers who maintained the palace grounds and the Maharaja's apartments.

With Mrs Gandhi's machiavellian de-recognition of the princely order at the end of 1970 and the concomitant loss of the privy purse that had been guaranteed to his father by Mahatma Gandhi, Virbadhrasinh found the upkeep of the palace he hardly lived in any longer a terrible drain on his severely diminished income. The ten acres of wooded gardens, which had been the pride of Nilambag, were necessarily neglected, becoming overgrown and dead. The once vibrant and elegant palace lay grim, dusty and mouldering.

The Maharaja resisted turning his family home into a commercial establishment until 1983 when, after building a smaller house for himself at one corner of the grounds, he entered into an arrangement with ITC-Welcomgroup to renovate and open Nilambag as a hotel. The conversion was supervised by engineer Virendra Mital who worked from the original palace plans to retain the integrity of the building. A water filtration plant was installed, the dead gardens were revived and re-landscaped, and the interiors were totally refurbished using furniture and fittings that had been left in the palace.

In 1986 Nilambag Palace was opened as a hotel.

WANKANER

WANKANER

The town of Wankaner, thirty miles to the north of Rajkot in the modern state of Gujarat, was the capital of a Rajput principality of the same name in Jhalawad, a dynastic territory in Kathiawar first established in the 12th century by a tribe from Sind known as the Makwana, a word which may well have derived from the Greek word Makedonia, leading some to believe this race to have descended from the armies of Alexander. The Makwana migrated to the Kathiawar peninsula in 1090 and settled in Patdi on the north-eastern edge of Saurashtra, the capital of a territory of 1,600 villages granted by the King of Anhilwad to their leader, Harpal Dev, who, through his knowledge of the unseen, had cured the ruler of a demonic insomnia.

The name Jhala attached to this tribe and their land through Shaktimata, the wife of Harpal Dev, who is believed to have possessed transcendental powers and has accordingly been deified. Her legend has it that one evening she was resting upon a balcony above the courtyard of her husband's fortress, looking down upon their three young sons at play, when a rogue elephant crashed through the compound gates, charging toward the children. With one long supernatural stretch Shaktimata snatched her sons from the path of the raging beast. 'To snatch' in Gujarati is *Jhalwu* and the clan named themselves thus in memory of their matriarch's miraculous rescue.

The Mughal and Afghan onslaught on Gujarat in the sixteenth century forced the Jhalas westward where they re-established their capital at Halvad. Wankaner was a filiation of Halvad founded in 1605 by Sultanji, the son of Prathiraj of Halvad, in an attempt to capture the kingdom he believed to be his by right of primogeniture. The Halvad throne had been usurped by Sultanji's uncle, Askaran, while his father languished to death in a Mughal prison cell in Ahmadabad.

Sultanji had taken a vow that neither he nor his descendants would complete the Hindu ceremony of four marriage rounds until Halvad was retaken. He raised an army from the forces of his maternal grandfather Jam Jasaji of Nawanagar, marching east until he came upon a high hill from which the fortress of Halvad could be clearly seen across the plains. He made his camp upon this strategic rise and ventured out from there with raiding parties to wrest surrounding territories from his enemy's lands, cutting out an independent state from Halvad which was ultimately known as Wankaner.

For generation after generation the armies of Wankaner laid siege to the fortress of Halvad, making life so vexatious for the Jhala clan that in the eighteenth century they were finally driven to establish a new capital further east at Dhrangadhara, which gave the name to their modern princely state. But for all their aggression, Sultanji and his descendants never managed to occupy and hold Halvad, and in fulfilment of their ancestral vow, the Wankaner dynasty has never to this day completed the four rounds in their marriage rituals.

The feud between the two Jhala houses continued, albeit with diminishing intensity, until Colonel Walker of the British East India Company circulated the peninsula in 1807 and pledged the combative Kathiawar states to peace and territorial integrity. Even then it took another century for the bad blood between these sister clans to finally subside.

RANJIT VILAS PALACE

The capital of Wankaner was built at the foot of the rise from which Sultanji initiated his campaign of conquest. It is here, halfway up this hill, that Ranjit Vilas Palace looms over the otherwise unassuming Gujarati township in scrambled, Euro-Oriental immensity.

The hillside site was first developed in the 1870s during the reign of Raj Sahib Bane Sinh (1860-81), who built a moderately sized residence to which he moved from the traditional mid-town palace of his ancestors. The later Ranjit Vilas Palace, which stands adjacent to the original not so very tiny building and completely dwarfs it, was conceived, designed and built by Bane

Sinh's son, the last ruling Prince of Wankaner, Maharana Raj Sahib Amar Sinh (1881-1947) who reigned with beneficent, autocratic energy over his tiny state for sixty-seven years.

Born in 1879, Amar Sinh ascended the Gadi at the age of two upon the death of his father. According to established practice, a Regency Council was constituted by and under the supervision of the Political Agent at Rajkot to rule the state on behalf of the infant prince through the duration of his minority. Like Maharaja Ganga Singh of Bikaner, Amar Sinh was raised and meticulously shaped in the British mould, receiving his education at Rajkot Princes' College, and like Ganga Singh, the young ruler of Wankaner State grew into a stalwart of Empire and an exemplary ruler according to the British ideal. After graduation from Rajkot, the summer before receiving his full ruling powers in 1899, the young Raj Sahib was taken on a grand European tour – a journey which awakened in the prince an abiding love of architecture and a yen to build.

Upon his return to Wankaner Amar Sinh took up residence in his late father's hillside palace but almost immediately set himself to putting his own architectonic stamp on the site. Between 1900 and 1907 the ruler built a new palace contiguous to the old which he called Amar Vilas, in honour of himself. This was, however, but an intermediate step, a mere *entr'acte*, while the ruler worked out his grand design. Dictating his ideas to the Chief Engineer of Wankaner State, the prince threw absolutely everything he liked into this new composition – every architectural element, every motif he fancied from his travels and books brought back from Europe, every innovation, every Doric, Victorian, Ionian, Saracenic, Gothic, Art Deco, Palladian, Beaux Arts touch which would make his palace on the hill an inimitable projection of a ruler whose personality was, like the building itself, out of scale with his diminutive nine-gun, second-class state. It took him twenty years to do it.

The foundation stone was laid for the new palace of Wankaner in 1907 by Amar Sinh's dear friend and distant cousin, Ranjit Singh of Nawanagar, 'the Prince of Cricket', who had in his illustrious career as champion batsman for England in the last decade of the nineteenth century and through the turn of the present century, become the most famous Indian of his day, known throughout the sporting world as 'Ranji'. In 1907 Ranji ascended to the Gadi of his state and one of his first ceremonial duties as Jam Sahib of Nawanagar was to lay this foundation stone. So, in a lovely departure from the normal princely narcissism of naming, the Raj Sahib Amar Sinh called his new palace Ranjit Vilas, in honour of his friend.

Ranjit Vilas Palace was constructed of red sandstone quarried in Wankaner, with a liberal finishing of creamy Italian marble imported from the Carrara quarries, punctuated by black Belgian marble and trellis-work of pure white Indian marble. The masonry and intricate stone carving was all carried out by local craftsmen who worked from adapted European patterns. The new palace was under perpetual construction for seven years and on the verge of completion when the First World War broke out in 1914 and armies were marshalled from throughout the Empire to fight the Germans.

Captain H. Wilberforce-Bell wrote that 'the Kathiawad chiefs without exception proved their loyalty by placing the whole of the resources of their States at the disposal of the King Emperor'. In an extraordinary act of Imperial fealty, Raj Sahib Amar Sinh and Jam Sahib Ranjit Sinh also offered themselves up for military service, serving together at the French front as honorary officers of the Indian Army. For this gesture Raj Sahib Amar Sinh was elevated by a grateful King-Emperor to the royal rank of Maharana.

Throughout the duration of the war Ranjit Vilas Palace was an empty and unfinished shell and work was only taken up again after 1918 when the complicated and expensive process of finishing and furnishing this king-sized Indo-European structure was initiated. All the essential fittings of modern palaces in India had to be imported. Yet Wankaner was a small state with an annual income of a few lakhs of rupees and the Maharana could not afford to order everything at one time. Moreover, unlike less responsible rulers who vampirized the treasuries of their states for the sake of self-glorification, Amar Sinh never abused his authority by exceeding his privy purse. Therefore Ranjit Vilas Palace was finished in stages.

The first year after the war was taken up with painting and decoration. In each succeeding year another phase was undertaken: plumbing, electrics, lighting, ornamental ironwork, furniture. Almost all the architectural fittings, including the stained-glass windows, the ornamental bronze entrance and the enormous clock-tower bell, were imported from England. The gigantic crystal chandeliers were Venetian and the enormous oriental carpets were hand-loomed especially for the palace in the city of Mirzapur in what is now Uttar Pradesh. The furniture itself was custom-made by the Bombay firm of John Roberts & Co., the favoured furniture-maker of the Indian princes of the day.

This long-drawn-out process took until 1927, throughout which time the palace remained unoccupied. It was another year before the Wankaner ruling family moved from the not-so-very-old adjacent palace of Amar Vilas to their new residence. The son and successor of Maharana Amar Sinh, Maharana Raj Sahib Pratap Sinh, who was born in 1907, the year construction on Ranjit Vilas Palace was begun, remembers growing up with the palace, and perhaps it is fitting that the first ceremony to take place in Ranjit Vilas was his marriage in 1928 to Rani Rama Kumari of Dungarpur State.

There were many other palaces in the Raj which were much larger and more spectacular than Ranjit Vilas but by virtue of its location in a tiny state of only 101 villages and a single small town for a capital, and by its audacious, unbridled eclecticism and eccentricity, this is among the most distinctive princely residences constructed in the early twentieth century. It is an angular symmetrical edifice of three floors beneath a gabled roof and a marble-domed central clock tower flanked by similarly domed subsidiary turrets and hypostyle pavilions. The palace is utterly without the usual kind of restraint and stylistic uniformity that even the weirdest architects and engineers of the period exercised. In the mammoth central drawing room alone there are round imposted arches, Saracenic arches, baroque lancet arches, pedimented Corinthian portals and Art Deco doorways. The Italian marble ballustraded double staircase, ascending-descending in a disorienting angular spiral might have been inspired by an Escher etching.

The exterior is a hypertrophic *mélange* of elements, a pandemonium of windows, arches and loggias, with a central projecting *porte-cochère*, a common and totally European innovation allowing visitors to alight from car or carriage at the entrance to the palace beneath a roof, shielded from sun and rain. The new palace is connected to the old by a long covered passageway.

Life in Ranjit Vilas Palace was on the whole quiet and uneventful. Set as it was amidst the royal game preserves, the prince and his progeny indulged in their passion for the *shikar*, adding to the overwhelming glass-eyed menagerie, fixed in pacific ferocity along the interior walls of the palace. There was also breeding of the unique Kathiawari horse with its vertical ears which turn forward when the animal focuses its eyes on a frontal point. There were dinner parties and tea parties but traditional ceremonies were still carried out at the old palace in the town.

Maharana Amar Sinh continued to make regular visits to Europe, attending the Coronation of King George VI in 1937 as one of twelve officially invited princes, and he continued to build. He expanded his garden house (see page 89) and constructed Wankaner House, his fabulous Bombay residence which after Independence was sold to the American Government for their Consulate General. He built schools and hospitals and numerous other public buildings. Maharana Amar Sinh was a hands-on ruler who turned up daily at his office in town to direct the affairs of his state. He was a popular autocrat and as a result of his efficiency and beneficence Wankaner was never subjected to the nationalist agitation that raged around India and in Gujarat in particular.

There was no avoiding the outcome of Independence from Britain, however. Maharana Pratap Sinh remembers that by the end of the war 'we knew we were going to lose everything. The writing was on the wall.' There was no way around the fact that Wankaner, along with all of the Kathiawar states, would be absorbed into

the Indian Union. Only Junagadh, whose Muslim ruler understandably and quite irrationally declared that his small peninsular state well inside Indian territory would become part of Pakistan, resisted and was forced to flee to his chosen country at the threat of police action. The subsequent treaties with the Central Government ensured that the private properties of the Maharajas were inviolable, but the former rulers were subjected to land-ceiling restrictions and thus the surrounding hills which formed the royal hunting preserves had to be given to the government and the palace estate was considerably reduced in size.

Maharana Amar Sinh died in 1954, seventy-three years after assuming power over Wankaner, five years after losing it. His son, Maharana Raj Sahib Pratap Sinh, who had been groomed all his life to rule, when the time came, could not.

The Wankaner family remained in their amazing palace while India changed. The Maharana's son, Dr Digvijay Sinh, an environmentalist, politician and world traveller, who served for nine years as Director of the Indian Tourism Development Corporation (ITDC), made a tour in 1971 to eleven European countries in order to study the conversion and operation of Europe's stately homes and palaces as hotels. The following year Dr Sinh opened the six-room guest annexe at Ranjit Vilas and the twelve-room garden house of Purna Chandra Bhavan to paying guests as a means of promoting tourism in Gujarat.

Throughout the 1970s and '80s Dr Sinh's increased involvement in politics prevented him from developing the family properties but they have remained in casual operation with Maharana Pratap Sinh and his wife in residence, graciously hosting visitors by private arrangement on advance notice. It is very informal: literally living and dining with the courtly no-nonsense Maharana and his warm-hearted wife in their monumental hereditary palace, which remains almost exactly as it was in 1928 when it opened, carved silver beds, Venetian chandeliers and all.

To stay at Ranjit Vilas Palace as a personal guest of its princely proprietor is to enter into another realm, an evanescent world barely removed from the aristocratic gentility of the Raj – fading, fading away . . .

PURNA CHANDRA BHAVAN
Oasis Palace

During the reign of Raj Sahib Bane Sinh (1860-81), most likely sometime in the 1870s, a simple single-storey bungalow in colonial style was built within the perimeters of a cultivated tract set upon the flatlands some two miles distant from the ruler's hillside residence, presumably for his rest and pleasure. The bungalow was referred to as the Garden House.

The Raj Sahib's son and successor Amar Sinh (1881-1947) continued to use the Garden House as a personal resort and, also, increasingly, as accommodation for his guests. In 1917 the Raj Sahib presided over the marriage of his daughter to Purna Chandra Bhanja Deo, the Maharaja of Mayurbhanj (in Orissa) and, during their days in Wankaner, he set up the newly wedded couple in the Garden House, which he renamed Purna Chandra Bhavan, in honour of his son-in-law.

In the early 1930s Maharana Raj Sahib Amar Sinh built an extension to Purna Chandra Bhavan. It was in fact an entirely new white colonial palace, adjacent to the original bungalow, and intended as the Wankaner State Guest House. Constructed under the supervision of Mr Shah, Chief Engineer of Wankaner State, the new Purna Chandra Bhavan consisted of two large suites and four other bedrooms, along with the usual public rooms, with elaborate imported Art Deco furnishings and a superb indoor swimming pool.

More impressive than the palace itself was the excavation and construction of the only *baoli*, or step-well, erected in India during the twentieth century. The ornamental step-well within the garden of Purna Chanda Bhavan was covered by a two-storey white pavilion and descended three storeys beneath the earth. Stone stairways gave access to galleries and resting rooms recessed into the subterranean walls, giving cool refuge from the dusty summer heat of Kathiawar. A fountain exploded from the well below, shooting a spray of water two storeys up into the interiors to moisten the atmosphere with refreshing mists.

In his old age Maharana Raj Sahib Amar Sinh intended to retire to Purna Chandra

Bhavan after transferring power to his son, Yuvraj Pratap Sinh, the present Maharana Raj Sahib of Wankaner.

'He used to go for a few days,' remembers Pratap Sinh, 'but he felt cut off there', and never settled down to live in his garden palace.

Pratap Sinh gifted Purna Chandra Bhavan to his own son, Dr Digvijay Sinh, who began to take in paying guests there in 1972 in order to encourage tourism in his district. With its conversion into a privately managed commercial motel, he changed the name to Oasis Palace.

CENTRAL INDIA

ORCHHA

The haunting palatial vestiges of Orchha cover a craggy eminence some ten miles south of Jhansi in a green and rock-strewn tangle of scrub jungle on the left bank of the winding River Betwa. These ravishing remains form the abandoned capital of the kingdom of Bundelkhand, ruled by Bundela Rajputs from the Gaharwar clan of Benares, who trace back their ancestry to Lord Rama and beyond to the Sun itself.

The name Bundela is said to have originated in the eleventh century from Hemkaran who, hounded from Benares by his brothers, approached the shrine of Vindhyavasini Devi with five human heads as a sacrificial offering and was invested with the title 'Pancham Vindhyela' by the bloodthirsty goddess, promising the warrior a glorious future. Vindhyela became Bundela and attached itself to the tribe of Hemkaran. In their western diaspora into central India the Bundelas finally reached Orchha in 1501 when their chief Rudra Pratap moved his capital thirty-five miles from Garnkundar and began to build Ramji Mandir, the first of Orchha's fortified palaces.

The kings of Orchha had a turbulent history unavoidably interlocked with the Mughal empire, culminating in the reign of Bir Singh Deo (1605-27) who transformed Orchha and its sister-city Datia into architectural treasures. Bir Singh Deo's

dominion precisely parallels that of Emperor Jahanghir, his Mughal benefactor, and in many ways these two contemporaries had much in common: both were second sons with pretensions to succession; both were cold-blooded, cruel, ambitious and brilliant; and both rulers became great patrons of art.

While his brother Ram Shah (1592-1605) ruled uneasily in Orchha, Bir Singh Deo expanded his compensatory *jagir* through a relentless series of lightning raids into Mughal territory, earning him the name of *Dang*, or bandit, for his brutal rapacity. He also earned the anger of the emperor, who sent forces in pursuit of the renegade warlord. Dogged by Akbar's men, the Dang cast in his lot in 1601 with the emperor's rebellious second son Salim, who must certainly have seen something of himself in the ambitious Rajput.

The Mughal prince's most powerful enemy at court was Abu Fazal, Akbar's friend, biographer and heresiarch of the emperor's eclectic cult, who had set himself against Salim's succession. Bir Singh Deo made an audacious and effective play for the prince's favour, when he murdered Abu Fazl, sending his decapitated head as a gift to Salim.

In a raging fury Akbar sent force after force to hunt down and capture the assassin but Bir Singh Deo managed to elude his pursuers until Akbar's death in 1605 and Salim's ascension to the throne of Delhi as Emperor Jahanghir.

In recompense for his bloody offering Jahanghir deposed Ram Shah from the Orchha Gadi and elevated Bir Singh Deo to the throne of Bundelkhand. The Emperor personally journeyed to Orchha to invest his vassal with a ceremonial palanquin, drum, flag of state – and the sword of Abu Fazal. In honour of his overlord Bir Singh Deo began constructing Jahanghir Mahal across from Raj Mandir, the palace built upon an island in the River Betwa between 1554 and 1592 by his father Madhukar Shah.

Jahanghir Mahal was the first of fifty-two major forts and palaces in central India Bir Singh Deo built during his twenty-two years upon the Gadi. His ruthlessly attained but benevolently spent raj was the pinnacle of Bundelkhand history. Succeeding kings of

Orchha continued their collaboration with the Mughals, but without the special affinity that existed between Jahanghir and Bir Singh Deo, their position within the empire inevitably slipped. With the decline of the Mughals, the Bundela Rajputs of Orchha and its sister principality Datia (gifted by Bir Singh Deo to his son the year before his death) suffered the Maratha onslaught and the rising fury of Jat peasant armies. Finally, in 1783, Orchha was forsaken as the Bundela rulers removed to Tikamgarh to escape the incessant threat of Jat raiding parties.

The once powerful kingdom had become partitioned into petty principalities and by the 1860s, when the French traveller Louis Rousselet reached its ancient walls, it had become 'nothing but a township in the raj of Tehri, where a few hundred peasants vegetate beneath the shadow of its palace'.

But Orchha is an exquisite antiquity, suspended in another age with only the river and the encroaching jungle to remind one of the continuum of nature, and the choked roadside approaches to remind one of the roiling banality of the present.

SHEESH MAHAL

Orchha is unusual in that unlike other Rajput capitals with a single fortified palace which evolved internally from one generation to the next, according to the needs and caprices of each ruler, separate palaces were newly constructed in proximity to one another. In Orchha there are three large independent palaces representing three distinct periods. The first palace was Ramji Mandir, begun by Rudra Pratap in 1501 and continued into the reign of his successor Bharti Chand (1531-54). The second palace was Raj Mandir, built upon an island within the River Betwa by Madhukar Shah (1554-92) throughout the period of his reign and possibly into that of his son Ram Shah (1592-1605). The third palace is Jahanghir Mahal, constructed in honour of the Mughal emperor by Bir Singh Deo from 1605, on the site of an earlier structure built around 1586. All three palaces are square courtyard structures with plain crenellated exterior walls crowned by *chattris*.

Set back between Raj Mahal and Jahan-ghir Mahal, Sheesh Mahal (Palace of Mirrors) was constructed in the early eighteenth century during the reign of Udait Singh (1689-1735), long after the fortunes of Orchha had declined, as a rest pavilion for the ruler's private use. This relatively small and simple rectangular palace forms an ell-extension to the massive Jahanghir Mahal and struck Louis Rousselet when he passed through Orchha in 1867 with its 'heavy appearance'. Built on an entirely different plan from the earlier, more magnificent palaces, Sheesh Mahal contains an open terrace above a wide hall flanked by pavilion apartments including two rooms inlaid with mirrors after the fashion of Amber Palace in Rajasthan, which has inspired its name.

Because of its smaller, more manageable scale and relatively recent vintage Sheesh Mahal was used as a pleasure resort by the rulers of Orchha until Independence in 1947, when it was taken over by the newly formed state government, eventually passing to the Madhya Pradesh Tourism Development Corporation, which converted the palace into a guest house with characteristic insensitivity. The renovations undertaken have been crude and haphazard and much of whatever character there was has been mutilated. What is more, most of the antique furniture, oriental carpets and chandeliers which had been left in the palace when the Maharaja handed the property over have disappeared. Only the monumental bath tubs and a few scattered pieces of semi-antique furniture left in place betray a trace of its most recent raj. Even so, the setting is incomparable, enveloping the visitor in the haunted majesty of the antiquities of Orchha.

Far left Huzoor Mahal at Nilambag was first built in 1875. The hand-carved Burmese teakwood entry arch was added in 1940.

Left and below Built over a period of 20 years, Ranjit Vilas was named after Jam Sahib Ranjit Singh of Nawanagar, the famous 19th century cricketer known in Britain as 'Ranji'.

Above First built in the 1870s as a garden house, the main palace of Purna Chandra Bhawan was built in colonial style by Maharana Raj Sahib Amar Singh in 1930 with art deco interiors.

Right After he'd built his mammoth neo-classical Jai Vilas Palace in 1875, Maharaja Jayaji Rao Scindia found he didn't much like it, so he set about building smaller palaces more to his taste. Usha Kiran was one of these.

Above In 1920 the strict vegetarian Maharaja of Mysore had E.W. Fritchley design Lalitha Mahal to house his meat-eating European guests. The result was what Philip Davies has called 'nothing less than a bold attempt to transpose St. Paul's Cathedral to a South Indian setting'.

Left Even after indepence, into the 1960s when the last Maharaja Jaya-Chama-Wadiyar, served as Governor of Mysore, Lalitha Mahal served as the official guest palace of Mysore.

Above Spectacularly located upon a headland bluff overlooking a beautiful inlet, Kovalam Palace was built sometime between 1924 and 1931 during the regency of Maharani Setu Lakshmi Bai to serve as a royal retreat for the Travancore family.

Right Bolghatty Palace was built by Dutch merchants in 1744 from stone and teakwood at the tip of Mulakukadu (Bolghatty) island.

GWALIOR

The Maratha Confederacy was formed upon the farmlands of Maharashtra between the Deccan plateau and Upper India with the revolutionary aim of overthrowing the Muslim emperors of Delhi and re-establishing the supremacy of Hindu India. Unlike Rajput war-lords of Kshatriya stock, grandly attributing their origins to a theogony, the Marathas were – proudly, defiantly – herdsmen and cultivators from the lowly Sudra caste, first inspired and unified by a seventeenth-century peasant firebrand named Sivaji, who became their patron saint.

Muslim iconoclasm under Aurangzeb's long reign reinforced Maratha resolve against the Mughals. Aurangzeb barely managed to hold in check these threatening proletarian hordes and in the anarchic aftermath of the Emperor's death, they spilled out across India in campaigns of conquest. Burning with revivalist zeal, the Maratha armies were, as one observer noted, 'more indefatigable and destructive than myriads of locusts'.

The secret of their power lay in their ascetic peasant simplicity. Although the Rajputs remained brilliant military commanders, they were soft Sybarites by comparison with these rough, low-caste chieftains. The Marathas had no court-life and still lived close to the earth. The greatest of these peasant war-lords to emerge in the eighteenth century was Mahadji Scindia (1761-94), who in 1771 fulfilled the dream of the Marathas by conquering Delhi and placing the Mughal Emperor Shah Alam under his protection. The Scindias were the strongest of four great Maratha dynasties who ranged across the plains of central India from Baroda to Gwalior venturing forth in every direction to wrest away the land from the Mughals and their Hindu quislings. Indeed, it was the Maratha onslaught that drove most of the Rajput dynasties to make protective treaties with the British East India Company.

By the beginning of the nineteenth century the Scindia chief had become, according to the French traveller Louis Rousselet, 'the most powerful native sovereign of Hindostan'. Mahadji Scindia first reigned from Ujjain but in 1810 his son Daulat Rao (1794-1827) established an alternative tent-camp capital two miles from the ancient city of Gwalior which was known as Gwalior-ka-Lashkar – the Camp of Gwalior.

This new settlement evolved into what Rousselet described as 'one of the finest cities in India' and achieved a particular magnificence when Jayaji Rao Scindia (1843-86) constructed one of the most fabled and fabulous European palaces in princely India. The primeval plainness of the Marathas had unavoidably changed in Gwalior to a pageant of grandeur, courtliness and colour.

USHA KIRAN PALACE

In the winter of 1843 while the young and sonless ruler Jankoji Scindia lay upon his deathbed, his Dewan, Sambhaji Rao Angre, galloped through the streets of Gwalior urgently searching out a successor to prevent the acquisitive British East India Company from annexing their kingdom on the grounds that its sovereign had died without an heir. The Dewan rode into a neighbourhood inhabited by the closest corollary branch of the Scindia family and encountered a group of young boys shooting marbles on the street. He watched their game intently as an eight-year-old by the name of Bhagirath Shinde (the surname from which Scindia derives) made a spectacular shot from a great distance to hit his target marble. Angre perceived this feat as a propitious signal from the gods. He rode up beside the child, reached down, swept him up on to his horse and charged off toward the palace to arrange an eleventh-hour adoption. The boy was invested as heir-apparent (all the while protesting that he had been deprived of the marble he had won, even trying to run away to collect it) only hours before Jankoji Scindia expired. The ascendant ruler's name was changed to Jayaji Rao Scindia.

Within months of the boy's sudden accession Gwalior was ruthlessly reduced through the swift and cynical machinations of the British under Governor-General Lord Ellenborough, from an independent kingdom to a feudatory of the East India Company, ruled by a Regency Council presided over by the British Resident who could overrule any collective decision at will. It was reported that during the child Maharaja's subsequent mandatory audience with Ellenborough 'he had wept most of the time'. This incomprehensible, traumatic loss at the inception of his unanticipated reign left an indelible mark on Jayaji Rao Scindia's still unformed character. According to Rajmata Vijayaraje Scindia, her husband's grandfather 'developed an exaggerated respect for British might, British cunning, British capacity for intrigue. No one could oppose them.' By the time he was invested with circumscribed ruling powers in 1854 he had become:

an enigmatic character, given to weighing the odds too much before acting, preferring silence to speech, devious and secretive, yet managing to give the impression of a happy-go-lucky prince who enjoyed the good things of life, music, hunting and pageantry. He reminds me of the Roman Emperor Claudius as portrayed by Robert Graves, for he was the same size and shape and even had Claudius's tendency to stammer. Both had developed an uncanny capacity for survival.

Jayaji Rao Scindia and other minority rulers of his generation were raised under British domination without being acculturated by British upbringing and education. Their successors were conscientiously westernized by British nannies, British tutors and in the Princes' Colleges set up for this purpose, but Jayaji Rao and his contemporaries grew up under British rule without altogether absorbing its values and sensibilities. This complex ambivalence was reflected in the building of Jaivilas Palace, far and away the most grandiose European princely building constructed during the last decades of the nineteenth century.

Gwalior was justly famous for the wildlife in the Maharaja's teeming game preserves, particularly the tigers. To bag a tiger in the jungles of Gwalior became one of the most prestigious sporting achievements in the Raj and almost a duty for an incumbent viceroy or a high-ranking English aristocrat.

Viceregal tours of Indian India usually included up to one thousand people who were traditionally accommodated in temporary tent cities set up in proximity to the native prince's palace with electricity, and every other Western amenity except solid walls. Most Maharajas let these arrangements suffice but aristocratic traffic to Gwalior was becoming so heavy and Jayaji Rao's penchant for spectacle so highly developed that the Scindia decided to build another palace (there were already three in the precincts of Gwalior City) so enormous that an entire viceregal retinue could be accommodated within its compound.

To accomplish this he commissioned one of his most trusted courtiers, a sardar, or nobleman, by the name of Lieutenant-Colonel Michael Filose, known in Gwalior as Mukel Sahib. Michael Filose was the descendant of Jean Baptiste, an Italian soldier of fortune who had served as an officer in the army of Mahadji Scindia and who had supported the regime of his son, Daulat Rao Scindia. Michael Filose was the namesake of Jean Baptiste's son who, when Daulat Rao accused him of disloyalty, instantly killed himself by cutting his own throat with his sword.

The Scindia sent Mukel Sahib on a tour to all the capitals of Europe with instructions to study royal architecture and to purchase without any consideration for expense all the fittings and materials necessary to make a palace of unprecedented majesty and modernity in India. Filose imported chandeliers, tapestries, mirrors, paintings, furniture and fabrics by the ton.

The result was a mammoth neo-classical *mélange*, interpolating Doric, Tuscan and Corinthian elements with references to Versailles and the Place Vendôme in Paris, around a floor plan based upon that of an Italian palazzo. The palace structures covered an area of over one million square feet and included a Corinthian Durbar Hall ninety-seven feet long, fifty feet wide and forty-one feet in height with a hand-made carpet covering five thousand square feet, woven in place by inmates of the Gwalior jail. A pair of the largest chandeliers ever fabricated were hung from the vaulted ceiling. Each of these gigantic Viennese lighting fixtures was forty-two feet high,

with 248 candles and weighing three tons. Huge wall mirrors replicated their astonishing incandescence in a cataclysm of light. The building of the Maharaja's new palace set the ruler back nineteen lakhs of rupees.

The Scindia's first guest in his new palace was the most prestigious a prince could hope for: His Royal Highness the Prince of Wales, the future King Edward VII. The Prince of Wales arrived in December 1875, stayed four days, bagged a respectable number of tigers and, by all appearances, departed satisifed and duly impressed with the Maharaja's hospitality and his spectacular accommodation (Michael Filose received a knighthood for a job well done).

After the royal entourage packed up and moved on to its next destination Jayaji Rao was left with what Yvonne Fitzroy later described as 'a pantomime palace with its vast chandeliers, its glass fountains, glass banisters, glass furniture and lustre fringes' and found that when all was said and done he did not much like it. The rooms were far too large for his still intrinsically Indian tastes. The scale and acoustics of the durbar hall were entirely unsuitable for the intimacy of classical Indian singing or a nautch performance. Nor were any of the other two hundred rooms, cluttered with stuffed and upright Franco-Italian gilt and crystal furniture, appropriate for a traditional gathering of Hindustani princes who reclined comfortably upon cushions arranged around an open room.

The Scindia was still far too Indian to enjoy living in the palace he had built for the benefit of his British masters and almost immediately he began to build himself alternative residences and pleasure pavilions more to his taste. Chief among these was Moti Mahal, built according to the Maharaja's own specifications along the lines of a traditional Indian palace with narrow passages and small, low-ceilinged chambers. Moti Mahal, and not Jaivilas, became Jayaji Rao Scindia's permanent residence. The Maharaja also constructed Vishram, Vijay Bhavan, Ram Bagh, Raj Mahal and, in the early 1880s, a small palace immediately adjacent to his Jai Vilas complex called Nao Talao, which means Nine Tanks, for a series of interconnecting ornamental ponds within its grounds.

Nao Talao, like all the secondary palaces of the Scindia, was not designed by Sir Michael Filose but by the Maharaja himself with the help of a state engineer. The original palace was a rude, eccentric synthesis of Eastern and Western design ideas with twin flat-topped octagonal towers that looked as if domes had been arbitrarily sawed off, and a wide external staircase which swept directly from the gardens to the first-floor entrance. Carved *jaali* screens and sandstone work in the Gwalior style added an indigenous touch to this capricious pastiche. Nao Talao became a favourite resort of Jayaji Rao Scindia by virtue of its proximity to Jaivilas palace with its elaborate lakes and pleasure gardens. On the grounds of the palace a small bungalow called Ragha-Bagh was built. It was in Ragha-Bagh that the Maharaja died in 1886.

He was succeeded by his son Madhav Rao Scindia (1886-1925) who converted Nao Talao into an official guest house for elite European visitors to Gwalior. When his son Maharaja Jivaji Rao Scindia (1925-47) ascended the Gadi he wished to distance himself from the suffocating influence of his mother, who resided in Jaivilas. Moreover, the young Maharaja had the relatively simple tastes of his grandfather and chose to live in the relatively simple mini-palace just one hundred yards from Jaivilas.

Nao Talao was totally renovated for its royal occupant between 1938 and 1939. A lift was installed and the external stairway was torn down and replaced with a more conventional covered porch with a double staircase leading to the first-floor suites.

When the Maharaja's lovely Nepalese bride from neighbouring Sagar, Shrimata Lekha Devi, arrived in Gwalior in 1941 to become Maharani Vijayaraje Scindia, it was to Nao Talao that she moved and took up residence in a purdah area set up for her on the second floor. Her husband's quarters covered the first floor and ADCs occupied the ground floor of the palace.

In 1944, with the birth of the Maharaja's second daughter Usharaje, the garden palace of Nao Talao was renamed Usha Kiran, in her honour. The small palace of Usha Kiran remained the principal residence of the Scindias until the Maharaja's death in 1961.

SOUTHERN INDIA

MYSORE

THE MODEL

Mysore with its industrial and engineering schools and its Technical Institute just begun, its green parks and substantial buildings, its asphalted drains, its standpipes along the streets, and its clean neat air . . .
H. F. Prevost Battersby, *India Under Royal Eyes*, 1906

Mysore received its name around 1524 in remembrance of the prehistoric destruction upon Chamundi Hill of the rampaging minotaur Mashisura, but its reputation and identity are of far more recent vintage. It was not this mythological cataclysm nor the footprints of Rama, Lakshmana and Sita said to have sanctified its fertile earth, nor the mystic union its rulers celebrated with their goddess, nor even the widely known hunting of wild elephants – the *khedda* – that commended this southern Indian principality. Rather, it was the westernizing imprint of the Englishman, with his asphalt roads, Technical Institutes and fastidious standpipes along the streets, which transformed Mysore into the model of 'enlightened progress' and modernity.

The penultimate ruling Maharaja of Mysore, Sri Krishna-Raja Wadiyar Bahadur IV (1894-1940), was a devoutly orthodox Hindu who nonetheless managed to strike an extraordinary balance between his atavistic piety and a cosmopolitan modernism in his approach to governing what was commonly regarded as India's most enlightened and progressive Native State. In his religious devotions he was uncompromising but in the administration of Mysore he was an absolute pragmatist.

Although characterized as rigid in his Hinduism he appointed a Muslim, Sir Mirza Ismail, as his Prime Minister simply because Sir Mirza was a superb, modern-minded administrator. Moreover, as Mahaswami of Mysore, the state's High Priest of Hinduism, the Maharaja might have been expected to discourage transoceanic travel as it was believed to break caste, yet Mysore was the only princely state to have sent ambassadors to European capitals.

The Maharaja himself refrained from crossing the seas for forty years and when finally he did make his European tour, he would never eat with Europeans. Indeed, it was said that the Hindu king would ritually bathe following any contact with a white Westerner. Instead, he brought his store of holy water from the Ganges for purification, he brought his own cooks and he always set aside two rooms in whichever hotel suite he took over: one for a temple and one for a vegetarian kitchen.

This blend of stark orthodoxy and flexible sophistication led directly to the creation of the Lalitha Mahal Palace.

In the early decades of this century the Raj was in its richest and most delirious period and Mysore State was one of the largest and loveliest jewels in its Imperial Crown. Swarms of Europeans descended upon the princely city which had become the very model of the modern Indian state with all the requisite development accomplished through European technology and European expertise. Naturally, the ruler was required to accommodate his colonial guests and sincerely wished to extend hospitality to them. The rub was

that religious belief restricted him from contaminating his own palace of Amba Vilas, no matter how spacious, with the cooking of flesh. But he had no more wish to offend his visitors than he had to offend his gods.

Thus in 1920 the Maharaja commissioned the architect E.W. Fritchley to design a special palace to accommodate his carnivorous guests. Fritchley conceived the palace on a ridge in the shadow of Chamundi Hill as something akin to an Edwardian hotel which, as Philip Davies observed, 'was nothing less than a bold attempt to transpose St Paul's Cathedral to a South Indian setting'. The cornerstone was laid in 1921 and a white classical structure rose up in spectral incongruity on the flat Mysore terrain 'like some evanescent dream palace from the heat haze of the South Indian plain . . .'.

Set upon a beautifully landscaped eminence some four miles from the city, Lalitha Mahal was built at a cost of over twenty-four lakhs of rupees and took the remainder of the decade to complete, although it began to function as a guest palace as early as 1926. It was a massive white symmetrical structure spreading 325 feet across the rise between two domed towers rising 92 feet above the ground. A central dome, 133 feet from floor to finial, dominated the complex, surrounded by four secondary towers reaching to a height of 85 feet. The entire edifice extended back 225 feet from its colonnaded façade of coupled Corinthian columns.

A grand central entrance opened on to a wide, dividing Italian marble staircase with a mirrored half-landing which reflected the city of Mysore. The staircase was flanked on the right-hand side by an ornate state ballroom featuring a sprung dance floor, and a state banquet hall on the left. There were cloakrooms and bedrooms, a billiard and card room and a decorated reception hall which measured 50 feet by 32 feet ranged along the corridor opposite these two main ceremonial halls.

Aside from the ornamental staircase there was an electric lift to transport guests to the first floor which formed the principal residential section of the palace, replete with its own private dining room and reception rooms. The northern wing of the first floor

was taken up entirely with the viceregal suite. The southern wing contained suites for officers and ADCs in the entourage.

The management of the Lalitha Mahal was impeccable. Every need and desire of a guest was ministered to with meticulous care. Mysore State guests from this period remember that the moment a room was left unoccupied at any time, day or night, it was completely re-made: clothes were pressed and hung in closets, shoes shined, sealed bottles displaced those newly opened on the private bar, used glasses were instantly replaced, ruffled sofas re-fluffed, cigarettes and cigars replenished, ashtrays emptied and washed, sheets changed, beds made and furniture polished. The service was effortless, immaculate and, for those unaccustomed to such ministrations, almost unnerving.

Lalitha Mahal remained the official Guest Palace of Mysore State well into the 1960s, when its last ruling Maharaja, Jaya-Chama-Raja Wadiyar, served as Governor of the state. One of US Ambassador John Kenneth Galbraith's journal entries from his tenure in the Kennedy era indicates that Lalitha Mahal, even in its post-Independence operations, retained much of its original princely splash:

If one favors medieval splendor, this may be the last place in the world to sample it. We are ensconced, as guests of the Maharaja (and Governor) of Mysore, in the Lalitha Mahal, a large marble-domed palace about two miles from the main palace . . . Our suite consists of four or five large high-ceilinged rooms opening at each side on a spacious verandah. We get to it via a vast marble staircase which leads up from the state dining room and drawing rooms, all of suitable elegance.

As a Mysore State property rather than a private holding of the Wadiyars, Lalitha Mahal was subsequently placed under the authority of the Archaeological Department and for a while its use as a museum was considered. The palace was then transferred to the Karnataka State Tourism Department and in 1974 the Indian Tourism Development Corporation (ITDC – Ashok Group) took it over to convert into a hotel. A thirty-two room annexe to the original structure was built in 1980 and in 1983 the central government hotel inspection committee awarded Five-Star status to the Lalitha Mahal Palace Hotel.

Of all the palaces of India, the Lalitha Mahal Palace is among the most suited to its role as a luxury hotel. As Philip Davies writes, 'It is an ideal use, for the interiors remain unspoiled with a magnificent suite of principal rooms, complete with stained glass lanterns, ornate plasterwork and finely-chased metalwork.'

The Palace is in appearance, if not always in service, much the way it was in the glory days of the British Raj.

RAJENDRA VILAS PALACE

The mythology of Dravidian Hinduism relates the tale of Chanda and Manda, two demons set loose upon the land, soon exterminated by the goddess Parvati, who assumed their conjugated name as Chamundi and made her home upon a hill. Her effigy is revered by the rulers of Mysore, who have taken Sri Chamundeswari Devi as their tutelary deity and dynastic guardian and in the holy season of Dassera seek for mystical union with her divinity, reaching this theophany in a ritual of ascetic contemplation and flamboyant pageantry which culminates at her temple near the summit of the sacred hill some three miles from their capital.

For the British agents of Empire ruling over Mysore in the early nineteenth century it was the cool, salubrious climate on Chamundi Hill and its ravishing panoramic vantage point, and definitely *not* its Hindu holiness, which induced them to make the gruelling 1,000-foot ascent to its summit through thorny jungles infested with porcupine and wild-pig. Once there they were above the flustering heat of southern India and could gaze, goddess-like, down upon their recently conquered kingdom. Chamundi Hill quickly became a favoured refuge for the colonial elite administrating Mysore State.

It was the Resident of Mysore, Mr Arthur (later Sir Arthur) Cole who first built a bungalow on the crown of Chamundi in 1822 to escape the seasonal heat. When Colonel Walter Campbell made a blistering climb up Chamundi on an early morning in 1833 to see the cottage there, he found

A comfortable English-looking country house . . . nothing remarkable about it except that it was fitted up with fireplaces, which gave it a very homely and un-Indian look; and that, hanging in the entrance hall, I discovered the most splendid specimen of a sambar's head I have ever seen [a large asiatic deer with three pointed antlers and long coarse hair at throat]. The horn was 18 inches round the burr, and large in proportion. I have seen many large heads, but never one at all to compare with this.

On 16 March 1834, the British Governor-General of India, Lord William Bentinck, made a visit to Mysore and took up residence for three days in this comfortable, unremarkable English house with the splendid sambar trophy in it. On the second day of the Governor-General's stay Maharaja Krishna-Raja Wadiyar III (1799-1868) made his obeisant way up Chamundi Hill to the door of the bungalow to pay his respects to the man who, three years earlier, had stripped him of administrative control over his state for reasons of incompetence. Lord Bentinck evidently enjoyed his stay at the Chamundi bungalow because in October of the same year he chose to stop there again on a return visit to Mysore.

It is not clear precisely when this property reverted to the use of the Maharajas of Mysore, although most probably the Residents and Commissioners who managed the state relinquished their claim on the bungalow sometime after Chama-Rajendra Wadiyar X (1868-94) was invested with full ruling powers in 1880. During his brief reign, or that of his successor, Maharaja Krishna-Raja Wadiyar IV (1894-1941), the homely, un-Indian looking house, became known as the Palace Bungalow.

Maharaja Krishna-Raja Wadiyar IV approached the mystical dimension of his princely station with the deepest gravity and undoubtedly appreciated the proximity of the Palace Bungalow to the abode of his deity. In the aftermath of Dassera ceremonies the Maharaja would take rest briefly there before returning to his Palace and on the eve of the Chamundi Chariot Festival he would return to his bungalow to prepare himself to take part in this traditional event. Aside from these festive responsibilities, the Maharaja would frequently take refuge in the Palace

Bungalow to rest, meditate, to catch up with his paper work and, no doubt, to contemplate his prospering kingdom from on high.

The Maharaja took to spending so much time atop Chamundi Hill that in the early 1930s it was decided to rebuild the bungalow as a bona fide palace. Foundations were laid sometime between 1932 and 1934 but the Maharaja's advisers had overlooked one crucial factor: the bungalow and the palace that was to replace it had been located upon a site higher than the Chamundaswari Temple. According to Hindu tradition secular buildings should never be erected above those that are sacred. Human beings, even those like the Wadiyars who have been touched with divinity, should not live above the gods. The inhabitants of the mountain and devotees of the temple openly demonstrated against the building of the palace and construction was brought to a standstill for a considerable time.

By the late 1930s palace authorities had managed to overcome local opposition to the project and by 1939, though still under construction, Rajendra Vilas, as the palace was now called, was well enough along to be described – somewhat inaccurately – in a commemorative book published on the occasion of the visit of Viceroy and Marchioness Linlithgow;

The new house has two floors with living apartments and four side towers and a central tower rising 80 feet above the ground level; all the towers being finished with domes. The architecture is somewhat on the style of old Rajputana Palaces with a blending of modern ornamentation. This structure has a dignified, elegant and attactive elevation and is surrounded with natural landscapes and rock gardens.

Actually, it is a strange agglomeration of styles and really nothing at all like the old Rajputana palaces. It is, rather, like a white Italianate mansion with oriental towers tacked on. The interiors are thoroughly European with a central Italian marble staircase, ornamental wrought-ironwork by McPherson's Saracen Foundry of Glasgow, ballrooms, suites and Burmese teak-panelled libraries, and a dining room upholstered in red velvet. The splendid sambar's head has been replaced by that of an equally splendid elephant.

For all the trouble and effort that went into the building of Rajendra Vilas, Maharaja Krishna-Raja Wadiyar IV never stayed there. He died in 1941 with the palace sitting empty and incomplete upon its summit. His nephew and successor Jaya-Chama-Raja Wadiyar (1941-7) ascended the Gadi of Mysore and oversaw the completion of the palace between 1942 and 1944.

Thereafter, Rajendra Vilas became the residence of the Maharaja's aunt and was used as a rest-house for the Maharaja at the Dassera ceremony during which, his son remembers, the family would reside for three full days, but with Independence and the eventual de-recognition of the princes in 1971, the mystical transference of divinity on Chamundi Hill became a private affair.

In 1975 Srikanta-Datta-Narasimha-Raja Wadiyar, Jaya-Chama-Raja Wadiyar's son and heir, converted the palace into a hotel and placed it under the management of ITC's hotel division, Welcomgroup. In 1984 Mr Wadiyar himself took over the running of Rajendra Vilas as part of his own chain of hotel properties.

OOTACAMUND

LIKE AN ENGLISH PLACE

Ootacamund is prettier than I had expected, but is just like an English place, such as Leatherhead. Got a very good breakfast, beefsteak and claret; afterwards, slept a wink, and then wrote letters. A curious place is 'Ooty'; houses stuck all about the hills, and trees everywhere, which is not what I was led to expect . . . 'Ooty' is far more varied and perhaps more picturesque than Coonoor, but is so English as to be, I think, utterly undrawable.
Edward Lear, *Indian Journal*, 1874

Long before the utterly undrawable lay over of Mr Edward Lear, 'Ooty' had become the most completely realized colonial illusion conjured in the British Raj: a meticulously transplanted concoction of English countryside set up in the Nilgiri mountain range of southern India, replete with English oaks and English apple trees, hedgerows and country lanes, sweet peas and begonias, hollyhocks and Ayrshire roses, dandelion weeds and rounded downs, and stuck about with quaint, gabled cottages with quaint suburban names like 'Cedarhurst' and 'Glen View' (and scathingly characterized as 'cow houses' by Richard Burton, a young officer who came in 1847 to the bustling hill station to convalesce before embarking on explorations closer to his oriental tastes in Africa and Arabia). But most English of all in Ooty was the cold, cold air.

It was the unexpected English climate of Ootacamund which struck its first 'discoverers' in 1818. Two vigorous young colonial officers, Mr Whish and Mr Kindersley, assistants to the Collector of Coimbatore, were tracking deep and up into the jungle-covered Nilgiris in pursuit of an errant band of tobacco smugglers when they came upon an open, fertile plateau some 7,000 feet above the sea.

Accustomed as they were to the sweltering heat of their lowland outpost, the officers were flabbergasted by the icy nights and the 'English' landscapes and rushed down the mountain with effusions of praise for this new-found territory which they duly related to their superior, Mr John Sullivan, the Collector of Coimbatore and future Father of Ootacamund.

Mr Sullivan took his two assistants at their word and the following year made a journey of his own into the Nilgiris to confirm what he suspected. The Collector was electrified by the bracing Englishness of Ooty and by the miraculous recovery of his companion, a French naturalist who had arrived a wreck and revived within a day upon the high, rolling hills of the Nilgiri plateau. With the zeal of a convert, Sullivan managed to convince his masters in Madras that it would make a perfect health resort for the British in southern India.

In 1821 the Government of Madras began excavating a pass toward the highland plateau and by 1823 Mr Sullivan had moved his family up into the highlands, built the first house there and – his lucripitous wits about him – was furiously purchasing every patch of land he could lay his hands on from its unwitting aboriginal owners, the Todas, building cottages on his newly acquired plots and selling them off for heavy profits. To the increasing chagrin of his colonial employers, Mr Sullivan ran his burgeoning hill station like a feudal lord until finally, in 1830, Madras installed a Military Commandant to oversee control of what was by this time a flourishing health resort.

By the 1870s almost every finishing touch had been added to the Englishness of Ooty and the Government of Madras had settled down for six months of every year in this 'Queen of Hill Stations'. Even Viceroys down from Simla gushed enthusiasm for this paradisiacal reminder of home as did Lord Lytton, who rhapsodized of 'Hertfordshire lanes, Devonshire downs, Westmorland lakes, Scotch trout streams . . .'.

So utterly English – and so utterly undrawable.

FERN HILL PALACE

By the 1840s Ootacamund had for at least ten years been the unofficial hill resort for British officialdom of the Madras Presidency and thus had been subject to a welter of subdivision, development, sale and re-sale as throngs of colonials threw up country bungalows for their sojourns in the south, then sold them off to others seeking refuge

from the seething summer heat, who disposed of them in turn when their terms of service in southern India had reached completion.

It is not known precisely when, in all this land boom, the site of Fern Hill Palace was circumscribed (perhaps it was one of Mr Sullivan's speculative tracts) but there are two suggestions as to who first settled on the property. One report has it that Captain F. Cotton built the first house on the site in 1844. The first recorded resident, however, was a Mr J. Groves and, although there is no documentation confirming this, an early citizen of Ooty contended that it was he and not the captain who had constructed the first house, in 1842. Whatever the truth may be, the Government of Madras did issue Mr Groves a lease for his piece of land in 1846 and it is known that he retained the property for nine more years before he sold to Major-General Stratton the house he had by this time named Fern Hill Bungalow.

The major-general kept his summer cottage until 1861 when he sold out to Mr W.H. Wapshare and Mr E. Copleston, for 500 rupees. Sometime in the next nine years Mr Copleston sold his share of the property to a Mr Macfayden. It is quite probably during this period of partnership that Fern Hill was temporarily re-named Moone-sami's and served as one of Ooty's earliest country club-hotels. Subscription dances and 'miscellaneous entertainments' were held at Moonesami's until, according to Sir Frederick Price, Ooty's painstaking turn-of-the-century historian, 'the floor proved so rotten that dancing on it was found to be dangerous, and gaieties at Fern Hill had to be abandoned'.

In June 1870 the partners transferred title of their property (for the handsome sum of 6,000 rupees) to Lieutenant-Colonel Rose Campbell, who held his purchase briefly before selling out to Mr J.A. Boyson.

Through all these changing hands Fern Hill must have worked up something of a reputation, for the house was known to have hosted an impressive parade of Governors of Madras, including Lord Harris, Sir William Denison, Lord Napier and Lord Hobart. It may have been the superb location that attracted these distinguished guests, for Sir Frederick Price deemed 'the views from its grounds of the downs and Kundas ... the most beautiful in Ootacamund'.

Certainly the reputation of the estate and its spectacular setting drew the first princely resident to the British resort. On 12 September 1873 the twelve-year-old Maharaja Chama-Rajendra Wadiyar X of Mysore (1868-1894) purchased Fern Hill from its owner (Mr Boyson) for 10,000 rupees and the same year made his first move to Ooty in the company of his guardian Colonel G.B. Malleson.

Maharaja Chama-Rajendra Wadiyar spent a decade renovating his property. By 1884 Fern Hill had been transformed from a large colonial bungalow to an enormous rambling country palace superbly finished with carved Burmese teak and featuring a new magnificent ballroom over-arched by a high-vaulted ornamental papier mâché ceiling. This ballroom had two overlooking galleries. One gallery, veiled by lace curtains, was used as a kind of purdah area for women of the household. An identical gallery on the opposite side of the hall was used for the court orchestra.

In the time of Chama-Rajendra Wadiyar's successor, Maharaja Krishna-Raja Wadiyar IV (1894-1941), this ballroom served a second and more serious purpose as a mini-durbar, when the Maharaja would meet with the many Mysoreans living in proximity to Ootacamund whose families had emigrated to the Nilgiris from Mysore over several centuries.

The original 'Fern Hill Bungalow' structure, including its Mooneswami's extensions, was greatly enlarged, forming the zenana wing occupied by the Maharaja and his wife and their personal staff. The opposite, newly erected wing, was for the princely children and their servants. There were also dozens of service buildings and staff quarters ranged around the 410-acre estate including an indoor badminton court.

Princely guests and distinguished Indians were accommodated in Bhawani House, a spacious guest cottage set some distance from the palace, and lesser Indians and Europeans such as the British Resident at Mysore, were put up at the smaller but equally comfortable Mowbray Cottage.

Philip Davies describes the reconstructed Fern Hill Complex as:

a riot of carved bargeboards, ornamental cast-iron balustrading, trelliswork and verandahs set in a compound studded with firs, cedars, palms, and monkey puzzle trees. The house is painted red oxide with green painted timberwork, and it is the culmination of the Swiss chalet style which pervades much of the architecture of Ootacamund.

The Maharaja of Mysore was the first native prince to own a residence in Ootacamund and by the turn of the century over sixty other princes from throughout India had followed suit and settled for the summer in the southern Indian resort. Fern Hill crested the centre of an expanding circle of estates coalesced round an open area which came to be known as Rajah's Square.

Although Maharaja Krishna-Raja Wadiyar IV (1894-1941) made regular visits to Fern Hill throughout his long reign, he rarely stayed for more than a week or two at a time. The Wadiyar ladies and other members of the royal family seem to have spent considerably more time in Ooty, staying on throughout the season.

In 1894 Fern Hill Palace became the starting point of the famous Ootacamund Hunt, first established in 1844, in which imported English foxhounds chased hapless jackals around the Nilgiri hills. The Maharajas of Mysore presided as official hosts of the annual event – Ooty's most prestigious – until 1941 when the Hunt was discontinued because of the war. The Mysore royal family continued to visit Fern Hill Palace with semi-regularity until the late 1960s. Mollie Panter-Downes visited the Nilgiris in 1966 and recorded her impressions of the fading hill station and its princely precincts:

Another day, still on the track of the really high life as it used to be lived in Ooty, I go to take a look at the neighbourhood of Rajah's Square, where some of the princes' 'palaces' were built, including that of Highness Mysore, as Miss Guthrie refers to the Governor [Maharaja Jaya-Chama-Rajendra Wadiyar IV] . . .

Whatever the Square may have seen in the past, today, when I visit it, it is full only of sunlit emptiness and a great deal of nature at its most beautiful, for nowhere else do the trees soar more nobly to lace themselves in green Gothic aisles overhead, or the lawns – nature charmingly tamed for the rich – more carefully match themselves to

emeralds than in this exclusive neighbourhood of self-consciously grand entrance gates, through which one gets glimpses of well-watered parterres . . . But I am disappointed by what I can make out of the princely 'palaces', since I had hoped for something truly Indian and exotic, instead of which these large mansions have from afar a comfortable English air, providing a flash of gables and hints of white-balustrated balconies and garden seats and glassed-in nooks that would not be out of place among the pines and rhododendrons of Ascot.

People have told me of the old days of princely entertaining in Ooty, when the catering for a ball or a reception might be ordered from some famous firm in distant Calcutta, to give added chic to the occasion. Then the entourage of such an establishment would certainly include numerous relatives and hangers-on, and the big families of children were likely to have an English comptroller to direct the education of the young princes, and a Scottish governess and a nannie, uprooted in her grey coat and round felt hat straight out of Hyde Park, as well as ayahs for infants. The maharajahs who come up now for the best months of the year live less showily . . . Rajah's Square and the other houses of the rich have not yet become museums, but their mode of life, perhaps, is changing.

Though the Governor is 'at home' to Ooty with garden parties during the season, the days of really lavish entertainments must surely be over.

Whatever princely entertainments did remain at Fern Hill Palace when Miss Panter-Downes was passing by its gates were ended suddenly in December 1970 when the princes were de-recognized by presidential order and their privy purses unceremoniously cancelled. Maharaja Jaya-Chama-Raja Wadiyar came to Ooty once in 1971 to dismiss his staff, settle his accounts and oversee the closure of Fern Hill Palace. He never returned. The last ruling Maharaja of Mysore died in 1974, leaving the vast Mysore estates to his young son, Srikanta-Datta-Narasimha-Raja Wadiyar, who in 1974 set about converting Fern Hill Palace into a hotel which opened for business in 1975.

COCHIN AND TRAVANCORE

It is a land in which it seems always to be afternoon. No one is poor, no one is energetic. Here in the uttermost recesses of India old habits linger that have long been abandoned elsewhere ... Cochin and Travancore live upon their fish and their cocoanuts.
Perceval Landon, *Under the Sun*

The southern Malayali kingdoms of Cochin and Travancore ran along the raging, luxuriant coastline of Malabar, stretching from Trichur to the tip of India with their rice paddies and coconut palms, their spices and the natural harbours and backwaters that attracted traders from China, Arabia, Portugal, Holland and finally Britain, seeking black gold (pepper) and empire. With their trade these alien races brought missionaries and religion to this peaceful and receptive people so that *viharas*, churches, synagogues and mosques multiplied among the indigenous Dravidian temples – dawn ringing with a diversity of horns, bells and cries of piety. Mostly though, this ancient land of Malabar, which its Malayali inhabitants called Kerala, was a fount of Brahmanic faith where, in the words of Pierre Loti, the high caste would 'come from the surrounding countries, and from those forests where they live on fruit and grain, absorbed in mystic dreams and disdainful of the things of this world' to celebrate their sacred rites under the reverent patronage of theistic Hindu kings.

Indeed the creation of this coastal territory is mythically attributed to the hand of Parasu Rama, the Brahmin incarnation of the god Vishnu who, it is said, threw his golden sacrificial axe (*Parasu*) from Gokarnam to Kanya Kumari (Cape Comorin), and watched the waters recede between these points, revealing this restful, resplendent land – a gift from the Arabian Sea. Although scholars have scoffed at the veracity of this legend, geologists and geographers believe that some seismic or volcanic cataclysm did suddenly uncover Kerala from beneath the seas in a postdiluvian period concurrent to that of the avatar.

Travancore emanated from the medieval kingdom of Venad which expanded in the eighteenth century to contain the entirety of southern Kerala. The kings of Travancore traded with the British throughout the seventeenth century and first made treaty with the Honourable East India Company in 1723. The onslaught of the Mysorean forces of Haidur Ali and Tippu Sultan sealed the bond and in 1795 Travancore formally became a British protectorate.

In this same year the French conquest of Holland stimulated the British to seize all Dutch colonies in India, including the protectorate of Cochin which centred round a magnificent natural harbour formed suddenly in 1341 from a violently irrupting flood and eventually displacing Cranganore as the primary port of Malabar. Once tributary to the Zamorin of Calicut, the Raja of Cochin made alliance with the Portuguese following the arrival of Vasco da Gama in 1948. In 1663 Dutch East India Company forces captured Cochin from the Portuguese and established their dominion in Kerala. With the defeat of Holland and Dutch surrender in Cochin the port and its surrounding territories came under the control of the British; a rule which was finally ratified under the Paris Convention of 1814 when Cochin was formally ceded to the British East India Company.

Meanwhile the Malayalis of Malabar, the sweet, dark citizens of Cochin and Travancore, continued to linger in their ancient ways, worshipping their variegated gods, warding off the evil eye, savouring the Kathakali pantomime, holding to their habits and – quietly, without fanfare – plunging into education to emerge at the end of the Raj as the most literate of all Indian societies, promulgating Communism and still living on their fish and their coconuts.

BOLGHATTY PALACE

In 1663 Dutch East India Company forces captured Cochin, installed their own puppet ruler as Raja and evicted the Portuguese. The Dutch were now in control of the finest natural harbour in spice-rich Malabar and in command of its fabulously profitable trade in ginger, cloves, nutmeg, cocoa, mace and, most important of all, pepper – 'black gold' – then the most precious commodity on earth. In 1666 wide tracts of land along the coast and on islands within the harbour were acquired by the new colonial power and Dutch mercantile lords began to build palaces on the picturesque backwaters of Cochin. By 1781 nine islands had come into the possession of the Dutch. One of these islands was called Mulakukadu in the local language of Malayalam, subsequently Europeanized to Bolghatty. At the tip of the southern end of this island, in an area called Ponnikkara, a stone and teakwood villa with a spacious room projecting into the backwater was built by Dutch merchants in 1744. This villa was subsequently extended, lush gardens were landscaped around it and the villa, or palace as it now was, became identified with the island itself. Historians record that the gardens of Bolghatty Palace became a popular picnic resort used by the Dutch gentry.

It is not known exactly what Bolghatty Palace was used for after 1795 when the British East India Company superseded the Dutch in Cochin, but the property seems to have reverted to the Raja. In 1909 the palace and its extensive grounds were given over to the Indian Government to house the British Resident for a fixed rent of 6,000 rupees per year. Shortly after the Residency was established at Bolghatty Palace, the British traveller Perceval Landon visited there and left a vivid description of the island which is as valid today as it was in his time:

The leafless white branches of the champaks throw a tangled shadow like black lace upon the moon-whitened turf of the Residency lawn; overhead there is a sound of a gong in the tops of the casuarinas; and all round, through the warm movement of a sultry night breeze, sweeps in the lap and the trickle of the lagoon against the tufa blocks at the water's edge. Across the lagoon the rare lights of Cochin speckle the low, misty line of dense cocoanuts, and the antiphone of some invisible rowers back from Ernakulam in the very moon's pathway is timed by the ground bass of their thudding tholepins. If ever there were a land of peace it is here in Cochin, where Vasco de Gama's keels first foundered in the soft sand of the bar, and the soil of India was broken by the earliest of those Renaissance 'venturers who were to change the face of the land . . .'.

With the British withdrawal from India the Residency was closed and Bolghatty Palace became the property of the state, eventually coming under control of the Kerala Tourism Development Corporation, which opened the property as a tourist hotel.

KOVALAM PALACE
Ashok Halcyon Palace

In other regions of the world it seems as if human life flocked instinctively towards the sea. Men construct their dwellings by its shores, and their towns as nearly as possible to its waters; they are jealous of the smallest bay that can contain ships, and even the smallest strip of coast.

Here, on the contrary, it is shunned as something dead or void. This sea is but an abyss that cannot be crossed, that serves no purpose, and but inspires terror. It is almost inaccessible, and no one ventures on it. Before the endless line of breakers, and along the endless extent of sand, the only human trace that I can see is an old granite temple, lowly and rude, with worn columns, half eaten away by salt and spray. It is placed here to appease and exorcise the restless devourer which imprisons Travancore, and which, calm as it is this evening, will shortly, when the summer monsoon commences, rage furiously during an entire season.
Pierre Loti, *India*, 1906

Perhaps it was an atavistic sense of terror that prevented the Maharajas of Travancore from building upon their raging, magnificent coastline. It is certainly one explanation that could be put forward as to why the beautiful, craggy white sand inlet of Kovalam, ten miles south of Trivandrum, remained deserted well into the 1920s.

Kovalam Palace was constructed upon a headland bluff high above the turbulent surf sometime between 1924 and 1931 during

the seven-year regency of Maharani Setu Lakshmibai, who reigned throughout the minority of her nephew, Maharaja Chitra Tirunal (1924-49), the last ruler of Travancore, possibly for an invalid member of the Travancore family. The structure is of European style with an exposed stone façade which projects the incongruous impression of a miniature Gothic palace (with indigenous touches) plunked down in the tropics, surrounded as it is by spindly, coconut groves ruffling in the sea-winds. The palace was used as a summer retreat at the crest of a large, gated hill compound dotted with smaller bungalows for staff.

After Independence the entire property was acquired by the government and the land was eventually developed as a tourist resort. One of the annexe residences became the Kerala State Government Guest House. Kovalam Palace was renamed Halcyon Palace and incorporated into the Kovalam Ashok Beach Resort complex designed by Charles Correa and run (abysmally) by ITDC. Recent renovations have been undertaken to upgrade this charming stone anachronism looming over the low-slung, sloping, moss-stained modernist concrete holiday haven, canting the palmy hillside straight down to the cove below.

THE HOTELS

AUTHOR'S NOTE

The hotel industry in India differs from its counterparts in Europe and America in the wildly unpredictable standards of facilities and services offered and the sometimes radical (and sudden) changes in management, for better or for worse. This lack of continuity makes it almost impossible to record an abidingly reliable evaluation of any but the most established hotels in India. Since there are no more than five or six properties of that category included in this book, we are dealing with a series of moving targets. Palace hotels in India are a relatively recent phenomenon and many of the properties treated in this volume are in an experimental stage and verging on change.

The presence of the three outstanding private hotel management groups – Taj, Oberoi, and ITC-Welcomgroup – which dominate the industry and offer a high standard of professional services, only accentuates the mutability of the palace hotel business in India. Aside from the palace properties they presently manage, these companies have all become involved with other princely palaces which, for a variety of reasons – mostly, but not always, revolving around money – either did not ultimately become hotels or are being privately developed and operated by the families themselves. One of these companies managed a number of palaces for a Maharaja over a short period of time until a dispute with the owner forced it to withdraw. These properties have, in consequence, rapidly deteriorated in both services and facilities, yet guide books written during the brief tenure of the management company have recorded a positive impression, leading innocent travellers to let themselves in for a vexatious stop-over. On the other hand, a number of properties that are not very well run at present are in the process of coming under the management of one of these professional groups and by the time this book reaches the market may well have improved considerably.

Some palaces are entirely dependent upon the presence of the proprietors themselves. For example, we intended to include the marvellous Udai Vilas Palace in Dungarpur which was for a number of years informally opened to paying guests by Maharana Lakshman Singh, one of the last and most respected ruling princes in India. Before we departed for our field work we came to learn that His Highness had passed away earlier in the year and that Udai Vilas Palace had been closed to visitors, so we had to leave the property out. Perhaps it will be opened again by one of the Maharana's heirs. Perhaps not.

In my comments on each property I have tried to give an indication of what to expect, based upon my own fleeting experience in these palace hotels. I have limited myself to generalities because specifics can change very swiftly in India. None of this should be taken as gospel. What I might appreciate, you might not. At the same time, it should be understood that in certain instances I was given preferential treatment because I was the author of a book and have come away with a better impression than an ordinary traveller, treated ordinarily, might come away with. We tried to minimize this bias by turning up unexpectedly in many cases, but there is inevitably a certain degree of distortion.

I have studiously avoided commenting upon food because by and large Indian hotel cuisine, even the best of it, presents problems for the Western traveller. Western food is usually very inferior in even the finest hotels in India. Traditional Indian food needs to be made fresh and carefully spiced; conveyor-belt curry cooking is rarely, if ever, palatable. Hotel buffets with their oily masalas simmering away for hours on end can be the most unsettling suppers imaginable. This is not to say that you will not have wonderful culinary experiences in India but I am not going to make any promises as to when and where.

Having covered myself thus, I would say that almost all the hotels presented in this book offer, at the very least, adequate accommodation and some are positively superb. Furthermore, what many lack in

amenities is more than made up for in ambience.

Basically to sojourn in India's palace hotels is an adventure – an opportunity to look out upon vistas that were arranged for kings, to walk down hallways that once echoed with the whisperings of courtiers and concubines, to sleep beneath a canopy once reserved for viceroys, and to venture forth into the recesses of India – to its antiquities and village life – so that one might experience this awesome country with an intimacy and susceptibility never possible in a concrete block.

If you are among the adventurous take note of all that follows.

NATIONAL AND REGIONAL HOTEL MANAGEMENT COMPANIES

Taj Group of Hotels

Apollo Bunder
Bombay 400 039
India
UK reservations:
St James's Court Hotel and Apartments
Buckingham Gate
London SW1E 6AF
England
Tel: 071-828-5909
Toll Free: (UK) 0800 282699

USA reservations:
The Taj Group
230 Park Avenue
Suite 466
New York, NY 10169
USA
Tel: (212) 972-6830
Toll Free: (USA) 1-800-458-8825

ITC-Welcomgroup

Welcomgroup Maurya Sheraton Hotel
and Towers
Diplomatic Enclave
New Delhi 110 021
India
Tel: 3010101, 3010136
Cable: WELCOTEL
Fax: 3010908
Telex: 031-65217 WELC IN

UK reservations:
Tel: (toll free) 0800-282-811

USA reservations:
Welcomgroup ITC Ltd
342 Madison Avenue
New York, NY 10173
USA
Tel: (212) 986-3724
Tel: (toll free-USA and Canada)
800-223-0888
Telex: 426083 ITCL-UI

Oberoi Hotels

7 Sham Nath Marg
Delhi 110 054
India
Tel: 2525464
Telex: 66303/78163 OMDL IN
Fax: 2929800

UK reservations:
Tel: 081-788-2070
Telex: 23116
Fax: 081-789-5369

USA reservations:
Tel: (toll free) 800-223-1474
(212) 682-7655

ITDC-Ashok Group

Ashok Reservation Service
Ashok Hotel
Chanakya Puri
New Delhi
India
Tel: 600121
Telex: 031-72333
or:
SD Enterprises Ltd
Wembley
Middlesex
England HA9 0PA
Tel: 0903-3411
Telex: 94012027 SDEL D
or:
Golden Tulip/KLM Reservation Offices
Worldwide
ASRA ORIENT
Frankfurt
Germany
Tel: (069) 253098
Telex: 413 451 ASRAD

Rajasthan Tourism Development Corporation (RTDC)

Usha Niwas
Kalyan Path
Police Memorial
Jaipur - 302 004
Rajasthan
India
Tel: 79252/65076
Telex: 365 2469 RTDC IN
Cable: AATITHYA, JAIPUR
Manager, Accommodation-Package
Tours
Rajasthan Tourism Development
Corporation
Chandra Lok Building
36 Janpath
New Delhi - 110 001
India
Tel: 3321820/3322332
Telex: 31 63142 RTDC IN

Kerala Tourism

Director of Tourism
Parkview
Trivandrum
Kerala
India

GAZETTEER OF HOTELS

RAJASTHAN

UDAIPUR

Lake Palace Hotel
(Jag Niwas)
Pichola Lake,
Udaipur – 313 001
Rajasthan
Telex: 033-203 LPAL IN

Reservations: see Taj Group of Hotels.

Accommodation: 85 rooms and Special Suites.

Five-star deluxe. An incomparable property with adequate to exquisite rooms, good, professional service, well managed in best Taj style. Recommended.

Shivniwas Palace
Udaipur – 313 001
Rajasthan
Telex: 033-226 IPAL IN

Accommodation: 17 suites. 1 Imperial suite, 2 Royal suites, 6 Historic suites. 8 deluxe suites. 14 rooms. All centrally air-conditioned and heated. All with attached baths and telephones.

In every way by far the finest palace hotel in India – elegant, beautifully run, with wonderful rooms. All the efficiency of a five-star hotel without the impersonal quality. Very highly recommended if you have the means.

Laxmi Vilas Palace Hotel
Udaipur – 313 001
Rajasthan
Telex: 033-218

Reservations: See ITDC-Ashok Group.

Accommodation: 54 rooms (45 double with air-conditioning, 4 double without, 4 suites, 1 Maharani suite) all with telephone, attached bath, television, video and refrigerator.

Decent second-rank hotel in an outstanding location overlooking Fateh Sagar Lake with pleasant old rooms and a nice swimming pool. Service is mediocre.

Shikarbadi
Goverdhanvilas
Udaipur – 313 001
Rajasthan
Telex: 033-227 BADI IN

Accommodation: 25 double rooms with attached bath, heating and cooling.

Originally a royal hunting lodge, the property is efficiently managed and provides comfortable lodgings in an entirely different atmosphere from the other Udaipur properties, geared to outdoor recreation and relaxation.

JAIPUR

The Rambagh Palace
Bhawani Singh Road
Jaipur – 302 005
Rajasthan
Telex: 364 2254 RBAG IN/365 2147 RBAG IN

Reservations: see Taj Group of Hotels.

Accommodation: 110 rooms and special suites. All rooms with telephones, attached baths with hot and cold water, channel music and colour television.

Five-star deluxe professionalism. Very comfortable and generally well managed. The recent renovation and redecoration of suites is very disappointing, having expunged their original character in exchange for chic, homogenized hotel décor with unconvincing oriental flourishes, at double the previous prices. Most annoying. Otherwise recommended.

Raj Mahal Palace
(Maji-ka-Bagh)
Sardar Patel Marg
Jaipur – 302 001
Rajasthan
Telex: 0365-313 JAI IN

Reservations: see Taj Group of Hotels.

Accommodation: 11 rooms and suites with telephones and attached baths.

Thus far, Raj Mahal Palace has been left untouched, thread-bare and down-at-heel, which in a way is appealing. The enormous suites contain some of the original furniture but have been stripped of the all-important bric-à-brac, leaving the kind of abandoned atmosphere one finds in many of the lesser princely palace hotels. It is well managed by Taj and the grounds are wonderful.

The Jai Mahal Palace Hotel
(Natani-ka-Bagh)
Jacob Road
Civil Lines
Jaipur - 302 006
Rajasthan
Telex: 365 2250 JMPH IN/365 2716 TAJJ IN

Reservations: see Taj Group of Hotels.

Accommodation: 120 rooms with central air-conditioning, attached baths, telephones, channel music, colour television, video.

Five-star. Well-managed, comfortable hotel with a beautiful garden and comfortable, if undistinguished, rooms; the newest of the Taj properties in Jaipur. The most interesting feature is an ambitious recreation of a Mughal garden in its grounds. A lovely place to stay.

Narain Niwas Palace Hotel
(Kanota Bagh)
Kanota Bagh
Narain Singh Road
Jaipur – 302 004
Rajasthan

Accommodation: 22 double rooms (13 with air-conditioning) with attached baths and telephones.

This is a lively, unpretentious operation in the midst of large gardens. The rooms are spacious and comfortable, with fine period decoration and eccentric turn-of-the-century Raj furniture. To sit out upon the verandah in the evening is a particular pleasure. Recommended.

Kanota Fort
(Kanota Garh)
Kanota Village
Jaipur District

For information contact Narain Niwas Palace (above).

This village fort is primarily used as spill-over accommodation and for special occasions.

Samode Haveli
Samode House
Gangapole
Jaipur – 302 002
Rajasthan

The only drawback to this wonderful haveli hotel is that it is set in an obscure district deep inside a part of the city nobody seems to be familiar with. Once there, this is the most relaxing hotel in all of Jaipur to spend time in. The front verandah is lovely and it has a dining room as fabulously decorated as you will find in India. Highly recommended.

Achrol Lodge
(Achrol Kothi)
Hari Bhawan,
Jacob Road, Civil Lines.
Jaipur – 302 006

Reservations: By mail or telephone.

Accommodation: 6 large rooms with dressing rooms and attached baths, plus tent and camper space.

Conveniently located and set amidst lush and spacious gardens, this is a simple but very pleasant place to stay, without the sometimes frantic atmosphere one finds in other of the more commercial palace hotels.

Hotel Mandawa House
(Mandawa Dera)
Sansar Chandra Road
Jaipur – 302 001
Rajasthan
Telex: 365 2342 CMDW IN

Built in 1896 by Thakur Baghwat Singh of Mandawa. Opened by the Mandawa family in 1989 in the wake of their success with Castle Mandawa in Sheikhawati.

Hotel Bissau Palace
O/S, Chandpole
Jaipur – 302 016
Cable: HOBI

Accommodation: 27 rooms (25 doubles, 2 suites) all with attached baths, air-conditioning, telephone.

Built in 1919, first opened as a hotel in 1972, this was once the best second-rank hotel in Jaipur but has since been eclipsed by Narain Niwas and Samode Haveli. Still a nice place to stay, with an interesting library-cum-museum and pleasant gardens.

Khetri House Hotel
O/S, Chandpole
Jaipur – 302 016

Accommodation: 6 double rooms, 4 single rooms, 1 double suite, 2 deluxe suites. All with separate baths.

Khetri House was first opened as a hotel in the early 1950s and might have been really elegant back then. These days, however, the hotel, which is managed by a local bureaucrat, is a dim, depressing dump despite its period décor, surrounded by dusty, unkempt gardens. Definitely a last resort.

SAMODE
(25 miles from Jaipur)

Samode Palace
Samode
District Jaipur
Rajasthan – 303806

Reservations: Manager Reservations
Samode House
Gangapole
Jaipur
Rajasthan – 302 002

Accommodation: 20 rooms.

This is one of the most dynamic and creative palace hotel operations in India, constantly improving and expanding. An experience well worth going out of one's way for.

RAMGARH
(28 miles from Jaipur Airport)

Ramgarh Lodge
Jamuva Ramgarh
Jaipur 303 109
Rajasthan

Reservations: see Taj Group of Hotels.

Accommodation: 9 rooms with attached baths and hot and cold running water.

Lakeside hunting lodge resort of the Maharaja of Jaipur, 1930s vintage. Expertly run by Taj Group.

SARISKA (22 miles from Alwar, 65 miles from Jaipur, 125 miles from New Delhi)

Hotel Sariska Palace
Sariska – 301 022
District Alwar
Rajasthan

Reservations: 4/1, D.B. Gupta Road
Pahar Ganj
New Delhi

Accommodation: 31 rooms. 17 doubles. Plain, clean and decently run.

SILISERH

Lake Palace
Siliserh
District Alwar
Rajasthan

Reservations: see Rajasthan Tourism Development Corporation.

Accommodation: 11 rooms. 9 double rooms (6 with air-conditioning, 3 without). 2 single rooms. 5-bed dormitory.
One of the worst-run hotels of all the properties considered in this book and a genuine waste of a wonderful palace.

ALWAR

Phool Bagh Palace Hotel
Opp. New Stadium (near Moti Dungri)
Alwar – 301 001
Accommodation: 13 rooms.

Built in 1959 by the Alwar princely family and thus not really a Raj palace, but probably the only decent place to stay in Alwar.

NEEMRANA (75 miles from New Delhi on Delhi-Jaipur Highway)

Neemrana Fort
Post Office Neemrana
Behror
Alwar District
Rajasthan 301 705

Accommodation: 10 – 15 rooms, each decorated in indigenous Indian style.

The most fascinating and creative palace hotel project yet attempted in India. Set on a hillside with spectacular views of the plains, this fortified palace offers lovely but relatively Spartan accommodation and will most likely be under development for many years to come. Recommended.

BHARATPUR

Ghol Bagh Palace
Agra Road
Bharatpur – 321 001

Accommodation: 18 rooms (10 in main building including suites, 8 in annexe) all
with attached bath, none with air-conditioning.

Built in 1903 by Maharaja Kishan Singh of Bharatpur as a private hunting lodge at the same time as the adjacent Moti Mahal Palace. Slightly down-at-heel but comfortable.

SAWAI MADHOPUR

Sawai Madhopur Lodge
Ranthambor Road
Sawai Madhopur
Rajasthan

Reservations: see Taj Group of Hotels.

Accommodation: 16 air-conditioned rooms with attached baths, hot and cold running water.

Originally a tented hunting compound for Maharaja Man Singh of Jaipur. Well managed by Taj Group.

Castle Jhoomer Baori
Ranthambor Wildlife Sanctuary
Sawai Madhopur
Rajasthan
Tel: 2495

Reservations: see Rajasthan Tourism Development Corporation.

Hilltop hunting lodge built in the late nineteenth century by Sawai Madho Singh, originally with six or seven bedrooms.

KOTA

Brij Raj Bhavan Palace
(Raj Bhavan)
Civil Lines
Kota – 324 001
Rajasthan

Accommodation: 8 rooms (2 large doubles) all air-cooled and with attached baths.

Run (informally) as a guest house since 1964 the building itself is unexceptional but the site overlooking the Chambal River is outstanding and, being the private domicile of a prince, the décor is authentically aristocratic down to the last silver-framed photograph. The rooms are very comfortable, the views wonderful and the grounds lovely. Recommended.

PUSHKAR

Sarovar Tourist Bungalow
(Jaipur Haveli)
Pushkar
Rajasthan
Tel: 40

Reservations: see Rajasthan Tourism Development Corporation.

Accommodation: 40 rooms.

The former Pushkar resort of the Maharajas of Jaipur.

Hotel Pushkar Palace
(Kishangarh Haveli)
Pushkar – 305 022
Rajasthan

Accommodation: 31 rooms. 2 suites and 15 double rooms with attached baths, 11 double rooms with shared baths, 3 single rooms with shared baths. Plus one dormitory room with 12 beds.

The former Pushkar resort of the Maharajas of Kishangarh.

NAWALGARH (90 miles from Jaipur via Sikar, 160 miles from Delhi via Rewari Narnaul, accessible by rail)

Roop Niwas Palace
Nawalgarh – 333 042
District Jhunjhunu Sheikhawati
Rajasthan

Reservations: Tel: Jaipur – 68726/62987

Accommodation: 20 double rooms with attached baths.

Although this kothi is relatively modern, the rooms are spacious and comfortable, the grounds are pleasant, and the presence of its quietly dignified proprietor Rawal Madan Singh, who built it in 1930, was a treat.

DUNDLOD (100 miles from Jaipur via Sikar, 155 miles from Delhi via Dharuhera and Rewari, and accessible by rail)

Dundlod Qila
P.O. Dundlod
District Jhunjhunu Sheikhawati
Rajasthan – 333 702
Reservations: Dundlod House
Civil Lines
Jaipur – 302 006
Cable: Dera Hotel

Royal Excursions
C-7 Friends Colony
New Delhi – 110 065
Telex: 316-3122 IMMA IN

Accommodation: 10 double rooms with attached baths.

Dundlod Qila was a pleasant surprise. The rooms are clean, comfortable and atmospheric, the Dundlod family and their retainers are gracious and we were able to witness more of village life in all its purity and beauty than in any other place except Rohet, in Jodhpur State. Recommended.

MANDAWA (105 miles from Jaipur, 155 miles from Delhi, accessible by rail)

Hotel Castle Mandawa
(Mandawa Garh)
Mandawa,
District Jhunjhunu Sheikhawati
Rajasthan – 333704

Reservations: Mandawa House
Sansar Chandra Road
Jaipur 302001
Telex: 365 2342 CMDW IN

Accommodation: 36 rooms at Castle – all with attached bath (14 cottages in desert camp ½ mile from the Castle.)

The fort is wonderful, the rooms are good, the service is all right, but the hotel has been in operation for quite a while and as a result the whole atmosphere has taken on a more artificial and touristic quality. The newly constructed desert camp is quite pleasant.

BIKANER

Hotel Lallgarh Palace
(Lallgarh Palace)
Bikaner – 334 001
Rajasthan

Accommodation: 40 rooms (38 double, 2 single) all with attached baths (air-conditioned in summer and heated in winter).

A ten-star property with two-star services. The hotel is run by a charitable trust and, as such, is without the polish of a professional operation. Still, Lallgarh Palace is a genuinely extraordinary palace and is a magnificent place to visit, if even for a day.

Hotel Gajner Palace
Gajner
Rajasthan

Reservations: Lallgarh Palace
Bikaner – 334 001
Rajasthan

Accommodation: 24 rooms (8 in main palace, 16 in annexe) all with attached baths.

The same unprofessional service one finds in Lallgarh but the location is utterly captivating and rooms in the main palace are authentic and unretouched. Definitely worth a visit.

JODHPUR

Welcomgroup Umaid Bhawan Palace
(Umaid Bhawan)
Jodhpur – 342 006
Rajasthan
Tel: 22316/22516/22366
Telex: 0552-202 UBP IN

Reservations: see ITC-Welcomgroup.

Accommodation: 95 rooms and suites with telephones, attached baths, channel music, television, video, refrigerators.

This is the most staggering palace hotel in India, kept in superb condition by ITC-Welcomgroup under the careful supervision of Maharaja Gaj Singh, who lives within the complex. Absolutely unmissable.

Ajit Bhawan
Near Circuit House
Jodhpur – 342 006
Telex: 552-277 AJIT IN

Accommodation: 50 rooms: 12 in main palace, 38 in garden bungalows and stone tents.

Ajit Bhawan is one of the most entertaining palace hotels you will find in India. It was here that the village safari concept was pioneered. The best part of the facility in which to stay is the tourist huts scattered around the grounds like hobbit houses. The effect is Disneyesque, kitsch and utterly artificial but, by God, it works.

POKARAN (70 miles from Jaisalmer, 105 miles from Jodhpur)

Fort Pokaran
(Bala Garh)
Pokaran
District Jaisalmer
Rajasthan
Tel: 71

Reservations: Pokaran House
P.W.D. Road
Jodhpur – 342001
Rajasthan

A beautiful fourteenth-century fort which ultimately passed into the hands of the Champawat clan who became the thakurs of Pokaran. Ideally situated as a rest-stop at the Bikaner-Jaisalmer-Jodhpur crossroads. Facilities need development but Fort Pokaran is still well worth a stop-over, if for nothing else than to visit the small family museum.

KHIMSAR (60 miles from Jodhpur)

Welcomgroup Royal Castle
(Khimsar Garh)
PO Box Khimsar
District Nagaur
Khimsar
Rajasthan

Reservations: see ITC-Welcomgroup.

Accommodation: 14 rooms, air-cooled and with attached baths.

Khimsar Garh was constructed in the fifteenth century by Rao Karamsi, a junior son of Rao Jodha of Jodhpur and became the headquarters of the Karamsots, a sub-clan of the Rathors. Khimsar Royal Castle, as it is now called, is off the beaten track but once there, it is a very pleasant place to stay, with fine large rooms, good service and decent food. The village is nothing much to see, however.

JAISALMER

Hotel Jawahar Niwas Palace
Jaisalmer – 345001
Rajasthan

Reservations: Manager
Hotel Jawahar Niwas Palace
Post Box No. 1
Jaisalmer
Rajasthan

Accommodation: 18 rooms: 6 deluxe rooms, 9 double rooms, 3 single rooms, all with attached bath.

This is a large, European building without much sense of ever having been in royal hands but it is a nice facility, set right at the edge of the desert.

ROHET (25 miles from Jodhpur Airport, 145 miles from Udaipur)

Rohet Garh
Village and P.O. Rohet
District Pali – 306 421
Rajasthan

Reservations: Rohet House
P.W.D. Road
Jodhpur – 342 001
Rajasthan

Accommodation: 15 rooms, including 3 suites.

We were astonished by this place. The fort itself (seventeenth century with early-twentieth-century additions) is well run and comfortable – nothing spectacular on its own – but the village when we were there was dream-like. The villagers are possessed of phenomenal innocence and beauty and the Rohet family take one to the heart of village life in a way that would be almost impossible to access on one's own. How long this enchantment will last is hard to tell. Rohet is also a convenient rest-stop between Jodhpur and Udaipur. Definitely recommended.

RANAKPUR (60 miles from Udaipur, 85 miles from Mount Abu, 100 miles from Jodhpur)

Maharani Bagh
Orchard Retreat
Ranakpur
Rajasthan

Reservations: General Manager
Maharani Bagh
c/o Umaid Bhawan Palace
Jodhpur
Rajasthan

Accommodation: 5 double rooms. Royal tented camp can be organized on grounds.

Originally a nineteenth-century royal garden of Jodhpur's rulers, it is still used by present Maharaja Gaj Singh but now

opened to the public. Not a palace but a lovely royal resort.

GHANERAO
(close to Ranakpur)

Ghanerao Royal Castle
Ghanerao – 306 704
District Pali
Rajasthan

Accommodation: 16 rooms: 12 double, 4 single.

Ghanerao Durg was first built in 1627 as a border outpost within Udaipur State. This is a nice surprise once you negotiate the winding, narrow side-scraping road into the depths of the village. Contains an especially charming marble pavilion and pleasant rooms. It is not a professional operation but pleasant and relaxing nonetheless.

MOUNT ABU (20 miles from Abu Road Railway Station; Nearest airport Udaipur – 110 miles; 150 miles to Ahmedabad.)

Palace Hotel
(Bikaner House)
Delwara Road
Mount Abu – 307 501
Rajasthan
Telex: 0365 2700 ABUIN 008

Mount Abu is not the aristocratic resort it once was, but pretty enough for day-trippers and overnighters. The palace, first built around 1895 and renovated between 1924 and 1927, is beautifully located in lovely grounds. The rooms are enormous, the furniture is original and the management is made up of retainers of the Bikaner royal family.

HIMACHAL PRADESH

SIMLA

Chapslee
Simla – 1
Himachal Pradesh

Coming into Chapslee is like entering a rich Edwardian time-warp. Of all the properties we visited, this was the most perfectly preserved without in any way seeming like a museum. Every tapestry, every piece of princely bric-à-brac is in place, every silver frame and big brass bed. It is, in fact, the private home of Ratanjit Singh of Kapurthala and his wife Srimata Pronoti Deoi of Assam. Gracious, pleasant and very highly recommended.

Woodville Palace
Raj Bhawan Road
Simla – 171002
Himachal Pradesh

Accommodation: 12 rooms. 7 doubles, 5 suites (all with attached baths).

Although more commercial and thus less authentically antiquarian than Chapslee, this hotel has more spacious and beautiful grounds and is a perfectly charming place to stay. Recommended.

CHAIL (30 miles/2 hours from Simla)

Palace Hotel Chail
District Solan
Himachal Pradesh

Accommodation: Maharaja Suite, Maharani Room, Prince and Princess Room, plus 16 regular rooms. 5 cottages. 5 log huts. Also Himneel Hotel with 6 doubles and 6 family sets.

Not much of a building to begin with and stripped of its original furnishings, this is a dismal hotel (another state-run tourist development operation). Nevertheless, the location is incomparable and the grounds are vast. Popular with honeymooners. Not particularly recommended.

KULU VALLEY

Hotel Castle
(Nagar Castle)
Nagar
Himachal Pradesh

Accommodation: 12 rooms; 10 doubles, 2 family suites.

Reservations: Himachal Pradesh Tourist Information Office, Kulu or Manali

We arrived at Nagar unannounced after midnight and approached the only illuminated house around which, we found, was inhabited by bhang-smoking Scandinavians. They pointed us to the darkened, grave-like castle next door and we roused a fabulously inebriated watchman, wild-eyed and staggering, who let us into big, rugged and surprisingly comfortable rooms. The early morning views from the balconies and main courtyard of the castle overlooking the Beas River Valley are indescribably majestic and beautiful. Recommended.

KANGRA VALLEY

Palace Motel
(Al Hilal – Taragarh Palace)
Tehsil Palampur, District Kangra
Himachal Pradesh

Accommodation: 14 rooms; 10 doubles, 4 singles.

An unpretentious, enchanting rest-stop surrounded by leafy gardens.

JAMMU AND KASHMIR

SRINAGAR

Both these hotels were closed during 1990-91. It is advisable to check before travelling to the region.

The Oberoi Palace
(Gulab Bhawan)
Gupkar Road
Srinagar – 190 001
Kashmir
Telex: 201 LXSR IN

Accommodation: 105 rooms; 26 single, 59 double, 20 suites (all with attached baths).

A five-star operation with very comfortable rooms, spacious gardens and much of the insularity from the Muslim populace of the valley that Maharaja Hari Singh strived to achieve. Whether that is desirable for a visitor to Srinagar is a matter of personal taste.

Lake Pavilion
(Kotar Khana)
Dal Lake
Srinagar
Kashmir

Reservations: The Manager, Lake Pavilion Estates,
3 Nyaya Marg, Diplomatic Enclave
New Delhi – 110 021
Tel: 301-5291/301-1744

A lovely location, no doubt about it, but incredibly pricey, with a certain snob appeal, geared as it is to clientele who probably would not deign to stay in a house boat.

JAMMU

Hari Niwas Palace
for information write to:
3 Nyaya Marg, Diplomatic Enclave,
New Delhi – 110 021

Accommodation: 25 rooms and suites

Built by Maharaja Hari Singh around 1925 adjacent to his father's palace, Amar Mahal, which is now a museum. It is a plain, white, entirely European structure spectacularly set high above the River Tawi.

GUJARAT

BHAVNAGAR

Welcomgroup Nilambag Palace
(Huzoor Palace at Nilambagh)
Bhavnagar – 364002
Gujarat

Reservations: See ITC-Welcomgroup.

Accommodation: 14 rooms and suites.
Dining hall (Continental and Indian),
garden tea lounge, banquet and conference facilities, laundry/dry-cleaning, library, spacious grounds.

We thoroughly enjoyed our stay in this hotel. Run by the Maharaja's private staff under the ITC-Welcomgroup umbrella, this is an excellent hotel with a relaxed atmosphere, friendly service and spacious, comfortable rooms. Promising and recommended.

WANKANER

Ranjit Vilas Palace
Wankaner – 363621
Gujarat

Reservations: write well in advance to:
Dr Digvijay Sinh
Secretary
The Palace
Wankaner – 363621
Gujarat

Accommodation: 6 rooms in palace guest house annexe, all with attached baths.

The palace is spell-binding on its own although the guest annexe accommodation would benefit from some upgrading. Eminently worth a side-trip to Gujarat.

Oasis Palace
(Purna Chandra Bhawan)
Wankaner – 363621
Gujarat

Accommodation: 6 rooms in main palace, including two suites. 6 rooms in palace annexe all with attached baths.

This is a property that has not been developed as much as it might, but it has great potential as a unique and first-rate resort. The rooms are attractive Art Deco and the palace is set within a lovely garden. Even as is, recommended.

CHORWAD (30 miles from Veraval, 45 miles from Junagadh, 245 miles from Ahmedabad)

Chorwad Beach Palace Resort
(Nawabi-ka-Bangla)
Chorwad
Gujarat

Reservations: Tourism Corporation of Gujarat Limited
H. K. House, off Ashram road
Ahmedabad-389 009
Tel: 449683/460640
Telex: 012-549 TCGL IN

Accommodation: 75 rooms in palace and recently built annexe and cottages.

This beach resort of the Nawab of Junaghadh might be an acceptable overnight stop if one happens to be passing by Chorwad. Otherwise, there is no much to recommend this run-down weather-beaten resort with an ugly annexe, miserable restaurant and mediocre service.

MADHYA PRADESH

MANDU (20 miles south of Dhar, 60 miles from Indore)

Taveli Mahal Rest House
(Taveli Mahal)
Mandu – 454 010
Madhya Pradesh
Tel: 25

Reservations: write at least two weeks in advance to:
Conservation Assistant
Archaeological Survey of India
Mandu – 454 010
Madhya Pradesh

Accommodation: 2 double rooms only.

Taveli means 'stable' and it is most likely that this palatial structure was originally for that purpose, although in the 1940s and early '50s it was converted during the reign of Maharaja Amash Rao Pawar of Dhar as a palace rest house. The advantage of this spartan rest house is two-fold: first, it is the only accommodation within the precincts of the ancient city and is set in a spectacular location, looking out upon the stunning Jahaz Mahal, or Ship Palace and the Kapur Talao, or Camphor Tank; secondly, at about 30p per person per night it is far and away the least expensive property covered in this book.

ORCHHA (12 miles from Jhansi, which is a railhead, 75 miles from Gwalior)

Sheesh Mahal
Orchha
Madhya Pradesh

Reservations: more than five days in advance through:
M.P. State Tourism Development Corp. Ltd.
4th Floor
Gangotri
T.T. Nagar
Bhopal – 462 003
Tel: 63552/66383/68563/64388/66342/ 65154
Textel: 0755-61629
Telex: 0705-275 TOUR IN
Cable: M.P.TOUR, BHOPAL

Accommodation: 8 rooms: 7 doubles, 1 single.

Matchless location overcomes all shortcomings.

GWALIOR

Welcomgroup Usha Kiran Palace
Jayendraganj Lashkar
Gwalior – 474 009
Madhya Pradesh

Reservations: See ITC-Welcomgroup.

Accommodation: 27 rooms and suites.

The best hotel in Gwalior and the most convenient. Well run by Welcomgroup with good rooms and lovely grounds. Recommended.

ANDHRA PRADESH

HYDERABAD

Ritz Hotel
(Hill Fort Palace)
Hyderabad – 500 463
Andhra Pradesh
Telex: 0425-6215

Accommodation: 40 rooms, doubles and suites, all air-conditioned and with attached bath, television, video, refrigerator and telephone.

Hill Fort Palace was built in 1923 by Sir Nizamat Jung. The Gothic design was apparently inspired by the poetry of Sir Walter Scott and Sir Nizamat's nostalgia for his Cambridge days. In 1931 the palace was purchased for Muazzam Jah, the second son of the Nizam of Hyderabad. After Independence it became the most ritzy hotel in Hyderabad but the Ritz has long since lost its lustre. It is run-down and inelegant with unregenerate 1950s décor and musty rooms. Not particularly recommended.

KARNATAKA

MYSORE

Lalitha Mahal Palace Hotel
(Lalitha Mahal Palace)
Mysore – 570 011
Karnataka
Telex: 0486-217

Reservations: See ITDC-Ashok Group.

Accommodation: 54 rooms and suites, air-conditioned and with attached bath, telephone, channel music, radio, 4-channel television and video, private balconies in most rooms.

This is an extraordinary property which is managed surprisingly well by ITDC, although not with the polish of Taj, Oberoi or Welcomgroup. The dining room is delightful. Definitely recommended.

Rajendra Vilas Palace
Chamundi Hills
Mysore – 570 018
Telex: 0846-230
Cable: PALASCHAIN

Accommodation: 29 rooms and suites.

This could be a wonderful palace hotel but, alas, it is not. The service is poor and the facilities have been allowed to deteriorate.

Plans for improvement have been on the cards for years.

KRISHNARAJASAGAR-BRINDAVAN GARDENS (10 miles from Mysore, 85 miles from Bangalore Airport)

Hotel Krishnarajasagar
PO Krishnarajasagar – 571 607
District Mandya
Karnataka
Telex: 0846-214

Reservation: The Ritz Hotels (Mysore) Limited
5 Jhansi Lakshmi Bai Road
Mysore – 570 005
Karnataka

Accommodation: 22 double rooms with attached bath and telephones.

This property is said to have been built around 1931 by the Maharaja of Mysore as a guest house, but I have my doubts about this as the building does not show up in photos from this period. More likely 1940s vintage. It is run-down and indifferently operated by the Ritz Hotel Group, but it is a hard hotel to pass up, set as it is above Brindavan Gardens, one of the most beautiful and impressive gardens in India. The evening illumination is justly famous. In spite of everything, a pleasure. Recommended.

KARAPUR (50 miles from Mysore airport and railway station)

Kabini River Lodge
Karapur
Karnataka

Reservations: Jungle Lodges & Resorts Limited
2nd Floor
Shrungar Shopping Centre
Mahatma Gandhi Road
Bangalore – 560 001

Accommodation: 14 double rooms with attached bath.

Well managed former hunting lodge of the Maharaja of Mysore, beautifully located with personable staff and comfortable rooms. For wildlife safaris and birdwatching.

TAMIL NADU

OOTACAMUND (Uthagamandalam)

Fernhill Palace
Ootacamund – 643 004
Tamil Nadu
Telex: 0853-246

Accommodation: 52 rooms, including Bhawani House and cottages. All double rooms with attached bath.

Another fantastic property owned and operated by the son of the last Maharaja of Mysore. This could be one of the premier palace hotels in India but, again, the owner's ambitious plan to transform the entire property into a dream resort has been imminent for many years and endlessly delayed.

Hotel Tamil Nadu
(Arranmore Palace)
Charing Cross Road
Ootacamund – 643 001
Tamil Nadu
Telex: 201

Reservations: Tamil Nadu Tourism Development Corporation
No 25, Dr Radhakrishnan Road
Mylapore
Madras – 600 004.
Tel: 842721/846843/849805/846825

Accommodation: rooms, suites and cottages.

Once the summer palace of the Maharajas of Jodhpur, Arranmore was sold to the state for a song in the 1960s (furniture and carpets included) and converted into accommodation for government guests. The property has subsequently been given over to the state Tourism Development Corporation and opened to the public. The staff is, according to bureaucratic form, surly and incompetent, and services are mediocre, but the property is surprisingly well kept up and its gardens are still quite lovely.

KERALA

THEKKADY

Lake Palace
Thekkady – 685 536
Kerala
Tel: Kumily 23

Built in the 1930s by the Maharaja of Travancore, Sri Chitra Triunal, after his establishment of Periyar as a wildlife sanctuary. Visitors naturally assume that the Lake Palace (a misnomer – it is but a medium-sized bungalow) was originally a hunting lodge. This is not the case. The Maharajas of Cochin and Travancore were strict vegetarians and adherents to the Hindu doctrine of Ahimsa which forbids the killing of animals. This is a lovely place to stay, not, however, very well run by Kerala Tourism Development Corporation (as distinct from Kerala Tourism which manages its properties much better).

COCHIN

Bolghatty Palace Hotel
Bolghatty Island
Mulavukad PO
Cochin – 682 504
Cable: RELAX, COCHIN

Accommodation: 5 large rooms in main palace (one air-conditioned, four with

fan) all with attached bath, plus 6 newly built cottages, all air-conditioned with attached bath.

This charming old island property surrounded by botanical gardens is marred only by the ugly concrete cylinders that pass for honeymoon cottages. Actually, they are the best kept part of the facility. The main building is still charming but there is a mustiness about the rooms which could be eradicated by some judicious redecoration and better management. Worth a stay, however.

TRICHUR

Government Guest House
(Rama Nilayam Palace)
Trichur
Kerala

Reservations: see Kerala Tourism.

Accommodation: 4 large double rooms in old palace with telephone, attached bath and air-conditioning (one room has television), palace annexe has 4 non-air-conditioned rooms with attached bath, new building has 24 rooms (11 air-conditioned, 13 non-air-conditioned).

This is a lovely mini-palace set in pleasant gardens with monumental bedrooms replete with some of the original semi-antique furniture (all obtrusively numbered to prevent theft) and gargantuan bathrooms. Government VIPs get preference for the four rooms in the old palace and the new annexe is drab, run-of-the-mill modern, so it is best to book ahead, specifying the older palace.

ALWAYE

Government Guest House
(Alwaye Palace)
Alwaye
Kerala

Reservations: see Kerala Tourism.

Accommodation: 10 double rooms with attached bath, none air-conditioned.

This nineteenth century riverside resort palace of the Maharaja of Travancore is

now a clean and decently run (by Kerala Tourism) government guest house. The rooms are palatially spacious although sparsely furnished (with original numbered semi-antique pieces), the grounds are large and lovely and the views of the Periyar are delightful. The hotel caters almost exclusively to local clientele and the services reflect this but at around £2 per night one has little cause to grouse.

Government Guest House
(Quilon Residency)
Asramam
Quilon – 691 002
Kerala

Reservations: see Kerala Tourism.

Accommodation: 8 large double rooms (3 air-conditioned, 5 non-air-conditioned, with fan). 2 single rooms. Private baths with old-fashioned English-style bathtubs.

Built by Colonel Munro, British Resident and Prime Minister of Travancore, in around 1811, during the reign of Rani Gauri Lakshmibai, as Residency and Huzoor Cutchery, or Seat of Government. Remained the Residency after government moved to Trivandrum in the 1830s. This is a beautifully situated property on Ashtamudi Lake with good recreational facilities for adults and children and Kerala Tourism budget prices (around £2). Great value for money.

KOVALAM (8 miles from Trivandrum, 9 miles from railway station, 12 miles from airport)

Halcyon Palace
(Kovalam Palace)
Kovalam Ashok Beach Resort
Trivandrum – 695 522
Kerala
Telex: 0884-216 KBR IN

Reservations: See ITDC-Ashok Group.

Accommodation: 4 double rooms.

An interesting building, recently renovated, which unfortunately is part of a poorly managed hotel complex.

FUTURE PALACE HOTELS

Kishangarh Fort-Palace
Kishangarh, Rajasthan

Achrol Fort-Palace
Achrol, Rajasthan

Soniwas Bagh
Samode, Rajasthan

Umed Bhawan Palace
Kota, Rajasthan

Bangalore Palace
Bangalore, Karnataka

Paschimahavini Palace
Seringapatam, Mysore, Karnataka

Lok Ranjan Mahal
Mysore, Karnataka

Hill palace of Nizam of Hyderabad
Ootacamund, Tamil Nadu

GLOSSARY

Achkan: *Long, high-collared coat.*

ADC: *Aide-de-camp.*

Atrium: *An open central court.*

Ayah: *A native nursemaid or nanny; a lady's maid-servant.*

Bagh: *A garden.*

Bargeboard: *A board projecting from the edge of a roof gable, frequently decorated or carved.*

Bhavan (Bhawan): *Building or house; palaces were often referred to simply as Bhawans.*

Begum: *Muslim princess, or wife of Nawab.*

Bighas: *A land measurement used in northern India. Approximately one-fifth of an acre.*

Bund: *A dam.*

Chajja: *A sloping stone projection similar to a cornice or dripstone blade which runs along the side of a building or over a door or window.*

Champawat, Chanpawat: *Rajput clan of the Rathor lineage.*

Chattri: *Literally, an umbrella. A dome upheld by pillars. A cenotaph.*

Chota Hazari: *Early-morning tea.*

Chowri: *A ceremonial fly-whisk made of a yak's tail and forming part of royal regalia.*

Cutchery (Kutchery): *Government office; Huzoor Cutchery was the administrative office of the state.*

Dassera: *Hindu festival in autumn celebrating Lord Rama's defeat of the demon king Ravana.*

Deodar: *Himalayan cedar.*

Deva, Devi: *A god, goddess.*

Devata: *A local, as distinct from a universal, deity.*

Dewan (Diwan): *A minister, usually a prime minister, although in some states there was a distinction between the two posts.*

Dharamsala: *A resting place.*

Diwan-i-Am: *Public audience chamber.*

Dormer: *A window set vertically in a gable projecting from the roof.*

Durbar (Darbar): *The court of a princely state; a public audience given by a ruler, including a viceroy, prince or governor; sometimes the word refers directly to the ruler.*

Durg: *A fort.*

Durrie: *A traditional floor covering of woven cotton.*

Finial: *A crowning ornament on top of a dome, spire or arch.*

Gable: *A triangular section of wall of a building from eaves to ridge.*

Gadi: *A cushion or princely throne.*

Garh (Gadh): *A fort.*

Ghats: *Literally, 'steps'; usually referring to a flight of steps leading down to the edge of a river or lake.*

Ghunghat: *A veil falling over the face.*

Haveli: *Literally, 'enclosure'; more specifically a town house or mansion with a courtyard.*

Holkar: *The title of the Maratha ruler of Indore.*

Howdah: *An open seat on the back of an elephant.*

Huzur (Huzoor): *Literally, 'the presence'; a term of respect traditionally applied to ruler of a princely state.*

Hypostyle: *A roof or ceiling supported by columns.*

Indo-Saracenic: *An architectural synthesis formulated by European architects, based on Mughal decorative motifs and European interior designs but employing a variety of architectural references.*

Jaali: *A pierced ornamental lattice screen, usually of stone.*

Jagir: *An hereditary landholding given by government or ruler, usually in return for or in recognition of services rendered.*

Jagirdar: *A holder of a* **jagir.**

Jamedar: *A guard or footman.*

Jampan: *A rickshaw.*

Jarokha: *A small projecting balcony.*

Jat: *Agrarian peasant clans which rose up in certain parts of northern India to form kingdoms.*

Kachhwaha: *Primary Rajput clan centred first in Amber and ultimately in Jaipur.*

Kanwar (Kunwar): *A junior prince, or heir-apparent to a feudal estate.*

Kathiawar: *Traditional name for Western Gujarat peninsula, also referred to as Saurashtra.*

Khalsa: *The resumption by the state of ownership of private property – either when the owner dies without issue or as a punishment for an offence against the state.*

Khud: *A steep hillside or precipice.*

Kiosk: *Term derived from the Turkish word for an open summer house or pavilion.*

Kothi: *A garden house or palace in the suburbs.*

Kshatriya: *The Hindu military and ruling caste.*

Lakh: *One hundred thousand.*

Mahal: *A palace; may refer to an entire palace or a single apartment within.*

Mahout: *An elephant keeper.*

Maji: *Literally, 'mother'; traditionally used to mean Queen Mother.*

Mandir: *Originally, a room; later indicated a palace and latterly a temple.*

Maratha (Marhatta): *A member of a confederacy formed from peasant cultivators of the Sudra caste in Maharashtra who rose up first in the seventeenth century under Sivaji and formed an empire in central India during the eighteenth century which was overthrown by the British.*

Mardana: *Men's quarters within a house or palace.*

Marwar: *The kingdom of Rathor Rajputs centred in Jodhpur.*

Mewar: *The kingdom of the Sisodia rulers, which was commonly referred to by the name of its last capital, Udaipur.*

Nagar: *A town.*

Nathawat: *A sub-clan of Kachhwaha Rajputs.*

Nautch: *A dance performance.*

Nawab: *Muslim prince or ruler; originally a governor of a town under Mughal rule.*

Niwas: *Abode; often referring to a small palace or an apartment within a small palace; sometimes indicating a garden.*

Nizam: *A ruler of Hyderabad, originally a viceregal role in the Mughal Empire.*

Paan: *The betel vine; a snack of betel nut combined with spices, wrapped in a green leaf and eaten after meals to aid digestion. Rulers would welcome guests with the presentation of paan.*

Pandit (Pundit): *A wise or learned Hindu.*

Porte-cochère: *A roofed structure extending out from the entrance to a building which covers a driveway and allows passengers to alight from vehicles beneath a shelter.*

Pugri: *A turban.*

Pukka: *Genuine, authentic, proper.*

Punkah: *A large cloth fan suspended from the ceiling and moved manually by means of a rope or long rods.*

Purdah: *Literally, 'behind the curtain'; a veil for women or the state of being veiled or in seclusion from men.*

Putta: *A title-deed.*

Qila: *A fortress.*

Raj: *Rule or government; often referring to British rule in India.*

Raja (Rao, Rawal, Rawat, Rana): *A Hindu prince, the basic title which was elaborated by Mughals and British into Maharaja, 'Maha' meaning 'great'. Therefore, during the British period a* **Maharaja** *or* **Maharana**, *etc. was superior in rank to a mere Raja or Rana, etc.*

Rajmata: *Queen Mother.*

Rajpramukh: *Governor of a former princely state or union of princely states between 1947 and 1956, when the largely ceremonial position was abolished.*

Rajput: *Literally, 'ruler's son'; a Hindu of the Kshatriya or warrior caste, according to myth claiming descent from one of four prototypical warriors created by Brahmins of Mount Abu to defend them from their enemies. Historians believe these warriors descended from central Asian invaders and possibly aboriginals inducted by Brahmins into Kshatriya. Almost all Hindu rulers of northern India are from one of the Rajput dynasties.*

Rathor: *Primary Rajput clan, ultimately based in Jodhpur.*

Rawala: *The women's private living quarters in a palace, the 'hareem', synonymous with* **zenana**.

Sadhu: *A wandering holy man.*

Sagar: *A lake.*

Sambar: *A large Asiatic deer.*

Sardar: *A leading nobleman in the court of a prince.*

Sawai: *Literally, 'one and a quarter'; a hereditary title given by Mughals to Rajput vassals. The most celebrated recipient was Sawai Jai Singh II, the founder of Jaipur.*

Sherwani: *A long coat.*
Shikar: *Hunting; shikari, a hunter.*
Sisodia: *A Rajput clan claiming descent from the sun.*
Swami: *A Hindu priest, scholar or teacher.*
Syce: *Groom.*
Takhallus: *A pen-name.*
Thakur: *A feudal chieftain similar to a medieval baron.*
Thikana: *The landholding of a* **thakur.**

Trabeated: *Constructed with horizontal beams or lintels upheld by posts rather than arches.*
Tripolia: *A triple gate.*
Uprajpramukh: *A deputy governor of a former princely state or union of princely states in India between 1947 and 1956.*
Verandah: *A covered and partly enclosed porch, balcony or gallery extending along the side of a building.*

Vilas: *A house; used by princes to refer to a pleasure palace or to an apartment within one.*
Yuvaraja (Yuvrawal): *Heir-apparent or Crown Prince. The female equivalent is* **Yuvrani.**
Zamandar: *A landholder or farmer;* **zamandari**, *a landholding.*
Zenana: *The women's private living quarters in a palace, the 'hareem', synonymous with* **rawala.**

BIBLIOGRAPHY

Achrol,
Annuals of the House of Achrol,
Scottish Mission Industries
Company, Ltd (Ajmer 1910).

Zahir Ahmed,
Life's Yesterdays,
Thacker & Co., Ltd (Bombay 1945).

Raza Alikhan,
Hyderabad, A City in History
(Hyderabad 1986).

**Charles Allen and Sharada
Dwivedi,**
Lives of the Indian Princes,
Century Publishing (London 1984).

Christopher Armstead,
Princely Pageant,
Thomas Harmsworth Publishing
(London 1987).

Maharaja of Baroda,
The Palaces of India,
The Vendome Press (New York
1980).

Sir William Barton
The Princes of India,
Nisbet & Co. Ltd (London 1934).

H.F. Prevost Battersby,
India Under Royal Eyes,
George Allen (London 1906).

Prabhakar V. Begde,
Forts and Palaces in India,
Sagar Publications (New Delhi).

Edward J. Buck,
Simla Past and Present,
Minerva Book House (Simla 1989).

Kalyan Kumar Chakravarty,
Orchha,
Arnold-Heinemann (New Delhi
1984).

Futeh Singh Chanpawat,
A Brief History of Jeypore
(Moon Press 1899).

Krishna Chartanya,
Kerala,
National Book Trust (New Delhi
1972).

Penelope Chetwode,
Kulu,
John Murray (London 1972).

Ian Copland,
The British Raj and the Indian Princes,
Orient Longman (Bombay 1982).

Sir Conrad Corfield,
article from unidentified newspaper,
'The Best Job I Ever Had', dated
January 1958.

Quentin Crewe,
The Last Maharaja,
Michael Joseph (London 1985).

**Geoff Crowther, Prakash A. Raj,
and Tony Wheeler,**
India – a travel survival kit,
Lonely Planet (Australia 1981).

Marquess of Curzon,
Leaves from a Viceroy's Note-Book,
Macmillan and Co., Ltd (London
1926).

Diwan Jarmani Dass,
Maharaja,
R.N. Sachdev (New Delhi 1987).

**Diwan Jarmani Dass and Rakesh
Bhan Dass,**
Maharani,
Deep Publications (New Delhi
1989).

Hugh Davenport,
*The Trials and Triumphs of the Mewar
Kingdom,*
Maharana of Mewar Charitable
Foundation (Udaipur).

Philip Davies,
Splendours of the Raj,
John Murray (London 1985).

Maurice Dekobra,
Perfumed Tigers,
Cassell & Company Ltd (London
1931).

Gayatri Devi and Santha Rama Rau,
A Princess Remembers,
Century (London 1984).

Marchioness of Dufferin,
Our Viceregal Life in India,
John Murray (London 1889).

Edward B. Eastwick,
*Kaisaranamah-i-Hind or Lay of the
Empress*
(private circulation only, London
1882).

S.M. Edwardes,
Ruling Princes of India – Bhavnagar,
Times of India Press (Bombay
1909).

James Fergusson,
*History of Indian and Eastern
Architecture,*
Munshiram Manoharlal, 1972.

Sir Kenneth Fitze,
Twilight of the Maharajas,
John Murray (London 1956).

Yvonne Fitzroy,
Courts and Camps in India,
Methuen & Co., Ltd (London
1926).

Rosita Forbes,
India of the Princes,
The Book Club (London 1939).

John Kenneth Galbraith,
Ambassador's Journal,
Hamish Hamilton (London 1969).

P.T. George,
Ceilings of Landholdings,
National Institute of Rural
Development (Hyderabad).

Pearce Gervis,
This is Kashmir,
Cassell & Company Ltd (London
1954).

D.V. Gundappa,
All About Mysore,
Karnataka Publishing House
(Bangalore 1931).

Thomas Holbein Hendley,
*The Rulers of India and the Chiefs of
Rajputana,*
W. Griggs (London 1897).

Yusef Husain,
The First Nizam,
Asia Publishing House (Bombay
1963).

Aldous Huxley,
Jesting Pilate,
Chatto & Windus (London 1927).

Muhammad Ibn Battuta,
Travels in Asia and Africa 1325-1354,
Routledge and Kegan Paul (London
1983).

Samuel Isreal and Bikram Grewal
(eds.),
India,
Insight Guides, APA Productions,
Ltd (Hong Kong 1985).

Samuel Isreal and Toby Sinclair
(eds.),
Rajasthan,
Insight Guides, APA Productions,
Ltd (Hong Kong 1988).

A. Padmanabha Iyer,
Modern Mysore,
Sridhara Printing House
(Trivandrum 1936).

A. Padmanabha Iyer,
Modern Travancore,
(Travancore 1941).

John Keay,
Into India,
John Murray (London 1973).

India Discovered,
Collins (London 1988).

Geoffrey Kendall,
Shakespeare Wallah,
Sidgwick and Jackson (London
1986).

Count Hermann Keyserling,
Indian Travel Diary of a Philosopher,
Jonathan Cape (London 1925).

Rudyard Kipling,
From Sea to Sea,
Vol. 1, Macmillan and Co., Ltd
(London 1919).

M. A. Laird,
Bishop Heber in Northern India,
Cambridge University Press
(Cambridge 1971).

Perceval Landon
Under the Sun,
George Bell and Sons (London,
early twentieth century).

**John Lawrence and Audrey
Woodiwiss,**
The Journals of Honoria Lawrence,
Hodder and Stoughton
(London).

Walter R. Lawrence,
The Valley of Kashmir,
Kesar Publishing (Srinagar 1967).

John Lord,
The Maharajahs,
Hutchinson (London 1971).

Sir Arthur Cunningham Lothian,
Kingdoms of Yesterday,
John Murray (London 1951).

Pierre Loti,
India,
T. Werner Laurie Ltd (London 1929).

Colonel G.B. Malleson,
The Native States of India,
Longmans (London 1875).

G.A. Mathews,
Diary of an Indian Tour,
(for private circulation only, Edinburgh 1906).

C. Achyuta Menon,
Cochin State Manual
(Cochin 1911).

K.P. Padmanabha Menon,
History of Kerala,
4 vols., Asian Educational Services (New Delhi 1982).

A. Shreedhara Menon,
A Survey of Kerala History,
S. Viswanathan, Pvt., Ltd (1988).

Thomas R. Metcalf,
An Imperial Vision,
Faber and Faber (London 1989).

R. L. Mishra,
The Forts of Rajasthan,
Kutir Prakashan (Mandawa, Rajasthan 1985).

Margaret Cotter Morrison,
A Lonely Summer in Kashmir.
Duckworth & Co. (London 1904).

Elizabeth B. Moynihan,
Paradise as a Garden,
George Braziller, Inc. (New York 1979).

Ray Murphy,
Edward Lear's Indian Journal,
Jarrolds Publishers, Ltd (London).

H.V. Sreenivasa Murthy and R. Ramakrishnan,
History of Karnataka,
S. Chand & Company, Ltd (New Delhi 1983).

Aman Nath and Francis Wacziarg,
Arts and Crafts of Rajasthan,
Mapin International Inc. (New York 1987).

Louise Nicholson,
India in Luxury,
Century (London 1985).

K.M. Pannikar,
His Highness The Maharaja of Bikaner,
Oxford University Press (London 1937).

Mollie Panter-Downes,
Ooty Preserved,
Hamish Hamilton (London 1967).

Constance E. Parsons,
Mysore City,
Oxford University Press (London 1930).

Baron Jean Pellenc,
Diamonds and Dust,
John Murray (London 1936).

Rajendra Prasad,
The Asif Jahs of Hyderabad,
Vikas Publishing House, Pvt., Ltd (1984).

Frederick Price,
Ootacamund – A History
(1900).

Maya Ram,
District Gazetteer of Rajasthan – Alwar
(India 1968).

N.S. Ramachandriah,
Mysore,
National Book Trust (New Delhi).

Barbara N. Ramusack,
The Princes of India in the Twilight of Empire,
Ohio State University Press (Columbus 1978).

Louis Rousselet,
India and its Native Princes,
Bickers & Son (London 1882).

Ashim Kumar Roy,
History of the Jaipur City,
Manohar Publications (New Delhi 1978).

Susanne Hoeber Rudolph and Lloyd I. Rudolph,
Essays on Rajputana,
Concept Publishing Company (New Delhi 1984).

Vijayareje Scindia,
Princess,
Century Hutchinson Ltd (London 1985).

Makhanlal Sen,
Valmiki Ramayana,
Rupa & Co. (New Delhi 1989).

Michael Myers Shoemaker,
Indian Pages and Pictures,
G.P. Putnam's Sons (London 1912).

Lieut.-Colonel H.L. Showers,
Notes on Jaipur
(Jaipur 1909).

Harnath Singh,
The Sheikhawats & Their Lands,
Raj. Educational Printers (Jaipur 1970).

Karan Singh,
Autobiography (1931-1967),
Oxford University Press (Oxford 1989).

Percival Spear,
A History of India 2,
Penguin Books Ltd (Harmondsworth 1982).

Robert W. Stern,
The Cat and the Lion,
E.J. Brill (Leiden 1988).

Edward Thompson,
The Making of the Indian Princes,
Oxford University Press (London 1943).

G.H.R. Tillotson,
The Rajput Palaces,
Oxford University Press (Bombay 1987).

The Tradition of Indian Architecture,
Yale University Press (New Haven and London 1989)

Lieut.-Col. James Tod,
Annals and Antiquities of Rajast'han,
Vols. 1 & 2, George Routledge & Sons Ltd (London – first edition 1829).

Anil Toshi,
Alwar at a Glance,
Kusum Prakashan (Alwar 1988).

Col. G.H. Trevor,
Rhymes of Rajputana,
Macmillan and Co., Ltd (London 1894).

Mark (Samuel L. Clemens) Twain,
Following the Equator,
Vol. 2, Chatto & Windus (London 1900).

Capt. H. Wilberforce-Bell,
The History of Kathiawad from the Earliest Times,
Ajay Book Service (New Delhi 1980).

William Hunter and Fanny Workman,
Through Town and Jungle,
T. Fisher Unwin (London 1904).

M.A. Yazdani,
Mandu, The City of Joy,
Oxford University Press (Oxford 1929).

INDEX

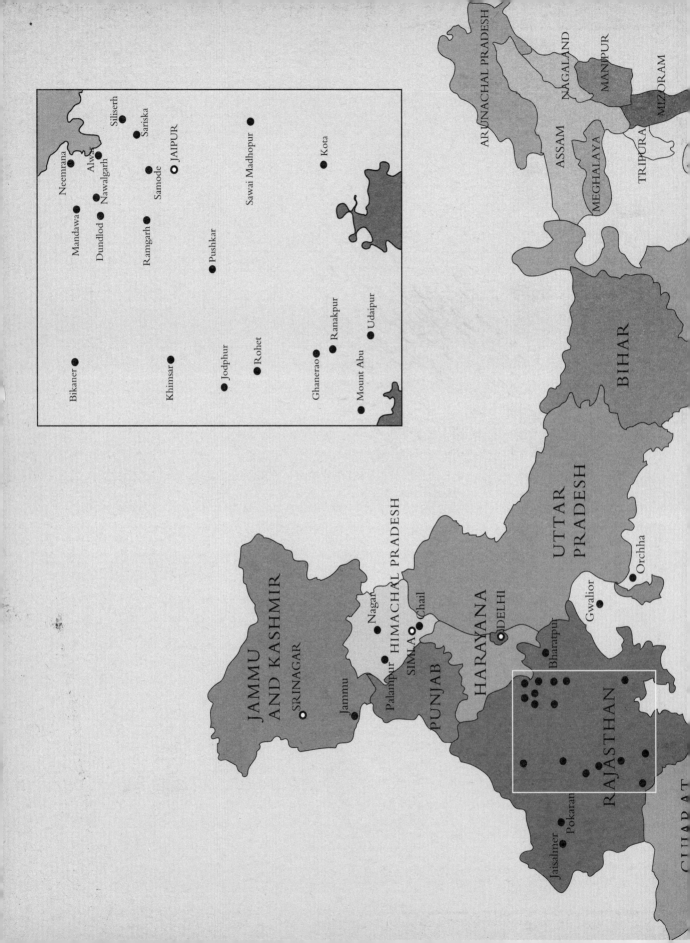

Neemrana
Siliserh
Alwar
Mandawa
Nawalgarh
Dundlod
Sariska
JAIPUR
Samode
Ramgarh
Kota
Sawai Madhopur
Pushkar
Bikaner
Khimsar
Ranakpur
Udaipur
Jodphur
Rohet
Ghanerao
Mount Abu

ARUNACHAL PRADESH
NAGALAND
MANIPUR
MIZORAM
ASSAM
MEGHALAYA
TRIPURA

BIHAR

UTTAR
PRADESH

Orchha

JAMMU
AND KASHMIR
SRINAGAR

HIMACHAL PRADESH
Nagar
Chail
DELHI
Gwalior

Palampur
SIMLA
HARYANA
PUNJAB
Bharatpur

Jammu

RAJASTHAN

Jaisalmer
Pokaran

GUJARAT